THE CRUCIBLE
OF CHRISTIAN
MORALITY

J. Ian H. McDonald

ROUTLEDGE

First published 1998
by Routledge
11 New Fetter Lane, London EC4P 4EE

Simultaneously published in the USA and Canada
by Routledge
29 West 35th Street, New York, NY 10001

© 1998 Ian McDonald

The right of Ian McDonald to be identified as the Author of this
Work has been asserted by him in accordance with the Copyright,
Designs and Patents Act 1988

Typeset in Garamond by Routledge
Printed and bound in Great Britain by Clays Ltd, St Ives PLC

British Library Cataloguing in Publication Data
A catalogue record for this book is available from the British Library

Library of Congress Cataloging in Publication Data
A catalogue record for this book has been requested

ISBN 0–415–11858–1 (hbk)
ISBN 0–415–11859–X (pbk)

CONTENTS

PREFACE

I am grateful to the editors and publishers for the opportunity to develop the present volume in relation to a series such as *Religion in the First Christian Centuries*. While it is the case that 'too often the religious traditions of antiquity are studied in isolation', this observation is doubly applicable to what is usually termed 'New Testament ethics'. The challenge is not only to recognise the interdisciplinary nature of the subject but to develop a method which accords with the logic of the study of religion, ethics and culture while relating to more specialised interests in the field. The success or otherwise of the attempt made in the present volume to address such a daunting task must be left to the reader to judge.

I have received encouragement and practical help from many quarters, which I can only inadequately acknowledge here. I am grateful to Richard Stoneman of Routledge and to the series editors, Deborah and John Sawyer, for putting the proposal to me, for helpful guidance in the preparation of the book and for accepting it for publication. I benefited from presenting some of the material in Chapter 6 to the ethics seminar of the Studiorum Novi Testamenti Societas (SNTS) at its Strasbourg meeting in 1995. In addition, some of the material contained in Chapters 5 and 6 first appeared in the article 'The crucible of Pauline ethics' in *The Edinburgh Review of Theology and Religion: Studies in World Christianity* 1997. I am grateful to the editor, Professor James Mackey, for agreeing so readily that I could reproduce selected material from that article in this book. Other debts are too numerous to mention, but I must gratefully acknowledge those who have materially assisted with the chores of book production. In particular, I should like to thank Mr Dennis Lambert and Mr Gee Lowe, postgraduate students in biblical ethics, who shared in the proof-reading and cheerfully survived being subjected to the substance of the book in seminars, and above all my wife Jenny, without whose constant encouragement and practical help the writing of the book amid all the pressures of academic life would have been even more difficult than it was.

Ian McDonald
Edinburgh
December 1997

INTRODUCTION

The title of this book signals several of its leading concerns. Its focus is on the making of Christian morality, one of the great moral traditions in world history. It follows the convention of using the term 'morality' of moral practice and discourse relating directly to it, while 'ethics' is reserved for secondary reflection on morality. Thus while a study such as this is part of ethical enquiry, its subject-matter is the developing moral ethos of the early Christian communities. The term 'crucible' indicates that the early Christian communities, in their various settings, were something of a melting-pot in which materials and traditions derived from a variety of sources – Jewish and Hellenistic, scriptural and messianic, charismatic and sapiential – were forged into a new and distinctive moral outlook. It suggests lively interaction, refinement, change and transformation, until a new product emerges, tested as by fire.

This type of approach may be contrasted with more traditional ways of studying 'New Testament ethics', a discipline which itself manifests several different varieties.

DIACHRONIC OR HISTORICAL MODELS

From the time that Hermann Jacoby published his *Neutestamentliche Ethik* in 1899, scholars have given attention to the moral teaching contained in the books of the New Testament. The impetus for much of this effort arose from the desire of critical scholars to shake off the shackles of traditional dogmatism and rediscover the historical roots of the Christian moral tradition. However, the nineteenth-century historical quest proved to be at least as vulnerable to ideological conditioning as its predecessors, and the 'Jesus of history' and 'Jesus as moral teacher' tended to reflect nineteenth-century idealism in a marked way. The work of Johannes Weiss and Albert Schweitzer presented a radical challenge to such procedures by highlighting the factor of eschatology in relation to both Jesus and Paul. Scholars had now to come to terms with the fact that the first-century social and religious context was radically different from that of the twentieth.

Essential tools for further research on the moral teaching of Jesus were found in source and documentary criticism, which concentrated on the earliest forms of written tradition, and subsequently in form and redaction criticism (*Formgeschichte* and *Redaktionsgeschichte*) which placed greater emphasis on the setting of the material in the life of the faith communities and on the relation of redactors or editors to it. To be sure, the centre of concern was frequently the historical Jesus or the *kerygma* – the proclaimed message of the churches – rather than moral studies as such, but some works concentrated on the teaching of Jesus (cf. Manson 1935), and studies in Pauline ethics also show development across the century (cf. Furnish 1968). A stream of more comprehensive studies of 'New Testament ethics' emanated from this critical epoch, including those of Schnackenburg (1975), Schrage (1988) and Marxsen (1993).

However, with the emergence of new evidence from antiquity and paradigm shifts in modern culture, the second part of the twentieth century brought a proliferation of new approaches. Qumran and Nag Hammadi,[1] for example, disclosed new data relating to Judaism around the time of Jesus and to Gnostic movements within or on the fringes of the Christian Church, thus greatly extending the scope of socio-historical studies in Christian origins, while twentieth-century thinking overcame the old subject–object divide and insisted on a much more participative culture. Theological and ideological emphases now included liberationist, feminist and ecological emphases, while the ethos of post-modernism encouraged a proliferation of viewpoints. In the excitement generated by this maelstrom, studies of the historical Jesus towards the end of the century evince even more variety, not to say partiality, than those of the nineteenth century castigated by Schweitzer. If 'New Testament ethics' had to be based on such shifting sands, there would indeed be a major problem for the ethicist. In face of such difficulties, it was useful to be reminded of Schweitzer's foundational work by J. T. Sanders (1975), although his concern seemed to be to refute popular non-contextual interpretations rather than to engage with modernity. J. L. Houlden gave a timely reminder of the importance of basing study on primary evidence, namely 'the thought of the writer concerned, or at most the circle he represents' (Houlden 1973: 4). He concluded that the teaching of Jesus, which is refracted through the church communities, does not offer a starting-point for the study of 'New Testament ethics'. Richard Hays plots the logical progression from the visions of the moral life in Paul and his successors to those reflected in the Gospels and other writings (Hays 1997: 13–185).

One of the problems of the historical approach is thus to determine how the diachronic progression should be described. Primary evidence reflecting the ethos of the early faith communities is clearly of great importance, and this ethos cannot be studied without reference to historical and contextual factors. It is misleading to treat the New Testament as if it constituted a world of its own, effectively divorced from its cultural setting (sometimes revealingly described as 'background'). However, 'New Testament ethics' is not only about history and context – or even theology. It has to do with the study of morality. What is the moral significance of these historical and contextual studies and the moral vision they enshrine? Hays attempts to address such problems by going beyond what he calls the descriptive task to find the coherence of the moral vision in three focal images: community, cross and new creation (Hays 1997: 187–205). While questions must be asked about the selection, his all-too-brief discussion crosses the line from the diachronic to the synchronic or thematic paradigm.

SYNCHRONIC OR THEMATIC MODELS

The synchronic approach lends itself to a theological and life-related appraisal of the moral dimension of the New Testament and, as Hays suggests, to finding the coherence of its moral vision. It has, in fact, a considerable pedigree. For instance, Lillie (1956) used a range of themes to relate 'the law of Christ' to modern problems; in a later book he not only considered questions of philosophical grounding but elucidated the New Testament attitude to law and justice, the State, wealth, work, marriage and divorce and children – issues which were effectively treated as themes (Lillie 1961). Spicq (1965) focused on life themes such as 'new being and new life', 'grace and glory', 'faith and fidelity', and 'love of God and neighbour' (to name only a few), in order to present a synthesis of materials drawn from a range of New Testament writings. Schelkle's procedure was somewhat different (1971–3). He adopted four formal categories: 'basic concepts', such as the obedience of faith, sin and grace, reward and punishment; 'basic attitudes', such as conversion and repentance, faith, hope and love; 'objectives', such as freedom, holiness and perfection; and a fourth general category, ranging from the discussion of virtue and the virtues to poverty and wealth, family, and civil government. Osborn (1976) used the notion of 'ethical patterns' as a guide to lead us through the diversity of the New Testament writings, the four main patterns being righteousness (or justice), discipleship, faith and love, together with the 'negative ethics' which form their obverse. Other examples are found in Lohse (1991). One of the inherent difficulties of the approach is the problem of selection, which may be governed by a wide range of theological and ideological considerations.

J. Matera (1996), whose study largely followed conventional diachronic lines, concluded his book by offering 'some overtures toward a more synthetic view of the legacy that Jesus and Paul bequeathed to the church' – a project which, he claims, would require another volume (Matera 1996: 248). He set out seven theses, of which the chief heads were:

1 The moral life of believers is a response to God's work of salvation.
2 Believers live the moral life in the light of God's coming salvation and judgement.
3 The moral life is lived in and with a community of disciples who form the church.
4 The personal example of Jesus and Paul instructs and sustains believers in the moral life.
5 The moral life consists in doing God's will.
6 The moral life expresses itself in love for God, love for neighbour and love for enemy.
7 The moral life is an expression of faith (cf. Matera 1996: 248–55).

These seven theses would appear to contain the potential for far-reaching discussion and represent a necessary complement to the diachronic approach adopted in the book.

The synchronic approach has much potential for exploring the moral world of the early Christians. The danger is that a thematic approach may do less than justice to the ethos and context of the moral communities on which it is dependent and thus become something of a detached or abstract study. Sometimes the notion of a 'timeless ethic' lingers in the background. How can such themes be adequately grounded in the context of the faith communities in which they were generated?

THE SOCIOLOGY OF KNOWLEDGE

While the diachronic or historical approach came to recognise the importance of the *Sitz im Leben* (or 'real-life context') of the New Testament material, sociological factors have come to play a more basic role in critical scholarship than was evident in *Formgeschichte* and related approaches noted above. It is now virtually axiomatic that human knowledge, perceptions and interpretations are determined by social factors. Consequently, social context, community setting and cultural patterns have a primary role to play in the discussion of moral understanding and value. To be sure, there are attendant dangers – not least the tendency to reduce the material to categories with which social science can deal (cf. Scroggs 1979) – but while these may not yet have been fully countered in theory, they can be largely obviated in practice if there is adequate awareness of them. No comprehensive study of 'New Testament ethics' has yet fully encapsulated this approach, although scholars such as Gager, Kee, Theissen and Meeks have made notable contributions. Meeks, for example, not only made a valuable study of Paul's social world (Meeks 1983) but extended this approach to wider intercultural concerns in *The Moral World of the First Christians* (1987). In *The Origins of Christian Morality* (1993), he presented what he called 'an ethnography of morals' and attempted 'to describe the moral dimensions of the subcultures of several varieties of the early Christian movement, seen within the larger complex culture of the Roman Empire' (Meeks 1993: 10). His 'bites out of early Christian moral culture' represent a highly defined form of the thematic approach. He avoids the term 'New Testament ethics' for several reasons. His field of reference is wider than the New Testament; the term is misleading because the first Christians 'who began to invent Christian morality' did not have a New Testament – an obvious fact often forgotten; and finally, morality and ethics have to do with people. 'Texts do not have an ethic; people do' (Meeks 1993: 3–4).

Meeks carefully distinguished between 'morality' and 'ethics' – which not all New Testament scholars trouble to do (as Matera (1996: 259, n.1) confessed, 'Throughout this work I use the adjectives "moral" and "ethical" interchangeably'). Of course, the terms do overlap and complete consistency is elusive. The attempt is made in this book to observe the distinction made earlier in this Introduction, which is broadly in line with Meeks' usage. A further term of importance is 'ethos', or the distinctive character or spirit of a community, people or culture (cf. Honecker 1990: 4–5).[2] Paraenesis, or moral exhortation, is primarily designed to reinforce ethos. In so far as community is basic to our study, 'ethos' is the leading term. This book is therefore concerned with the distinctive character or spirit of the early Christian communities, with the factors which reinforced it, and with its role in generating moral behaviour.

INTERPRETING THE SCRIPTURES

There is a hermeneutical or interpretative dimension to the business of 'inventing Christian morality'. The early Christian communities were, of course, attempting to respond to what they saw as the working of God in Jesus Christ, in whose ministry they believed the scriptures were fulfilled. Thus, virtually by definition, the interpretation of scripture operated at a fundamental level in the churches. That ancient hermeneutics were necessarily different from modern hermeneutics is illustrated by the fact that the New Testament scriptures had not yet come into being. 'The scriptures' were the scriptures of Israel, especially the Torah and prophets. As at Qumran, the scriptures were studied from a particular angle. The 'peshering' of scripture at Qumran involved a particular kind of eschatological interpretation which underscored the role of the community in the last days (cf. Lim 1997). The Christians' reading (or readings) of scripture, which also had strong eschatological elements, allowed them to see Jesus as the fulfilment of God's purposes in history, to appreciate Jesus' ministry more deeply, and to understand themselves as the people of God. In both cases, the scriptures translated into moral concern – for example, in the *Community Rule* at Qumran, and in the developing ethos of the churches. It comes as a shock to latter-day readers to discover that when the early Christians cited the love commandments, their reference was at least as likely to be to the teaching of the Torah as to the teaching of Jesus. In this scriptural concern, they were undoubtedly inspired by the example of Jesus who – whatever else he may have been – was an authoritative and radical interpreter of scripture.

Indeed, of all the roles he played that have been identified by modern scholarship, the most fundamental may well be that of biblical interpreter.

Scriptural interpretation was therefore an intrinsic element in the Christian community, as well as in Christian debate and controversy with groups who had different standpoints. One area to which it was fundamental was the development of Christology. The scriptures witnessed to Jesus as the Christ, and Jesus as the Christ brought new light to the scriptures. The cosmic vision of the churches was shaped accordingly. However, the centrality of scripture in community life could not but shape the ethos of the faith communities in a decisive way. The qualities inherent in faithfulness to God – in being the people of God – had to be reproduced in the life of the churches. The divine imperative inherent in the gracious indicative had to be heeded and reinforced. The scriptures were used freely for this purpose, strengthened and clarified by the teaching of Jesus. Converts from a pagan background, who brought with them their own range of moral assumptions, values and conventions, had to be inducted into and confirmed in this new realm of discourse. Hermeneutical acumen was also required in controversy. In what sense did the Christians obey the Torah? If they claimed to be faithful to God's requirements, why did they not observe the necessity for the circumcision of believers? Why did they not hold sabbath observance as normative? Why did they not observe the dietary requirements in scripture? These matters were not settled overnight. At almost every level, the churches were involved in searching, debate and decision.

THE DYNAMICS OF MORAL DISCOURSE

Our access to the debate is through primary moral and religious discourse in the New Testament itself. In other words, morality is concerned with people, but our access to them in their ancient setting is through texts. The texts involve the use of language as a form of social practice (cf. Appleby *et al.* 1996: 558). They are addressed to an interpretative community, structured to convey a coherent system of meanings, or to map a coherent picture of the world (Parker 1992: 10–12). New Testament discourse is complex in that it combines the language of morality (classified in the sociology of knowledge as 'control language') and the language of religion ('salvific knowledge': cf. Deeken 1974: 225). Part of our task is therefore to analyse or 'deconstruct' New Testament discourse in order to highlight the interaction between the cosmic vision which the writers share with the community ('salvific knowledge') and the ethos which the community and its members develop ('control language'). Another part is to identify the interaction between cosmic vision and action in the world, not least in relation to the governing authorities (cf. Winter 1994) and other authority structures, including the community's understanding of authority within its own fellowship. Discourse is inevitably concerned with institutions, power and ideology. The liveliness of the debate is reflected not simply in single texts but through the interaction of texts, which identifies different perspectives and issues that may have consequences far beyond the situations in question. Parker is at pains to emphasise that 'discourse analysis should bring about an understanding of the way things *were*, not the way things are' (Parker 1992: 21). Readers must beware of the danger of reading their own presuppositions into the material – an insidious temptation when dealing with morality. Nevertheless, it is possible to challenge the internal system of any discourse, to see how it relates to other discourses and to pursue the moral issues and values it promotes or denies.

COSMIC VISION AND MORAL PRACTICE

The cosmic vision of the early Christian communities was derived from the story of the people of God, crystallised in the story of Jesus. It was therefore compounded of many elements, including the notion of God as creator, the prophetic Word, the death and resurrection and glorification of the Christ, the Word made flesh, and so on. Not all may be cited at one time, but from this cosmic vision there emerged a coherent and distinctive way of life, responsive to the story the churches enshrined. This correlation is of supreme importance. It can work in both directions. If the ethos of the communities was defined by their distinctive story, their understanding of that story was enlarged by their common life and experience of the world. No one who understood the story of creation could despise God's creation; indeed, they could learn something of the creator from their experience of the creation (cf. Rom. 1: 19–21; 2.14–16). No one who understood the story of the coming of the Son as a servant, faithful unto death, could fail to hear the affirmation of humility in the sight of God and of self-giving for the sake of others. No one who knew the story and teaching of Jesus' ministry could doubt the importance of showing and promoting love, non-violence, human well-being and reconciliation in a world that was often unloving and violent; and in that mission one could learn more of Christ.[3]

A contrast is provided by the cosmic vision of Gnosticism and its relation to practice (cf. Rudolph 1984; Logan 1996). To the Gnostics, the world was an utterly alien order of being, the tragic result of a fateful event within the divine realm itself (such was their 'story'). Human beings need to come alive to the real nature of their imprisonment and to seek salvation from this alien material world, which is found in *gnosis* – at once self-knowledge and knowledge of God. This gnosis is mediated through the revealer, who calls people to realise where their true destiny lies. Gnosticism is thus about the process of spiritual liberation and realisation. Community ethics in the broad sense can be ruled out. A movement so inward looking and upward looking, and enshrining such hostility to the world, cannot but renounce the kind of concern for the world that is implicit in social ethics as generally understood in ancient and modern cultures. Their community ethic, which was described by Hans Jonas as 'a common solitude in a world become alien', focused on helping one another to nurture the divine spark within each being and so attain 'freedom'. This priority could take their praxis in apparently opposite directions. The *Gospel of Thomas* (among others) shows that the Gnostic ethical stance was the reverse of legalistic. External criteria were rejected in favour of an emphasis on inner motivation and disposition. Gnostics stood aloof from law, civil or religious, and earned for themselves the charge of being libertine or amoral. However, their world-denying perspective is perhaps more readily seen in ascetic tendencies, including abstinence from marriage ('the flesh') and from meat and other foods. Yet a principled ethic is endorsed by the texts from Nag Hammadi. Vice is seen as ignorance and indifference, while its opposite – moral practice – contributes to the spiritual quest. In short, their rejection of the world leads to a spiritual detachment from its contamination, while their view of the world reinforced their reading of the cosmos.[4]

It goes without saying that there are resemblances – real and superficial – between elements of Christian and Gnostic concern. Their essential differentiation lies in the nature of their respective cosmic visions and their impact on their understanding of community, morality and social obligation.

THE CRUCIBLE OF CHRISTIAN MORALITY

The use of the term 'crucible' is intended to suggest that interaction between tradition, text and context, between cosmic vision and life situation, was a feature of the moulding of Christian morality from the beginning and may therefore be expected to characterise Christian ethics today. As faith communities develop an ethos which translates into practice and is articulated in teaching, they generate moral reflection. This underlying thesis shapes the present book.

The first chapter focuses on the ethos of the Christian communities, expanding on some of the themes noted above – the relation of cosmic vision to moral understanding and practice, religious and doctrinal controversy, and paraenesis designed to reinforce and correct the ethos of the group. The primary evidence is supplied by letters and similar documents from the Pauline mission and other Diaspora locations.

The second and third chapters deal respectively with the place of scriptural interpretation (i.e., the 'Old Testament') and the tradition concerning Jesus in the making of Christian morality. Since we are interested in the earlier stages of the Christian church life, source material for the Jesus tradition is taken from the hypothetical document 'Q' (or the oral tradition it represents) and from Mark's Gospel, which is accepted as the earliest written Gospel. A few later developments relevant to the understanding of the Jesus tradition and its implications for faith and morality are also included.

The book, however, is not concerned simply with Christian origins but with Christian morality. Since morality has wide cultural implications, it is important to investigate leading moral issues which allow comparison and evaluation of relevant moral traditions. The fourth chapter is therefore devoted to the understanding of the person. Graeco-Roman philosophers discussed the role of the emotions in human life and even proposed therapeutic measures to cope with them. In the New Testament as in Judaism, the role of the passions is similarly discussed. Human life itself represents an interplay of elements. What then is a 'whole' being? How is Christian character to be described? What about the dark side of life?

In similar fashion, the fifth chapter explores the notion of community. An assessment is offered of community and communities in Graeco-Roman and Jewish life and their bearing on church life. The question of the distinctiveness of Christian community is discussed, not only in relation to the inner workings of church life but also in its interface with society through the household, with its institutionalised relationships and through its relation with the State.

The final chapter considers the notion of virtue or moral excellence that permeates Christian moral teaching. Comparative perspectives review the extent to which Graeco-Roman cultural values informed Jewish and Christian societies, and an assessment is made of distinctively Christian emphases which emerge from the interaction. As with the discussion of person and community in previous chapters, this exploration of moral excellence brings the discussion into active contact with primary concerns in Christian ethics – and perhaps also moral philosophy – today.

1

MORAL CONTEXT

The ethos of the early Christian communities

> Culture is not a plant sprouting from its seed in isolation; it is a continuous process of learning guided by curiosity along with practical needs and interests. It grows especially through a willingness to learn what is 'other', what is strange and foreign.
>
> (Burkert 1992: 29)

Every ethic has a context and is guided by practical needs and interests. No ethic falls complete from heaven – whether a religious ethic like that of Israel or the early Christian churches, or a philosophical ethic like that of Plato or Aristotle. An ethic also implies a community – a church, city or people – with a distinctive ethos or way or life, generated within the community itself as a response to what it perceives as moral reality. Such perceptions may differ, both within and outside the community. Variety of experience within the community can stimulate creative tensions.

Pluralism is by no means the prerogative of the modern or postmodern age. Many ancient cultures were acutely aware of pluralism in some form or other and adopted attitudes to it – whether positive, tolerant and inclusive or hostile, intolerant and exclusive. First-century Judaism was so diverse that some scholars prefer to speak of the 'Judaisms' of the period (Charlesworth 1990: 37). The Pharisees, Sadducees and Essenes were only some of the tendencies within it, and a messianic sect such as the earliest Christian community was simply another variant. Marginal groups can be tolerated if they are seen to reaffirm, or at least not to undermine, the centre of the tradition. If they are seen to change the centre of the tradition and to threaten a radical restatement of it, they may be deemed to have crossed the boundary and become intolerable within it. Such was the fate of the Christian movement.[1]

The Christian communities were thus born amid contention, and their moral understanding bears the marks of the struggle. Would Paul have attacked the notion of law quite so fiercely if he had not found himself confronted by 'Judaisers'? Would the Gospel records of Jesus' controversies with the Pharisees have been quite so bitter if the Christian movement and the continuing tradition of Judaism had not been so much at odds with each other, especially after the disaster of the Jewish War, *c.* 70 CE?

The tragedy is that the traditions had so much in common. The Jews, as Paul put it, 'are entrusted with the oracles of God' (Rom. 3.2). To them had been given covenant and promise. And Judaism had not been as inflexible as sometimes appears. Through the vicissitudes of its history from Maccabean times (or even earlier), it had learned much from its encounter with what was strange and foreign – especially from Hellenism. It had even diversified its own self-understanding. To be a Jew meant not only to be a member of a *genos*, an ethnic or national group into which one was born and sealed, in the case of males, by circumcision (the traditional understanding), but it could also mean to follow a distinctively Jewish way of life or culture, for which one could opt (cf. Josephus, *Contra Apionem* 2.210). The first is unchangeable, but the second offers a choice, especially when linked to the notion of salvation (Cohen 1990: 204–9). Hence, in principle and actuality, Judaism became open to outsiders through conversion and proselytisation, and there are hints in the New Testament of Pharisaic missionising (cf. Matt. 23.15). As the Jews came under increasing pressure from the Romans, though, the community became less open and more defensive. At this time, however, the Christians were engaged in their mission to the Gentiles. Since they claimed to be, or to be part of, the community of God's people and heirs to God's covenant and promise, the issue of circumcision, as well as respect for the Jewish law and customs, became a contentious one, reaching to the area of moral foundations. For the Christians, it was axiomatic that 'God is no respecter of persons'.[2] Logically, therefore, all were accepted on the same terms – whether Jew or Gentile, Greek or barbarian, circumcised or uncircumcised, slave or free, male or female (Gal. 3.28; Col. 3.11), or indeed rich or poor (cf. Jas. 2.1–7). The tension with Judaism was therefore acute and had implications for the Christian community itself.

As in Judaism, eschatological and millenarian expectation[3] served to intensify the vision, concentrate the mind, reinforce the community of the like-minded, heighten spiritual awareness and override worldly concern. Struggles with the world and its powers were accepted as the birth pangs of the coming age. Moral ambivalence is the unavoidable product of apocalypticism, with its preoccupation with the visions of the end. Its spirituality could be markedly otherworldly, involving an irresponsible neglect of this-worldly duties, as with some in Thessalonica (cf. 1 Thess. 5.1–11; 2 Thess. 2.1–12). It could engender a selfish luxuriating in spiritual excitement, negating its potential contribution to the building up of the worshipping community (1 Cor. 14 *passim*). It could impel the community to turn inwards upon itself, as in some phases of the Johannine community (cf. John 17.9, 14). But, as Richard Hayes has emphasised, it could also reinforce moral concern.[4] Generalisations about its moral consequences have to be carefully monitored. At times it could signal a pacific withdrawal from political struggle; at other times, it involved preparation for Armageddon.[5]

Judaism, with its long tradition of divine wisdom, and the Christian communities with their salvation motifs, both came to harbour an emphasis on *gnosis*, knowledge or enlightenment. Indeed, full-blown Gnosticism – a later phenomenon than the New Testament – had many points of contact in the ancient Near East and Greek culture, and was probably mediated to the Christian communities through Judaism. It must be emphasised that in the first century of the Christian era what is encountered is no more than its earliest foreshadowing; the substance was to emerge in the second and third centuries. Even in its early traces in Corinth, however, one can detect the focal emphasis on gnosis, accompanied by a claim to moral freedom. The 'enlightened' party were probably intellectually inclined and socially powerful.[6] The underlying motif was a discounting of the material world and immersion in the world of spirit. Its moral tendency, curiously, was to both extremes: to antinomianism, on the grounds that worldly duties impede the freedom of the spirit, and to asceticism, on the grounds that the material world, being evil, must be controlled by the enlightened. Its emphasis on salvation as an individual spiritual pilgrimage tended to engender a self-regarding spirit and a neglect of community values. Community existed only so far as it assisted the Gnostic to become free. Yet, in its concern for salvation, it had an appeal in Christian circles. Paul's response was to insist on the priority of Christian love (*agape*: cf. 1 Cor. 8 *passim*), as well as to counter its mythology.

Gentile culture and life-style was also a major factor. Judaism had learned much from Hellenism while preserving its distinctiveness. To be sure, the Jewish Diaspora communities bore the brunt of its onslaught. Reflective thinkers like Philo absorbed much of its philosophy while commending the higher wisdom of Moses. Apologists like the writer of 4 Maccabees linked the moral philosophy of Stoicism with loyalty to the law of Moses. The Christian communities distanced themselves from the pervasive immorality of Graeco-Roman society with sweeping condemnations of its vices (e.g. Rom. 1.29–31; 1 Cor. 6.9–10; Gal. 5.19–21). That these are more than the conventional rantings of moralists is borne out by 1 Corinthians 6.11 – 'And such were some of you'. Paul emphasised the cleansing that baptism signifies, together with the transformation embodied in the Christian faith, but it is not easy to divest oneself of engrained habits and assumptions about personal life and social conduct, and the Christian communities had to contend with a range of problems from that source, as 1 Corinthians itself shows. More cautiously, Paul accepted – as did Philo – that there was also in Gentile culture a recognition of virtuous conduct, which was worthy of consideration (Phil. 4.8), even if the fundamental parameters were derived from the moral tradition which the apostle taught (Phil. 4.9).

There can thus be little doubt the Christian communities were born amid conflict, yet no more stimulating environment could be found for the birth of a new moral and religious community. Issues abounded, and required solutions. The Christians were an increasingly independent movement with explosive potential for moral and religious creativity. Something of this kind took place in relation to the birth of Christianity. Thus we cannot understand the emerging faith and its new morality unless we look into the many-sided issues which were so hotly debated from its earliest days. The crucible of Christian ethics is a lively, if uncomfortable, place to be!

Our study begins with the traditions that show the leaders of the community engaging with some of the issues in question.

THE ISSUES FOR THE LEADERS

The mission of the early churches fell into several sectors. The mission to the Jews of the Diaspora and that to the Gentiles are the best known. As Paul reports, 'James and Cephas and John . . . gave to me and Barnabas the right hand of fellowship, that we should go to the Gentiles and they to the circumcised' (Gal. 2.9). Each of these missions had, or claimed, powerful figureheads, through whom we may find initial access to the ethos of their distinctive communities and the conflicts which shaped their ethic.

James and the church at Jerusalem

In the early decades of the Christian movement, James and the church in Jerusalem exerted tremendous influence and enjoyed considerable prestige. Luke probably oversimplified the situation when he made Jerusalem the launch-pad of Christian mission (Acts 1.8) and the locus of the apostles (Acts 1.12–14), as if the church in the beginning fanned out from that point by some centrifugal force. Jerusalem was not a strategic headquarters. The rapid spread of the movement in the Diaspora suggests that the Gospel may well have been carried in a variety of ways, not least through close contact between Galilee and Syria.[7] Paul, who was obligated for his baptism to Diaspora Christians in Damascus, made something of the fact that he did not go up to Jerusalem immediately and owed neither his conversion nor his commissioning to Jerusalem nor to Judean influence (Gal. 1.16–17). Yet he incidentally discloses the fact that the apostles were located there (Gal. 1.17), and that he eventually went up and met Cephas and James the Lord's brother (Gal. 1.19). Perhaps Luke's geographical scheme reflected the view of church origins which came to be widely held, even if it may not have been historically accurate.[8]

Jerusalem was certainly the centre of the Jewish world, the *axis mundi* and meeting-point for different types of Jews. In particular, it was the heartland of Judea and the target for Diaspora pilgrimage. Jesus himself made pilgrimage to it from Galilee. Hence diversity – to be specific, Jewish diversity – was part of its being, as various tendencies, generated within Jerusalem and also entering it from outside, asserted themselves. Paul encountered the 'Hellenists' there (Acts 9.29), the Jews of the Diaspora rather than the Jews or Jewish Christians of Judea (Gal. 1.22), but the 'Hebrews' were always a potent force.

Amid the diversity represented in the messianic community at Jerusalem, the hardliners were probably influenced by Pharisaic practice (Acts 15.5), and notably by conservative tendencies within it such as the school of Shammai, in so far as we can be guided by their insistence that Gentile proselytes should be circumcised. Two aspects are to be distinguished here. One is circumcision as a boundary-marker, the mark of belonging to the Jewish *politeia*. In this regard, the Jewish Christians affirmed their allegiance.[9] A second and more controversial point arose in relation to Gentile proselytes. Proselytising was not a constant practice among the Jews, who tended to be more anxious about their own separate identity, and after the disasters of the Jewish Wars the practice virtually ceased for a long time. In the period before the Wars, however, some Pharisees in particular were active missioners. As we have noted above, the change of policy was influenced by a change in the self-perception of Israel from being simply a nation and race into which one was born (a *genos*) to being a faith community and way of life to which one chose to belong.[10] Logically, proselytising cohered with the latter stance. It involved instruction and baptism to remove uncleanness. Did it also mean that Gentile converts had to be circumcised? The answer depends on whether one believes that the convert was being inducted into membership of the nation of Israel as well as into its faith. If the former, then circumcision is logically required; if the latter, then it is not. For a while, the issue probably remained less clear than the above analysis suggests, and the uncircumcised adherent possibly remained what the New Testament terms a 'Godfearer'.

James, as president of the church in Jerusalem, had to deal with more than the Pharisaic tendency. According to Acts 6.7, there was a priestly presence in the Christian community. While the Temple was the centre of the national cult, its condition since Maccabean times gave rise to extreme misgivings, represented by the Essenes of Qumran and reform movements within the priesthood itself; perhaps the Sadducees in their origin were precisely this kind of movement. An eschatological or millenarian cult might well attract some who related the 'Day of the Lord' to the restoration of the true Temple in a renovated Israel. Purity and freedom from pollution would be a continuing concern for them, translating into an emphasis on baptism, intense community life, prayers in the Temple and obedience to the Torah. This is already enough to make the life of the church president extremely difficult. An eschatological faith is readily seen as subversive by established bodies, whether religious or political – and religion was indeed political in Israel and, above all, in Jerusalem. To appear to challenge Temple authority was by no means free of political risk, while neither the Pharisaic tendency nor the Qumran community would have been impressed by the secularisation of the cult – its moral expression in the world, rather than mainly through specific rites or liturgical acts – which, paradoxically, the Christian movement implied. The 'otherworldliness' of eschatological hope has its roots and effects in this world. Moreover, a subversive hope had appeal to the out-and-out revolutionary, who in Israel might combine religious and political strands. There was possibly, therefore, a sensitive, if critical, relationship with the Zealot movement, which in the cauldron of Jerusalem in the decades before the Jewish Wars could be dangerous indeed.[11]

Within the Christian movement itself different tendencies had asserted themselves. James himself, 'the Lord's brother', represented the continuation of Jesus' family line, although he is also cited, by Paul as by the Gospel to the Hebrews, as a witness to the resurrection. The apostles ('the twelve') represented the disciple tradition and Jesus' proclamation to Israel (cf. Acts 6.2), and there may well have been other missionaries who claimed to have been commissioned by Jesus and who proclaimed the imminence of the Kingdom of God with charismatic zeal.[12] There were contrary tendencies. The fact that Jesus' family receives a relatively poor press in Mark suggests tension in the tradition. Peter's mission to the Diaspora seems at times to make a bid for independence from Jerusalem, causing James to take action to bring it back in line (the 'unfortunate incident at Antioch' involves Peter as well as Paul: Gal. 2.11–14). Disagreements between Paul and the Jerusalem church were disturbing to both parties. In addition to this was the fact that the more imaginative side of Judaism was developing tendencies towards a kind of gnosis, with problematic consequences for Jewish and Christian practice.[13]

That James, with his elders, managed to deal with the complexities of the Jerusalem situation and also to monitor developments in the wider church suggests that his title of 'the just' or 'the righteous' was well earned, but at a price. The political situation exploded in his face when the high priest Ananus opportunistically moved against him in 62 CE and brought about his death.

Peter and the Diaspora mission

Predictably, the issue of circumcision reared its head in the course of the early Christian mission. The reason was twofold. One was that the Christian community as a whole was oriented towards mission. Its messianic faith was concerned with salvation, with the call to repentance and decision, and with baptism and nurture in the faith community. Mission was a dominical command, as well as the logical expression of the community's very being. A fertile source of converts was precisely the semi-detached group of Godfearers found on the margins of the synagogue communities. The second factor was the basis of moral obligation within messianic faith. For the early Jewish Christian community, this was symbolised by 'Moses'. In words attributed to James, 'from early generations Moses has had in every city those who preach him, for he is read every sabbath in the synagogues' (Acts 15.21). We can certainly accept that the messiah was believed to have 'fulfilled' the scriptures and to have liberated them from the domestication and accommodation which scribes and Pharisees were held to have inflicted upon them (cf. Matt. 5.17–20), but 'Moses' or Torah remained a central symbol and a text to be interpreted (cf. Acts 28.23). The hardliners among the Jewish Christians argued that the Mosaic Law required every member of Israel to be circumcised and that if Gentiles wanted the benefits of membership they must comply: 'Unless you are circumcised according to the custom of Moses, you cannot be saved' (Acts 15.1; cf. 15.5). They made apparently unauthorised journeys to Antioch and perhaps beyond to insist on compliance – such at any rate was Luke's view.

There is no reason to suppose that the majority of Jewish Christians followed this line, nor that the 'Judaisers' whom Paul found so vexatious always came from this source.[14] The Jewish Christian mission or mission to the Diaspora which Cephas (Peter) and John led, was primarily aimed at the expatriate Jews, but it soon faced the problem of Gentile interest in messianic salvation. A solution to this problem was sought through activating other focal symbols in the Torah (such as the Abraham story) which interpreted God's relation to all his creatures.

J. D. M. Derrett has argued intriguingly that the symbol of Noah lies behind the vision and divine revelation ascribed to Peter in the Cornelius story (Acts 10.1–11.18). The basic image seems to be that of a sail sheet, secured by four ropes. If we assume, with Derrett,[15] that the sail is supported by a single mast, then we have a picture of an ancient ship, with an animal cargo. In short, we have Noah's ark, filled with all kinds of animals (as in Genesis), whether accounted clean or unclean. Peter is commanded to kill (the word means 'sacrificially slaughter') and eat, and he initially resists such an otherwise unauthorised action. Noah, however, was permitted to eat clean and unclean animals: 'Every moving thing that lives shall be food for you' (Gen. 9.3). The threefold divine voice declares all meat clean. With such divine authority, the praxis of the Jewish Christian mission may freely implement the tradition of Deuteronomy 12.15: 'You may slaughter and eat flesh within any of your towns, as much as you desire, according to the blessing of the Lord your God which he has given you; the unclean and the clean may eat of it, as of the gazelle and as of the hart' (cf. Deut. 12.20–22). The Deuteronomic permission operated if the designated sanctuary was too distant. How much more should it apply when the sanctuary has been superseded by the sacrifice of Christ (cf. Acts 20.28b)! As Derrett indicates, the divine declaration applies not only to the meat but to human association and community: 'God has shown me that I must not call any man common or unclean' (Acts 10.28). Peter, priest and prophet, thus establishes commensality with the Gentiles, for 'God shows no partiality' (Acts 10.34–35). Traditional taboos, for example about tanners and tanneries as well as Gentiles, no longer apply. Cleansing came by baptism and the Holy Spirit. Thereafter the emphasis was on respect for God and right action.

But what of the prohibition on eating the lifeblood (Gen. 9.4; Deut. 12.16)? This was a more difficult matter. Noah was specifically enjoined not to eat flesh containing blood. It is true that this prohibition related directly to the Temple cult: you shall 'offer your burnt offerings, the flesh and the blood, on the altar of the Lord your God; the blood of the sacrifices shall be poured out on the altar of the Lord your God, but the flesh you may eat' (cf. Deut. 12.27). If the Temple and the sacrificial system were superseded, did the prohibition of blood still apply? Three possible lines were open to the Jewish Christians as the mission expanded in the Diaspora and inevitably brought Gentiles into the community of faith. One was that of the Pharisaic Christians: all observances must be kept, so far as humanly possible. If our whole lives are sacrificed to God, it is precisely by keeping the law and taking ritual into everyday living that life is sanctified. Gentile believers must relate to Jewish requirements, including circumcision and the food laws, if they are to be numbered among God's people Israel. The second position related to the Noah symbol, God's covenant with all creation. By adopting a form of Noachide law, this response secured a means of coexistence and commensality with Gentile believers, cleansed by baptism. Any animal could be eaten, provided that the Noachide form of slaughter was followed. In the vision, Peter arguably related to such practice when he accepted divine authorisation to slaughter (that is, to kill in ritual fashion). The result was to rule out the meat markets of the Gentile world, which incurred the further disqualification of purveying meat which had in all probability been 'sacrificed to idols'. However, it is not clear that the command to kill in Peter's vision can bear the weight of this argument. This leads to the third option. The climactic word of God is, 'What God has cleansed, you must not call common' (Acts 10.15). God cleansed through baptism. Purity therefore concerned the baptised community; it was not a matter of food. As the Gospel tradition put it, 'not what goes into the mouth defiles a man, but what comes out of the mouth, this defiles a man' (Matt. 15.11; cf. Mark 7.15). Thus, none of Peter's contacts defile him: neither Simon the tanner, with whom no Pharisee would have associated, nor Cornelius the Gentile, nor the food that was being prepared. Indeed, according to the Acts narrative, Peter did not present the Noachide solution at the subsequent meeting in Jerusalem, but supported the Gentile case, which was the third option and more radical than the Noachide. In Christ there is a new creation. Jewish food laws were not obligatory, although one was free to relate to them as occasion demanded. This was essentially Paul's position. It appears that Peter, whose roots were not in Jerusalem, also accepted it, at least in principle – at Antioch he 'lived like a Greek', as Paul tartly reminded him (Gal. 2.14) – but the Noachide route might be expedient on some occasions.[16]

The schema Luke follows in Acts is in the main thematic, and it may be as well to follow up his narrative at this point. Predictably, Peter was challenged by the essentially Pharisaic 'circumcision party': 'Why did you go to uncircumcised men and eat with them?' (Acts 11.2). Yet the progress of the mission to the Jews of the Diaspora increasingly brought Greeks into the community (Acts 11.20), and Antioch in particular became a centre of 'Christianity' (Acts 11.26). Under continuing pressure from Pharisaic Christians, the Jerusalem church – 'the apostles and elders' – had to hold conference and give a ruling on the matter (Acts 15 *passim*). Peter presented the 'no partiality case'. Paul and Barnabas witnessed to the quality of the Gentile mission, but what part they had in the proceedings is not clear. James, as presiding elder, gave the sense of the meeting. The messianic age to which the prophets bore witness embraces 'all the Gentiles who are called by my name': that is, are called by baptism into the people of God. There are no further entry requirements, such as circumcision. The common praxis of the community, however, presupposes respect for certain Noachide parameters: the 'adultery' of idol meat and meat killed in unapproved ways (strangled or trapped, and containing blood). It may be, however, that 'adultery' should be taken literally. The 'decree' would then cover both pollution and morality.

Luke has, in fact, given a graphic account of a major issue for early church mission and polity. His theological scheme may disguise certain other aspects. Saul, the over-zealous Pharisee, would have been unlikely to persecute the early messianic believers because they baptised some Gentiles and brought them into line with Noachide practice. It may therefore be concluded that the Jewish Christian Diaspora mission already followed a liberal policy, at least in the Damascus or Syrian sector, and that it was this fact which so incensed Saul (Acts 9.1). Conversely, after his dramatic experience, it was this kind of Christian faith which Paul embraced. Hence Paul's gospel of radical freedom from the law may have been a relatively early phenomenon. If so, the declaration of Noachide requirements by James and the elders of Jerusalem seems to have been an attempt to modify existing practice in some quarters.

The complete reconciliation of Luke's account in Acts and Paul's in Galatians is by no means easy, but Paul's preoccupation was probably with the recognition of the validity of the Gentile mission and the manifestation of unity through the collection for the poor of Jerusalem (Gal. 2.1–10). On these matters, Paul was well satisfied. But the 'circumcision party' was not prepared to leave matters at that stage. Thwarted over circumcision, they challenged commensality at Antioch (Gal. 2.1–13).[17] Derrett wondered if Paul engineered the clash with Peter, a practice not unheard of in rabbinic circles where a point of difference existed.[18] It is more likely that the initiative came from outside, as Paul himself suggests. The consensus was that Antioch, if it wished commensality, should come in line with the Noachide requirements as the Jerusalem meeting had determined. Presumably the decision was taken less out of conviction (why had their practice been otherwise?) than for expediency. Paul was isolated; even Barnabas deserted him. The nub was that to change practice arguably meant for him not only an element of compromise but a retrogression which undermined the faith. It was nullifying the grace of God and deserting that radical obedience to the Gospel of Christ which Paul – and Peter – had practised among the Gentiles. 'If you, though a Jew, live like a Gentile and not like a Jew, how can you compel the Gentiles to live like Jews?' (Gal. 2.14). Peter, according to Luke, had given full support to the Gentile claim and apparently did not himself live by the Noachide requirements. In Antioch, the situation had been such as to permit this fuller liberty in the Gospel, until the challenge came from the 'circumcision party'. Antioch had then to come in line with general policy, Paul alone dissenting.

Paul and the mission to the Gentiles

When Paul had his remarkable encounter on the Damascus Road, he was set on the path of radical obedience to the messianic vision which would make him apostle to the Gentiles (cf. Gal. 1. 15–16). Paul himself was a Diaspora Christian, prepared when necessary to be flexible and accommodating (cf. 1 Cor. 9.20), but daring in his rethinking of the faith. Paul dared to say that he was no longer subject to the law as his fellow Jews understood it. While Diaspora Jews were not unaware of such tensions, Paul's case was more acute in that his 'conversion' was from an extreme expression of Pharisaism to a messianic faith which, in his hands, became an open missionary faith. As this developing movement began to pull down the barriers between Jew and Gentile, the reaction from traditional Jewry was fierce, for such a development posed a serious threat to Jewish identity and tradition. Even in Hellenistic times, the term *Ioudaios* retained its ethnic connotation while admitting those of other nationalities who accepted prescribed cultural or religious norms (Cohen 1990: 220). Many Jewish Christians would therefore have been unhappy with Paul's characterisation of himself as 'not myself subject to the law', even though he qualified that statement in terms of being 'subject to the law of Christ'. Indeed, in order to reduce tension between different groups of Christians, the mission to the Gentiles was expressly differentiated from that to the Jews (Gal. 2.9–10), but the cultural and religious ties were much too complex to allow such a facile division of influence. The two missions clashed in Antioch, with potentially devastating results for the Gentile mission (cf. Gal. 2.11–14). Paul clearly lost out at Antioch and moved his base of operations to Corinth. Meanwhile 'Judaisers', of whom there may have been different types, caused dissension in Galatia by countering Paul's teaching on the law and insisting on at least some forms of traditional Jewish practice. Any account of Paul's mission must take cognisance of the multicultural context of the churches – and dominant in the Diaspora environment was the perennial question of the place of Jew and Gentile in the people of God.

It must be acknowledged that the question of the origins of Paul's missionary faith and its break with Jewish practice is highly controversial today, and the debate continues.[19] A theological account by itself is insufficient; all is not explained by reference to justification by faith, still less by reference to Luther – Luther's context and frame of reference were quite different from Paul's. But a sociological account can be reductionist, as when it is argued that Paul and his followers abandoned parts of the law of Moses simply to make it easier for Gentiles to become Christians (cf. Watson 1986: 34). This sounds like a shrewd response to market forces: since the home market (the Jews) was impossibly restricted (as the alleged failure of early mission to Israel showed), they looked to world markets! However, when we posit 'the perennial question of the place of Jew and Gentile in the people of God', we are raising interrelated questions of a religious and sociological kind, which exercised Judaism as well as the new messianic movement (Cohen 1990: 204–23). If, as we have seen, it was possible to give different answers to the question 'Who is a Jew?', then it was equally possible to understand the people of God not in the restricted sense in which birth and nationality played a leading part, but as those who responded obediently to the God who revealed his will in history and experience, and cherished the hope of salvation thereby. For Paul the apostle, Abraham encapsulated this faith response (Rom. 4.1–25; Gal. 3.6–9), although it is to be noted that the Abraham story has always been a *crux* in Jewish as well as early Christian debate (cf. Vermes 1961: 193–227).

Within the fluidity of first-century Judaism, the Christians represented a messianic reform movement or sect,[20] identifying Jesus as the messiah and affirming his resurrected and transcendent status. As a messianic group, they believed – as did the Qumran sectaries – that they figured centrally in God's final plan of salvation, and the intensity of their faith lent it charismatic and apocalyptic features. Such eschatological intensity implied the need for a radical reorientation within the faith tradition of Israel, and consequently gave rise to tensions with upholders of traditional patterns. It is within this matrix that we must address the questions of the interpretation of Torah, the place of Moses as compared to Christ, and the identification and boundaries of the true Israel. This was the primary situation into which Paul was plunged on his 'conversion'.[21]

Paul's initial experience was born out of the complexities and problems of the religious context: the inter-community tensions, the clash of perspectives, and the notion of the elect people. In the messianically redefined people of God, Paul not only found his spiritual home but also contributed greatly to the articulation of its faith and life. This community baseline remains exceedingly important for understanding Paul's thinking and moral teaching. The language of cosmic vision and revelation – significant though they are – must not mislead one into thinking that Paul's theology came to him as a complete package, supernaturally gift-wrapped. In his letters, Paul was thinking *with* the Christian community about its own faith and life, and not least about the behaviour and conduct of members within the faith community and in society. Theory and practice constantly interrelate. Hence his moral teaching is not a simple deduction from a given theological standpoint, but emerges from participation in and reflection upon the faith and life of the believing messianic community. Only in this way can we begin to understand 'the theology and ethics of St Paul'.[22]

Paul did not have an easy ride in his ministry. On the one hand, there were opponents who questioned the apostolic authority which he claimed. He was not one of the Twelve nor did he have the family connections of James, and his encounter with the risen Christ fell outside the conventional range of 'resurrection appearances' which came to be recorded in some of the Gospels and presumably reflected thinking in influential circles. It is clear that his claimed special commissioning as an apostle and the credentials of his ministry were often under fire. The original mission of the Twelve and their successors was eschatological in tenor and called for the repentance of Israel in face of the imminent Day of Judgement (cf. Matt. 10.1–42). They were under strict orders as to life-style and message. Theirs was a message of eschatological warning related to the ingathering of Israel. The wider world might have recognised in them a likeness to the wandering Cynic preachers, except for the quality of faith that informed their message (Theissen 1982: 27–67). Their frame of reference was markedly different from Paul's, and Paul seems to have had a running battle with them just as he had, from time to time, to make real efforts to come to terms with Jewish Christianity in general and apostolic authorities in particular. On the other wing were threats from Gentile paganism (idolatry and immorality were key issues) and from early expressions of gnosis with their extremes of asceticism and antinomianism. Faced with such challenges, Paul had to emphasise the immediacy of his vocation – it came from Christ, without apostolic mediation – and he appealed to the evidences of grace and of the Spirit at work in his churches as validation of his apostolic work. It was of prime importance that the ethos of the churches reflected the Spirit of Christ.

In spite of the fact that he dealt firmly, if diplomatically, with charismatics at Corinth (cf. 1 Cor. 14), Paul's authority bore many features of the charismatic. His vision of the risen Christ – qualitatively different, he argued, from the more frequent types of charismatic phenomena, for it was part of the eschatological event which changed the worlds of Jew and Gentile – was for him self-authenticating. He might seek recognition, understanding and endorsement of his mission from the 'pillar apostles', but he did not in any sense derive authority for his vocation from them. This was the Lord's doing, and it was wondrous in his eyes! Paul fits Weber's description of the ethical prophet whose authority derives from the effectiveness and persuasive power of the revelation he proclaims (Weber 1965: 59, 139). Weber described charismatic leadership as operating particularly in a situation of crisis when traditional frameworks of meaning have been severely shaken. Paul recognised that while the pioneering Christian movement was destabilising in some respects in relation both to the religious and to the worldly order, it was also potentially creative. It was destabilising in relation to Judaism in that it radically reinterpreted the faith of Israel in such a way as to highlight the membership of Gentiles and was thus seen to undermine traditional parameters. In relation to Rome, it was potentially destabilising in that it affirmed a transcendent order beyond 'the powers that be'. It was creative in that it reaffirmed the roots of Jewish tradition in God, the creator of all, and the universal community of faith and covenant love as the divine goal of Israel's mission. In all these critical matters, the dialectical relationship between the leader and the group was essential for maintaining the creativity of the group and the renewal of the tradition, with a particular onus resting on the leader (cf. Kee 1980: 55).

John and the Johannine communities

John is in some ways the most elusive of the leading apostles. Paul gives first-hand evidence of his association with Peter in the mission to the Jews, especially in the Diaspora (Gal. 2.9), and Acts corroborates this (Acts 3.1, 4, 11; 8.14; cf. Luke 22.8). Discussion of Johannine origins and the composition of the 'Johannine circle' (Cullmann 1976) has led to a general recognition of a Johannine community, based in Asia Minor but with Palestinian roots. It appears to represent a distinctive sector of the mission, preserving characteristic traditions about Jesus and John the Baptist and being intimately involved in controversy with non-messianic Jews. It also seems to have absorbed a wide range of cultural influences, evident in the Gospel, epistles and the Apocalypse, which represent different phases of its life. The experience of persecution and dislocation has left its mark on the literature, not least on the Apocalypse and in the Gospel itself, with its strong 'hatred' for the world. The breach with Judaism was now complete (John 9.22; 12.42; 16.2), and relations with 'the Jews' hostile. This had consequences for community ethos and moral attitudes.

THE SHAPE OF THE TEACHING

In approaching the shape of moral teaching in the Christian communities, the question of method is important. We have chosen not to embrace a specific social science approach which might predetermine the outcome by its inherent presuppositions.[23] We shall therefore allow the structure of the teaching to emerge from its context, content, purpose and procedures. Our study so far has illustrated the overriding importance of cosmic vision and community ethos. These are leading categories in the analysis which follows. We are also concerned with the exercise of authority within the group, and with the attitude of the group to the world. Finally, we must also identify the type of moral discourse reflected in our sources.

Paul's moral teaching

Modelling 'the ethics of Paul' is not without its difficulties. Paul himself did not provide such a model. His writings were paraenetic and pastoral, addressing the needs of the churches of the Gentile mission and reinforcing their distinctive ethos. It is more accurate to speak of his moral teaching and the moral ethos of his churches than to imply a systematic model of Christian ethics. Yet while it is true that Paul, like his fellow apostles and teachers, was no moral philosopher, his teaching represents a form of moral discourse. It is therefore incumbent upon us to note the moral arguments and forms of persuasion which he does use in the course of his teaching.

There is, of course, the added problem of the authenticity of the letters ascribed to Paul. There is no place here for a detailed analysis of the problem, which is discussed in every commentary. It is admitted that perhaps all of Paul's letters have been subjected to a degree of editing, and that Colossians and Ephesians in particular of the so-called Pauline corpus may have acquired secondary features from the Diaspora mission. For our purposes, an interesting feature is their adoption of what appears to be a general pattern of moral duties (the so-called *Haustafeln* or household instruction) current in Christian circles in the Diaspora. The Pastoral epistles, which contain similar material, are later in general orientation and, while probably incorporating Pauline material, are best regarded as Diaspora products interpreting Paul's teaching to the churches.

Paul's cosmic vision

It was within the fellowship and mission of the Christian movement that Paul articulated his 'cosmic vision', which involved a reconfiguration of meaning and a reorientation of faith. Paul's initial vision crystallised the cosmic focus of the early church as a messianic, apocalyptic sect or group within Judaism. In their tradition and worship the churches hymned Jesus who, having fulfilled a servant ministry 'even unto death, death on a cross' (Phil. 2.8) – where could Paul have learned of this but from the Christian community? – was elevated as Lord of the cosmos.

> Therefore God raised him to the heights and bestowed on him the name above all names, that at the name of Jesus every knee should bow – in heaven, on earth, and in the depths – and every tongue acclaim, 'Jesus Christ is Lord,' to the glory of God the Father.
>
> (Phil. 2. 9–11, REB)

This view of the cosmic Christ is the ground for a universal faith, a universal obedience and a universal worship, while affirming the fundamental thrust of Israel's faith.[24] The moral thrust is unmistakable. The Christians are to internalise what they find in Christ Jesus: his humbling of himself, his readiness to serve God, his self-giving even to the point of death (Phil. 2.7–8). There is thus no room for selfish ambition or vanity (2.3). Obedience to God, so evident in Christ, will express itself in unity of purpose (2.2), willing service (2.14) and joy (2.18).

In the context of this world picture, Paul ascribed the moving force in the cosmic drama to divine justice (Gk. *dikaiosyne*; Heb. *tsedaqah*) and mercy or covenant love (Gk. *agape*; Heb. *chesed*), for which Abraham supplied the basic paradigm (cf. Gal. 3.6–9; Rom. 4.1–25). The Christian community-story (in all its particularity) was about access to God's justice and mercy through faith in Christ, the crucified and ascended Lord. To respond in faith to the God of the covenant now revealed in Christ was to be incorporated into the sphere of God's mercy and justice; it was to be 'justified by grace through faith'. *Dikaiosyne* in Paul is not a virtue one possesses, nor is it an absolute norm or principle, as in the Graeco-Roman tradition. Rather, it is an active transcendent reality, made known through the social relationship of a covenantal faith. As such, it must be taken 'on trust' and realised in social relationships within God's creation. In other words, its nature is participative and thus expressed in relationships with others – with God and other beings, even with creation itself. Furthermore, inseparable from divine justice is divine mercy (Heb. *chesed*) – 'God's love has flooded our hearts' (Rom. 5.4) – which enables the dynamic of divine grace to transform self and community, overcoming alienation and generating authentic humanness.

For Paul, this was the key to authentic freedom (Gal. 5.1). On no account must this freedom be surrendered to a reimposed legalism, which he describes as 'works of the law' (cf. Gal. 2.16), or a 'yoke of slavery' (Gal. 5.1). The divine dynamic has moved beyond this kind of particularism to a moral and spiritual freedom, not determined by selfish whim or desire ('an opportunity for the flesh' – a bondage of a different sort) but impelled by the divine Spirit (cf. Gal. 5.13, 16). In the biblical tradition the Spirit (Heb. *ruach*, Gk. *pneuma*) embodied a mighty power, evident physically in the fury of the wind and in the access of strength given to mighty leaders, and evident in cosmic terms in the creator Spirit brooding over the surface of the waters. The Spirit is therefore a power operating in creation itself and evident in the mighty acts of God. He is the endowment of the messiah, the anointed one, and Paul virtually identified Christ with the Spirit in scripture. The Spirit is thus seen as characterising the new and final age – there is a correlation between creation and new creation. The new life of the Spirit, however, presupposes identification with Christ. The motif of the cross is given moral application: crucifying the flesh with its passions and desires (Gal. 5.24), and rising with Christ to a new life (Rom. 6.4). The indicative and imperative are also organically related. The Spirit is a reality in the believing community, received in baptism; believers must therefore 'walk by the Spirit' (Gal. 5.25).

The divine–human transaction effected and symbolised in Christ can be articulated in terms of reconciliation. The fundamental perspective is reconciliation with God (Rom. 5.10), but Paul also sees Christ's completed work as abolishing the division of Jew and Gentile, constituted by the law, and establishing a new solidarity of faith – 'one new man in the place of two' (Eph. 2.15). Christ's reconciling work is cosmic, as well as communal in scope (Col. 1.20–21). To Paul and his churches has been committed 'the ministry of reconciliation' (2 Cor. 5.18), so that they are 'ambassadors for Christ' appealing to all to be reconciled to God (2 Cor. 5.20). Hence there is a corresponding drive for reconciliation, for the healing of the alienated and the establishment of peace, in Christian morality as in Christian mission.

Cosmic vision has dimensions which lend themselves to mythological expression. Thus the fall of Adam symbolised the universal moral disability of humankind, which the operation of law further illustrated and even 'multiplied' (Rom. 5.20). The whole of creation also suffers from the contagion of sin and its own decay, and like human beings themselves longs to be complete (Rom. 8.22). Hence in the Christian story we find not simply a new particularity or exclusiveness (*contra* Sanders 1993), but a witness to the divine in history, the ultimate in the conditioned, the universal in the particular. Paul recognised that human life had a fundamental involvement in forces far greater than the individual or the particular. These forces reflected the tensions within humankind, the duality of human experience: good and evil, faith and unbelief, hope and despair, empowerment and oppression. They could be described in a variety of ways: the Spirit and the devil or Satan, the spirit and the flesh, the spirit and the letter, freedom and bondage, life and death, or, for that matter, angels, principalities and powers. Such duality, however, denoted a dynamic rather than a static reality. As human beings, we are involved in an ever moving life situation in which the fundamental orientation of our life is critical. We are involved in a living process which builds up momentum. In this connection, it is important to note the affirmation of Christ's cosmic role. By his death and resurrection he broke the power of death and routed the demons (cf. Col. 2.15). The Spirit is the first token of the complete renewal yet to be. Thus there is hope, which inspires patience (Rom. 8.24–25). God had answered the deepest need of creation: the longing for freedom (Rom. 8.22–24). Thus Paul lives on – sometimes groaning inwardly (2 Cor. 5.2), sometimes with exuberance (Rom. 5.3–5) – but always sustained by the faith that God works for good in all human experience (Rom. 8.28–39).

Personal ethics and community ethos

Paul's cosmic view, while grounded in experience, was the matrix of his ethics. Within the interaction of cosmic view and human experience, the moral dimensions of personal and community life emerged in his dealings with the churches.

Baptism, while essentially a preparation for the new age, marked the bounds of the community. It was the rite of initiation, the seal of belonging to the people of God. Paul appealed to the imagery of baptism for an exploration of transformative ethics. Baptism means identifying with Christ in his death and resurrection (Rom. 6.3–11). Thus the power of death and the servitude to sin are broken, while the resurrection has moral as well as religious force. Believers embark on a new life (Rom. 6.4); like Christ, they are 'alive to God' (Rom. 6.11). But the will must be harnessed to the new realm of discourse. They must think of themselves as dead to sin and alive to God (6.11). They must put themselves at God's disposal as people who have been raised from the dead and dedicate their bodies as instruments for doing right (6.13). The Christian mystery is thus integral to Christian morality and the story of Christ, and it means giving wholehearted obedience to the received 'pattern of teaching'(6.17), the groundwork of a holy life (6.19, 22). Participation in the believing community is, for Paul, a transformative experience, as its liturgy bore witness (cf. Rom. 12.1).

The cosmic vision colours Paul's interpretation of human transformation – 'a new creation!' (2 Cor. 5.17). All the old barriers should therefore be no more (the indicative and imperative remain). The children of God know no barriers of race (Jew or Greek), social and economic status (slave or free), or gender (male and female), for all have been baptised into union with Christ (Gal. 3.26–29). As God's justice in the scriptures embraced the disadvantaged (cf. Zech. 7.9–10; Deut. 24.10–22) and the resident alien (Lev. 19.18, 34), so in the new communities there was a radical social initiative, combining the vertical relationship of transcendent justice and mercy with corresponding action on the horizontal plane, where barriers were all too real.

The Spirit represented the moral dynamics of the situation. In the churches it was taken as an immediate manifestation of the power and presence of God, the first instalment of the end-time. The Spirit was received at baptism as believers were incorporated into the 'body of Christ' (1 Cor. 2.13). Thus the new cosmic vision involved the generating of the virtuous life by the working of God's Spirit in human lives and human community. It is not that the moral content is blindingly novel. Everyone knew what was meant by 'the works of the flesh' (Gal. 5.16–21). Similarly, while 'love, joy, and peace' in particular have strong scriptural and eschatological connotations, most people would accept the 'fruits of the Spirit' as virtuous. As Paul put it, 'against such there is no law!' (Gal. 5.22). The Spirit is not against the law but expresses the dynamics of the covenant. The Spirit generated freedom, not licence, and prompted loving service, not in-fighting (Gal. 5.13–15). One can distinguish between the spiritual and unspiritual side of one's character. If we live 'according to the flesh' – according to the unspiritual side of our nature – we die; it is the Spirit that brings life and enables us to live as 'sons of God' who can cry 'Abba! Father!' (Rom. 8.12–15).

Thus when Paul touches on Christ as model (the *imitatio Christi*), the dominant focus is on participation in his death and resurrection. When he speaks of 'crucifying the flesh with its passions and desires', at least two dimensions emerge. One has to do with the idea, strongly held by the Stoics among others, that unrestrained passion and desire were destructive forces in life and had to be controlled. 'Self-control' is valued more highly than mere self-expression. But this control cannot be achieved by the will alone; the weakness of the will is a basic Pauline perception (cf. Rom. 7). One must be moved, inspired, energised, grasped by a new vision, such as the model presented by Christ. The second question concerns the notion of imitation itself. Paul offers himself as an example of following Christ's example (1 Cor. 11.1). The context here suggests that it is the character of Jesus' ministry that is the object of imitation. In it we find, not the wanton expression of unqualified freedom ('Christ too did not please himself': Rom. 15.3), but a concern for the interests of others and for the building up of community (1 Cor. 10.23–24; Rom. 15.1–2). Hence Paul's policy is to try to have empathy with and consideration for the standpoint and difficulties of people as different as Jews and Greeks, in order to further their salvation (1 Cor. 10.33). In this sense he believed he was setting a Christ-like example which his churches should follow. The model of the cross, however, is even more complex. It includes the notion of a spiritual 'dying' which must be accomplished before new life can emerge (cf. Rom. 8.12–13), and also a physical dying before the resurrection of the dead is effected through Christ (cf. 1 Cor. 15.20–23). The cross can also inspire those who suffer for their faith. Paul's central desire was to share Christ's sufferings in growing conformity to his death, for cross and resurrection are not to be separated (Phil. 3.10–11). There is undoubtedly an eschatological motif at work here. The sufferings of the faithful are part of the final struggle between good and evil.

In his letters, Paul characteristically addresses the saints. The word has a curious ring in modern ears, for whom 'saints' may denote canonisation and the glorious company of the blessed departed or, at the very least, those on earth who manifest an extraordinary degree of moral virtue. It comes almost as an anti-climax to realise that Paul used it to denote members of the church community – although his understanding of that community is crucial. Those whom he addressed had already identified with Christ in baptism (Rom. 6.3); they had put themselves at God's disposal; they had been raised from death to life; they were committed to a moral life-style (Rom. 6.13); they were obligated to live a holy life (Rom. 6.19). To be sure, the interplay of indicative and imperative runs through this whole line of thinking; the commitment to holiness has to be renewed constantly, and exhortation has thus to be a standard part of Christian rhetoric. As Ephesians puts it, the new nature which they have put on – created in God's likeness – expresses itself in the upright and devout life evoked by the truth (Eph. 4.24), and they must 'give no foothold to the devil' (Eph. 4.27). As noted above, worship and morality combine as Christians dedicate themselves to God as a living sacrifice (cf. Rom. 12.1–2).

The interaction of Paul's cosmic view and his moral awareness led to the affirmation of the trilogy of faith, hope and love (agape), which came to be known as the 'theological virtues'. All characterise the faithful; all are fundamental to human life. For the Christian community, faith in its particularity is response to the Gospel, to God in Christ. Implicitly – and here a universal aspect emerges – faith is related to those structures of trust which are fundamental to personal and community life as well as moral understanding, and without which life is futile and despairing (cf. Rom. 8.20–22). As for hope, Paul finds that the hope of the coming glory (Rom. 5.2) provides a new perspective on suffering. Christian hope provided 'a triumphant, rejoicing confidence' (Barrett 1991: 96), which linked suffering with endurance, endurance with tried character, and tried character with hope that will not prove false. Hope is therefore seen as the ground of human salvation (Rom. 8.24). Life is not simply a matter of empirical certainty. It has to reach out towards the future, in the expectation that things can be different and that we ourselves can change in order to see them differently. Ultimately, hope is the effective counter to despair. Love (agape) is the most fundamental of all. In the hymn of love (1 Cor. 13), Paul demonstrates that love must qualify many of the values cherished in the churches: *glosso-lalia* or rhetoric (13.1), prophecy, wisdom and faith (13.2), asceticism and martyrdom (13.3). Love transcends the 'goods' not only of the world but even of the community of faith, calling all towards perfection of character (13.4–7) and ultimate fulfilment (13.8–13).

Authority, discipline and nurture

We have already noted some features of Paul's view of authority and discipline, which broadly have three central points of reference. One was Christ the Lord, whose word was transcendent. The second was his commissioning as an apostle by the Lord. The third was the ethos he had cultivated in his churches, which he believed to reflect the Spirit of God. Thus Paul could, on occasion, cite a 'word of the Lord' as the authority which set out the basic agenda, whether of faith or moral practice: for example, that the wife should not separate from her husband nor the husband divorce his wife (1 Cor. 7.10–11), or concerning the resurrection to eternal life (1 Thess. 4. 15). This presupposed some kind of dominical tradition available to Paul and current in the churches (cf. 1 Cor. 15.1–4), although he appealed to it less frequently than might have been expected. When he cites, he makes a specific point. Thus when he introduced the narrative tradition of the last supper (1 Cor. 11.23–26), the context was the Corinthian tendency to form factions, evident even in the common meals. The model for their community's moral and liturgical practice was found in the dominical narrative. It is an act of *mimesis*: 'do this . . . '(1 Cor. 11.24–25), of remembrance or recollection (11.24), and of witness (11.26). To participate 'unworthily' (11.27) is to offend against the Lord and incur judgement as a form of discipline (11.27–32). Paul's argument is not without its cruder elements (cf. 11.30), but its purpose is clear. The common meal was not a time for self-indulgence, but for acting in community and sharing meaning (11.33).

Paul's apostolic authority was based on his commission from the risen Lord (1 Cor. 9.1; 15.8; Gal. 1.16). As the authentic interpreter of Christian tradition and 'the mind of Christ' (1 Cor. 2.16), he offered counsel on, for example, marriage and sexual relations (1 Cor. 7 *passim*, especially 7.7, 8–9, 12, 25, 32, 40). He thus treated received tradition on the indissolubility of marriage as the central principle and proceeded to interpret it by 'the Spirit of God' (1 Cor. 7.40) in relation to the given situation of mixed marriages in the church.

Paul also defined the ethos he expected in his churches: an ethos of mutual edification (1 Cor. 14 *passim*), which included respect for good order ('God is a God of peace'). Anyone who was spiritually minded, said Paul with an eye on the charismatics, must acknowledge that his advice was tantamount to a command of the Lord: 'if anyone does not recognise this, he is not recognised!' (14.37–38). The general practice of the churches also counted for something: on this basis, women should not speak in church (14.33–35)! In the last analysis, Paul insisted on conformity: 'If anyone is disposed to be contentious, we recognise no other practice, nor do the churches of God' (1 Cor. 11.16). Within the ethos of the churches, discipline must be exercised. A case of immorality at Corinth required the exclusion of the offender, 'in order that his spirit may be saved in the day of the Lord Jesus' (1 Cor. 5.5). The note of pastoral concern is evident, as also is the community's responsibility for exercising discipline over its members. There comes a time when love for the offender must be reaffirmed (2 Cor. 2.8). Paul respects the discretion of the community. 'Anyone whom you forgive, I also forgive' (2 Cor. 2.10). Paul is clear that he must not use his authority to 'lord it over' his churches; he is rather a co-worker with them (2 Cor. 1.24). He encourages tolerance and understanding of others' difficulties – for example, in the matter of eating meat or observing the Lord's day (Rom. 14.1–6). His policy is not to pass judgement on one another and not to put a stumbling block in another's way (Rom. 14.13).

Finally, nurture in the community follows a complex of deontological, teleological and relational procedures. In the household pattern, fathers are warned against excessive punishment of their children, which might be counter-productive. Rather, they should bring them up in the 'discipline' (*paideia*) and 'instruction' (*nouthesia*) of the Lord (Eph. 6.4). The former denotes the rearing or upbringing of a child, especially in relation to training or teaching or education, but it can also have the more limited sense of discipline or correction. The term *nouthesia* has overtones of warning but also suggests 'reminding'. Christian discipline, though strict, is essentially relational; it is about nurture in the culture of the faith community, which allows one to absorb its ethos and story and, above all, to 'learn Christ' (cf. Eph. 4.20).

Attitude to the world

Paul's attitude to the world is predictably complex. It is always conditioned by the notion of impermanence; 'the form of this world is passing away' (1 Cor. 7.31; cf. 7.29–31). The wisdom of the world has no roots (1 Cor. 1.20–25; 3.18–20). Christians are not to be enslaved by its philosophy, deceit, traditions or elemental principles (Col. 2.8). It is the home of the unrighteous whose carnal ways are the polar opposite of the way of the Christian community (1 Cor. 7.9–11). Yet Paul is not uniformly negative towards it. An embryonic 'natural theology' and 'natural law' motif appears in Romans as it does in the Psalms, and although it cannot be said to be prominent in Paul's thinking it does recognise moral perceptions among the Gentiles (Rom. 1.18–20; 2.14–16). The end might be close at hand, but meanwhile Christians must recognise that institutions such as the state, and the duty to maintain one's dependants, had a place in the divine economy (Rom. 13.1–7; cf. 2 Thess. 3.6–13). Paul's advice to his churches combined a realistic estimate of worldly values with a sense of responsibility as citizens in the world.

Moral procedures and criteria

This interplay of cosmic vision with personal and community *mores* provides a distinctive groundwork for Christian ethics. The initial claim that the latter is fundamentally different from moral philosophy in its procedures is justifiable on these grounds. Many of Paul's moral sentiments are expressed in hortatory form (*paraclesis*: cf. McDonald 1980), designed to reinforce community ethos. It does not follow from this, however, that Paul fails to use recognisable moral procedures and criteria. Briefly, these include:

1 A modified deontology[25] – Paul expressed obligation in terms of commandment, even 'the law of Christ'. No allegation of antinomianism can be sustained against Paul, although his enemies did their best. But for Paul moral requirement – 'deontology' in the strict sense – was no longer to be conceived in terms of the kind of 'covenantal nomism' which characterised Judaism (cf. Sanders 1977: 74, 236), nor in human regulations for the ascetic life, such as 'Do not handle, do not taste, do not touch' (Col. 2.21). In Paul the language of command and obligation, or 'deontology', was contextualised in, and thus modified by, one's relationship with Christ. The same applies to his characteristic juxtaposition and interrelating of indicative and imperative (Gal. 5.25), which seems to derive an 'ought' from an 'is', thus committing what is known as 'the naturalistic fallacy'. The latter, however, refers to an illogicality in proposi-

tional thinking. Paul is moving on a different plane. His discourse is religious and relational, and therefore responsive. The sense of obligation arises out of the religious and moral experience. The indicative denotes 'the grace in which we stand' and the creative energy of faith (Rom. 5.2); the imperative expresses the direction in which the energy impels. But the agent must decide to act accordingly. Moral dynamics – involving motive and motivation, and the overcoming of moral weakness and failure – are important in Paul. No ancient writer was more aware of the weakness of the will and the need for support, inspiration and grace to overcome it.

2   Teleological motifs[26] play a notable role in Paul's ethics: 'make love your aim'; 'reach out towards the prize'. In a religious context, however, the notion is not without paradox. A personal goal is set out in Philippians 3.12–14. The basic image is that of a race, with the prize set in a prominent position at the finishing line. The runner shuts out everything else and concentrates single-mindedly and with total dedication on the prize to be achieved. This image, however, is combined with another. The prize is not tangible, for it is 'God's heavenly calling in Christ Jesus'. But this has already been given by Christ and there is a sense, therefore, in which the faithful strive to attain that which they have already received! They must strive to make their own what they have already received in grace. Paul's mixed metaphors are not merely a matter of paraenetic style. The metaphor of the athlete was almost commonplace and made a point of individual effort and responsibility as against the notion that everything was handed to one on a plate, or the pietistic illusion that one has already attained perfection! Its limitation is that it seems to affirm individual effort alone and thus deny both the grace of God and the place of the church community in divine salvation. The corrective occasions Paul's mixed metaphor. Neither individual effort nor the notion of gift are to be denied. One must earn one's inheritance, work at one's calling, and realise more fully the inexhaustible grace already made effective in one's experience. A similar notion is expressed in Ephesians 4.1, where the basic image is corporate. All have been given gifts for the 'building up of the body of Christ' towards the goal of mature personhood (lit. 'to a perfect man': cf. AV), the standard of the full stature of Christ (Eph. 4.13). Growth in personhood is inseparable from growth in community[27] – once more, a significant departure from the

teleological motifs that commonly appear in philosophical discourse.

3   Consequentialist procedures are associated with the teleological. Paul points to the undesirable consequences of the kind of spirituality which is self-absorbed and does not build up the faith community (1 Cor. 14.4–6), that does not communicate (1 Cor. 14.16–19), or that may be accounted shameful behaviour (1 Cor. 14.35). In nurture within the family, as on public or social occasions, one must reckon with the effects of our actions on others (1 Cor. 8.9–13). Pastoral discipline has to be concerned with aims and consequences (1 Cor. 5.5). To persevere in marriage with an unbelieving partner may have good consequences for all the family (1 Cor. 7.14). Selfish action at the community meal leads to division and humiliation for others (1 Cor. 11.22). The criterion of consequences, of course, always presupposes values by which the moral quality of the consequences can be assessed. These are inherent in the values of the faith community, such as love of one's neighbour, but appeals are sometimes made to 'nature', custom or what is held 'shameful'.

4   Modelling, as noted above, is another important aspect of Paul's moral teaching, combining both deontological and teleological features as well as motivation. Paul uses a familiar rhetorical pattern to pick out contrasting values and so present a model to his charges (1 Cor. 4.16). Parodying their arrogant claims to fulfilment, wealth and royalty (a kind of debased 'noble vision'), he points out that apostles come at the other end of the scale, identifying with Christ's death, and with what the world counts foolishness (1 Cor. 4.8–10). In 1 Thessalonians 1.6–7 and 2.14, the focus is upon faithfulness in circumstances of active discouragement. The Thessalonian Christians followed the pattern of Christ, Paul and the Judean churches, and set an example for all to follow. In Philippians 3.17, Paul urges a communal imitation of his life-style and that of others who follow a similar way: 'You have us for a model'. He thus contrasts the Christian lifestyle with the way that leads to destruction, with the indulging of appetite, taking pride in what should bring shame, and a materialistic outlook. By contrast, the faithful must reflect in their actions the level of moral and spiritual maturity they have already attained (Phil. 3.15–16). This is as yet an imperfect maturity but one which derives the power it has from knowing Christ (Phil. 3.10), identifying with him in suffering and

adversity ('the fellowship of his sufferings') while being sustained by the hope of resurrection.

We turn now, briefly, to other examples of community ethos and moral teaching in the early churches.

Five Diaspora letter groups

The letters of James and 1 Peter are specifically addressed to the Diaspora (Jas. 1.1; 1 Pet. 1.1) and provide a useful contrast to the Pauline corpus. Hebrews represents a distinctive ethos, if not a distinctive ethic. The Pastoral epistles also show a marked development beyond the Pauline model. For our purposes here, the Petrine letters are treated as one group and the Pastorals as another. The letters of John present a useful commentary on the ethos of the Johannine churches.

The upheavals of the Jewish Wars saw the Jerusalem Christian congregation scattered. Many of them seem to have settled on the Syrian coast, near Antioch. It was probably out of this Diaspora situation that there came the Epistle of James, revised (even devised) by his devotees and addressed in his name 'to the twelve tribes in the Diaspora' (Jas. 1.1). Some suggest we should think in terms of an original deposit of Jacobean material, rewritten and incorporated within the letter as we now have it, the abiding memorial to a truly remarkable Jewish Christian leader, but such notions always contain a speculative aspect.[28] The issue of circumcision was no longer of great moment, although interpretation of the Mosaic Law and of religious purity are still to the fore. The context remains one of tension and contention.

When we turn to 1 Peter, the controversy over circumcision has also receded into the past, and even 'the keeping of the law' is no longer a major issue. The document takes the form of 'an apocalyptic Diaspora letter to "Israel"' (Michaels 1988: xlvi), but as with a number of Jewish specimens of the genre it need not have been written from Jerusalem (although many were). The location favoured for its writing is Rome ('Babylon', 5.13), and it is addressed to churches in Asia Minor (1.1). It presupposes a missionary situation, in which the past is left behind and Christians have to make their witness in an unsympathetic or hostile environment (4.3–5, 12–19). The recipients are assumed to be aware of their predominantly Gentile origins and their Jewish heritage in Christ, although they may literally be 'mixed' communities, as

Selwyn suggested (1964: 44). More importantly, the writer – whose Greek is good and whose thought is consistently Jewish – uses a coded type of discourse in which Christian experience is interpreted in Jewish terms. In other words, he is addressing the (largely Gentile) new Israel. It looks as if the older controversies have been left behind, and the mission to the Diaspora (even that term is allegorised: 'the exile') is in a later mode – although there is still a trace of Noah, if not of Noachides![29] As for time scale, the prominence it gives to enduring suffering reflects experience of bitter times, but the deference to institutions and the honouring of the emperor suggest a period of relative peace. It may therefore be placed at some point between Nero's time and that of Domitian. Such a date is after the martyrdom of Peter. The writing is thus pseudonymous, but in the master's name and for the benefit of the mission for which he gave his life. Pauline connections arise not only from the destination of the letter but also from the personnel apparently involved: Silvanus and Mark (5.12–13). However, attempts to classify it as 'deutero-Pauline' – as Schrage does (1988: 268–78), following a long scholarly tradition – are liable to misrepresent its true nature.[30]

Hebrews is a document of uncertain origin and distinctive content – not typically Pauline but related to the Diaspora mission. Discussion of authorship and provenance has been inconclusive. Barnabas, Apollos and others have been suggested as authors, but no case is provable. The phrase 'those from Italy send greetings' (13.24), even if it is part of the original document (which is doubtful), is ambiguous. Does it mean Christians in Italy sending greetings with the document, or Italians in exile sending greetings to fellow Christians in Italy? A Roman connection has been posited on the grounds of 1 Clement's familiarity with it. The title 'To the Hebrews' was known to Pantaenus and Tertullian but cannot be pressed too far. The Septuagint (LXX) is used throughout, and no trace can be found of Jewish concern with circumcision or food laws. The ethos of the document fits that of a Jewish Christian teacher of the Diaspora. The difficulties faced by Diaspora Christians in particular are strongly reflected.

The context of the Pastorals is that of doctrinal controversy with important moral implications. The details of the false teaching are lacking; some have held it to be a kind of gnosis mediated through Judaism (Barrett 1963: 12–16). The contradictory consequences for moral teaching were asceticism and antinomianism or plain immorality. Moreover, Paul's reputation had been sullied by some curious developments. Not unexpectedly, he was attacked by Jewish Christians for undermining the place of the law, but he had also been adopted by heretical teachers who claimed him as a true Gnostic. 2 Peter is explicit in the matter. Properly understood, Paul's letters convey divine wisdom, but 'there are some things in them hard to understand, which the ignorant and unstable twist to their own destruction, as they do the other scriptures' (2 Pet. 3.16). The Pastorals are therefore designed to reassert the balanced message and the authority of the apostle. Such an apologetic aim does not lend itself to the most exciting kind of presentation, but it appears to have been successful. C. K. Barrett has claimed that 'it is to some extent due to the Pastorals that, notwithstanding frontal attack and misunderstanding, the greater epistles of the real Paul held their place in the Canon' (Barrett 1963: 17–18).

The relationship between the Johannine documents is complex, but Gospel and letters recognisably belong to a related ethos (Brown 1982: 14–35; Smalley 1984: xxii). Apart from the alienation of 'the Jews', so evident in the Gospel, the problems of the polarisation of Jewish and Hellenistic Christians is still evident. In consequence, 'law' is still a difficulty, but so also is libertinism or even antinomianism. The moral concerns of the Johannine communities are therefore of considerable moment.

Moral teaching in the letter of James

In James cosmic vision is largely implicit, revealing itself only in a few telling phrases, although these could be the tip of a considerable iceberg. Thus its christology is often described as 'rudimentary', expressed only in phrases such as 'the faith of our Lord Jesus Christ, the Lord of glory' (2.1; cf. 1.1). Faith, so basic to the whole document, is theocentric rather than christocentric (3.9, 17; cf. 4.4–10; 5.11); God is lover of the poor (2.5) and vindicator of the oppressed (5.4), exercising providence over his creation (4.15) and answering prayer (1.5; 4.8; 5.14–18). In terms of eschatology, God will give the crown of life to those who love him, especially to those who have stood firm in trial (1.12). The judge is standing at the doors (5.7–9); the powers of the final age are already at work in the faithful, who are 'a kind of first fruits of his creatures' (1.18). Christians therefore live between the times, holding present and future in tension.

Personal and community ethics follow from this cosmic view and its consequences for the present time. Christians must show no partiality (2.1), but while in Paul this sentiment is addressed to rivalry between Jew and Gentile, in James it is addressed to rich and poor (1.9–11; 2.1–7). Some in the congregation know only too well the oppressive features of a culture where wealth talks, and where the poor are dragged into court without hope of redress (2.6–7; 5.6). Therefore, there must be no class distinction in church, no dishonouring of the poor and no adulation of the wealthy and influential – a hard lesson for a poor church to learn. The church must always remember the reality of the Day of Judgement, the redressing of the balances and the vindication of the righteous. Wealth and riches, as so often in the paraenetic tradition, are execrated because they are part of a quest for power, yet they are transient (1.9–11); they prompt arrogance, oppression and blasphemy, because their illusory power is wielded against the righteousness of God (1.9; 2.6–7; 4.16–17). Traders who think of nothing but profit are likewise pursuing an illusion, and judgement will come on them (4.13–5.6). But faith, or belief, possesses validity only so far as it leads to good action (1.22–27; 2.14–26). The wisdom of God must be shown in a good life (3.13). Scriptural examples reinforce the message (2.20–26) – including an interpretation of Abraham wholly different from Paul's.[31] Moral weight attaches to speech in particular (1.19; 3.1–12).[32] The writer underlines the solemn responsibilities of those who teach – almost to the point of discouragement (3.1). A church problem seems to be in view: 'from the same mouth come blessing and cursing. This ought not to be so' (3.10). Speech is closely related to anger (1.19), to bitter jealousy and selfish ambition (3.14), to fighting and quarrels arising from uncontrolled passions and covetousness (4.1–3). The recipients are warned against speaking evil against one another and usurping God's role as judge (4.11–12). Speech must reflect the divine wisdom, which is pure and peace-loving, gentle and open-minded, full of compassion and the goodness which wisdom produces, straightforward and sincere (3.17). Peace is the necessary context for generating righteousness (3.18). The faithful owe their salvation to God's word of truth (1.18); therefore they must not be false to the truth (3.14). They must be true to the 'implanted word', the message planted in the hearts, with its power to save (1.21). Let them not take oaths but give a straight 'yes' or 'no' (5.12). Those who are compromised – the 'double-minded' – must submit to God, be cleansed and purified, and be humble that God may restore them (cf. 4.8–10). Moral teaching and spirituality are thus closely related. Indeed, a concern for spirituality and pastoral ministry is reinforced in the latter part of the letter (5.13–20).[33]

The attitude to the world is distinctly negative. The world pollutes, renders unholy; the truly religious person avoids being tarnished by it (1.27). 'The world' represents the summation of evil. It evinces itself in the unrestrained tongue, with its destructive fire (3.6). If one is attracted to the things of the world – is its 'friend', in James' language – then one has made an enemy of God, for 'the world' is the source of the strife, envy, arrogance and wrongful ambition that destroy people and communities (cf. 4.1–10). One does not serve the world; one is called to show compassion for the needy in the world (1.27). Religion reinterpreted in these terms is 'to visit orphans and widows in their affliction, and to keep oneself unstained from the world' (1.27).

As far as moral discourse is concerned, the epistle is largely paraenetic – 'paraenetic through and through', according to W. Schrage.[34] It is concerned to reinforce moral conduct with moral instruction and exhortation, and is grounded in a faith which is often worked out amid trials and tribulation (5.7–11). There is an emphasis, therefore, on qualities such as steadfastness and constancy, which make for Christian maturity (1.2–8, 12), and on humility and meekness, controlling anger and resentment which are not consonant with God's righteousness (1.9). There is also, however, a focus on the divine command – 'the perfect law, the law of liberty' (1.25); 'the royal law' (2.8).[35] The immediate reference is to the command to love your neighbour as yourself (Lev. 19.18). It is the opposite of showing partiality, that is, discriminating against one of the parties, particularly the weaker, about whom the Mosaic Law was very concerned (cf. Lev. 19.9–10, 13–18). Leviticus 19 is part of what is sometimes called the law of holiness: 'You shall be holy; for I the Lord your God am holy' (Lev. 19.1). The language is covenantal; the moral requirement is part of the gracious relationship into which God has brought his people. It thus transcends legal requirement and casuistical debate. In this letter, there is a deep distrust of mere discussion, mere words. It is action that is required – in particular, loving action. This is the way to 'fulfil' the law; this is the perfect (complete) way. And this is freedom: to identify with the ethos of God's holy (cleansed, purified) people, and to act accordingly.

A contextual approach rightly pinpoints underlying controversies, with those, for example, who argued that every single law must be observed in full. James cites their battle-cry: 'For whoever keeps the whole law but fails in one point has become guilty of all of it' (2.10). The judgement will fall! But James urges, 'so speak and act as those who are to be judged under the law of liberty. For . . . mercy triumphs over judgement' (2.12–13). Live then in freedom as members of God's holy people, loving your neighbour as yourself. There is also controversy about different ideas of purity, whether the purity required of priest and Temple worshipper, the purity espoused by the Qumran community, the purity of Baptist sects or the purity of the ritually proper household (as with the Pharisees). For James and his church, the messianic community which places its trust in 'our Lord Jesus Christ, the Lord of Glory' (2.1) is the holy people committed in personal, social and community practice to love of one's neighbour. Holiness is now primarily a moral and relational quality, maintained through repentance, spiritual discipline and pastoral care in the community, including confessing sins to one another and praying for one another (5.16), and restoring the fallen (5.19–20). Such a holy people represents the first fruits of the age to come.

1 Peter and its moral teaching

1 Peter is largely concerned with the ethos of the faith community. In terms of cosmic view it reinforces the eschatological nature of the faith, to which the faithful have been brought by baptism (1 Pet. 3.21) and the resurrection of Jesus Christ from the dead. Theirs is an inheritance imperishable, giving cause for rejoicing even when life is difficult (1 Pet. 1.3–9). To this destiny the prophets bore witness; indeed, the Gospel has revealed 'things into which angels long to look' (1.10–12). Above all, they were 'ransomed . . . with the precious blood of Christ, like that of a lamb without blemish and spot' (1.18–19). By this sacrifice, destined from the foundation of the world yet revealed at this final climax of the ages, their salvation is secure. Thus is the Temple cult, with its notion or ritual purity, transcended and superseded. The response of the holy people includes praise to God and confidence in him (1.3, 21), love and reverence for Christ (1.8; 3.15), obedience (1.14) and community love (1.22). One of the features of the letter is its use of the Jewish scriptures (LXX), in which, as Selwyn has observed, the author is 'steeped' (1947: 24). He grounds the ethics of the community in the Holiness Code of Leviticus, citing Sarah as a model for Christian women. The letter has a number of similarities to the Epistle of James, although it has a more highly developed christology. Christ

died 'once for all', the righteous for the unrighteous – even the unrighteous of long ago (3.18–19). In the story of Noah, a few were saved through water. Now through baptism the faith community receives salvation, for it is 'an appeal to God for a clear conscience' through the risen Christ (3.21–22).

From the point of view of this study, however, the abiding value of the letter is in the direct link it establishes between eschatology and personal and community ethics. The faith community is characterised by holiness, a holiness which reflects the divine nature and is expressed in moral conduct (1.14–16). The community lives out the 'holiness code' so fundamental to Jewish liturgy and education (Num. 15.40), and is accountable to God who judges each one impartially (1 Pet. 1.17; cf. Acts 10.34). Built on the cornerstone rejected by human builders but affirmed by God, the community is a living edifice, a spiritual house. To it belong the prerogatives of faithful Israel, 'a chosen race, a royal priesthood, a holy nation, God's own people' (2.9). By God's mercy, its members have been raised from nothing to be the proclaimers of God's 'virtues', his mighty deeds (2.4–10).

This status imposes a corresponding community ethic. Growth within the community is a leading concern (2.2). Hence love for one another, rather than malice and guile, and growth towards salvation are the marks of the holy, moral community, 'for you have tasted the kindness of the Lord' (1.22–23). Leading qualities are empathy, brotherly love, kindness and humility. It has been justly observed that the emphasis in 1 Peter is on *philadelphia*, brotherly or sisterly love, rather than on *agape*, although the latter is not neglected. They should not repay wrong with wrong, but rather bestow a blessing (3.8–12). Members should be able to make a courteous and cogent defence of their faith as part of their witness to the outside world. Most importantly, they should seek to do what is right, even if it is costly (3.13–17). Again, in view of the nearness of the end, it is incumbent upon members to be responsible and prayerful, and above all loving, 'for love cancels a multitude of sins' (4.7–8). They should practise traditional hospitality and a proper stewardship of gifts, so that in everything God may be glorified (4.9–11). The elders should attend to pastoral care (5.1–4); the younger element should show deference and humility, and in due time they too will be exalted by God (5.5–6). Finally, watchfulness is needed. In an alien world, the devil is like a roaring lion on the prowl for prey. Resistance is a primary but demanding requirement, resourced through the solidarity of Christians facing the same experiences of suffering throughout the world. However, the exile has a homeland: the eternal glory in Christ (5.10).

Concerning relationship to the world, perhaps the most striking of the images characterising eschatological existence in 1 Peter is that of 'aliens and exiles' (2.11; cf. Elliott 1982). Indeed, the letter is ostensibly addressed to the 'exiles of the Diaspora' in Asia Minor (1.1), taking geographical exile to symbolise their eschatological condition. Aliens they are from the world of sensual gratification, to the surprise of their Gentile neighbours to whom proper witness must be given – a task which imposes spiritual and personal discipline (2.11–12; 4.1–6). This condition also governs their subjection 'for the Lord's sake' to the authorities, as it does slaves' submission to masters. Such conscientious submission, which may involve the acceptance of undeserved suffering, is endurable because it is undertaken in furtherance of God's will and with his approval, and because it accords with the pattern set by Christ himself (2.15, 20–25). Similar submissiveness on the part of wives may influence their husbands for good (3.1–6), while husbands' respect for their wives is not only because they are 'weaker' but because God's gift of life is something both parties share (3.7). Lack of respect would be inconsistent with devotional practice.

In terms of moral discourse, the most noticeable feature is the juxtaposition of indicative and imperative in the context of life in the faith community. 'Now that you have purified your souls by obedience to the truth until you feel sincere affection towards your fellow Christians, love one another wholeheartedly with all your strength' (1.22 REB). There is an induction into the faith community (cf. 2.2) which leads to a sustained encounter with community love (*philadelphia*), and in turn to the acceptance of the love command. The process of spiritual growth, together with the support of the community, enables one to 'abstain from the passions of the flesh' which characterise worldly behaviour (2.11). Maintaining good conduct among the Gentiles is virtually a debt of honour to the church, as is good service in one's capacity as citizen or subject, servant or family member. There is a norm of 'doing right' which is given with membership of the faith community, and when things are really difficult the example of Christ's patience in suffering inspires. Thus community practice is informed by christological and soteriological perspectives (cf. Schrage 1988: 269). The christological perspective entails the unity of thought and feeling, brotherly affection, kindliness and humility (3.8), and forbids repaying evil for evil (3.9).

Eschatological awareness serves to strengthen spiritual, moral and community life (4.7–11).

Moral teaching in Hebrews

Very briefly, the cosmic vision of Hebrews is fundamental to its position. God's revelation to his people reaches completion in Jesus Christ as Son and Priest – a claim substantiated by detailed scriptural exegesis. Jesus is superior to Moses, is a divinely appointed high priest 'after the order of Melchizedek' (4.14–5.10) and thus superior also to the Levitical priesthood. This high christology and soteriology, however, are specifically related to the human condition. The Son is transcendent, above the angelic order, but identifies with his brothers in faith and is merciful and faithful as their high priest before God (2.17). Moreover, since he himself has been tested in suffering, he is able to help those who are still under severe test (2.18).

There is therefore a close relation between cosmic vision and personal and community morality. The high priest in the heavens is able to sympathise with human weakness, having been tempted in every respect as his followers have been yet without sinning (4.15). What is emphasised in this connection is the worshipping community and the access it has to 'the throne of grace' in order to find mercy and grace to help in time of need (4.16). In Hebrews we find the closest correlation between christology, worship and morality. Through Christ the new covenant is established, when God's laws are 'written on the heart' and God's forgiveness cancels sin (10.16–17). Faithful worship opens 'a new and living way' to God (10.20–22); the community's confession of hope is firm and unswerving because God is to be trusted (12.23). There is point, therefore, in regular meetings, for the worshipping community develops a dynamic for love and active goodness (10.24) and for mutual encouragement (3.13). Faith is, of course, the linchpin and is fully documented from scripture (11.1–40). Christian community is therefore not merely empirical but comprises a 'great cloud of witnesses' who inspire the faithful to run with resolution, Jesus himself being the goal (12.1–2). It is a community of thanksgiving, reverence and awe (12.28).

The writer is well aware that the people he is addressing have encountered trials; they have had a hard struggle (10.32). Their attitude to the world is that it is a place of trial, and trials or temptations require to be faced with the determination and constancy of faith. Abuse and torment, imprisonment and loss of property are specifically mentioned (10.33–34). These now appear to be in the past, but the Christians still need endurance to do God's will and win through to the realisation of what he has promised (10.36). Falling away is a concern for the writer (6.6; 12.3). The concept of discipline is important for the Christian, especially when life is unpleasant and painful (12.5–13). The aim is not simply to overcome the challenge of a hostile world but, realising that this world and its values are passing away, to remain faithful to the end and receive the promised inheritance (6.12).

The moral discourse in Hebrews is strongly exhortatory or paraenetic. The moral admonitions are often general – against drifting off course (2.1), following an example of disbelief (4.11), being slow to learn (5.11) or laxity (6.12). Strong teleological perspectives are derived from christology and eschatology. The Christian life is compared to a race run with eyes fixed on Jesus (12.2). An appropriate aim is peace with everyone and a holy life (12.14). Here we have no lasting city but seek after the city that is to come (13.14). Certain consequences follow from this view, such as the need for determination, constancy and perseverance. Some actions are intrinsically right – love for fellow Christians (13.1; 10.24), hospitality, remembering those in prison, respect for marriage (13.2–4). Other acts are intrinsically wrong, such as living for money (13.5). The writer's main emphasis, however, is on the worshipping community, and therefore on a community ethic of mutual encouragement and watchful care. No one who forfeits the grace of God, no immoral person, can remain in the community to contaminate the rest (12.15–17). Through Jesus the community continually offers the sacrifice of praise. Its moral counterpart may be expressed as kindness and sharing. 'These are the sacrifices of which God approves' (13.15–16).

Moral teaching in the Pastorals

As has been suggested above, particular importance is attached to cosmic vision. The story of the creation and fall is used to insist that creation is good (1 Tim. 4.4) but spoiled by the sin of Adam and Eve – a story which is taken to underline the subordination of women (1 Tim. 2.11–14). There is emphasis on the salvation effected by God through Jesus Christ, on divine grace and on life and immortality through the Gospel (cf. 2 Tim. 1.9–10). Eschatological tension is affirmed. Salvation is both a future hope and a present reality through the Spirit (Tit. 3.5–7, though reference to the Spirit is less common in the Pastorals than in Paul's major letters). It is important that the true story of the Gospel be heard, not 'Jewish myths' and 'commands of men who reject the truth' (cf. Tit. 1.14), probably a reference to teachers of a Jewish kind of gnosis.

In terms of personal and community ethics, the general aim is presented clearly: 'love (*agape*) that issues from a pure heart and a good conscience and sincere faith' (1 Tim. 1.5). Since the church is a worshipping community, there is a correlation between worship and moral practice: 'a quiet and peaceable life, godly and respectful in every way' (1 Tim. 2.2). The Christian life flows from faith; conversely, righteous deeds do not earn salvation but express the working of the Spirit in the life of the baptised community (Tit. 3.6). In general, the simple life is commended, emphasising contentment and avoiding materialistic desires (1 Tim. 6.7–10). However, any attempt to interpret this teaching in ascetic terms is swiftly countered. Marriage should not be forbidden (1 Tim. 4.3); abstinence from food and wine is not enjoined (1 Tim. 4.3; 5.23; 6.17). Everything God has created is good, to be received and consecrated with thanksgiving (1 Tim. 4.4–5). Laws are to restrain bad conduct, and the Gospel endorses them (1 Tim. 1.8–11). The virtues commended in bishop and flock alike – characteristically broken down by age, sex and social position – are unexceptionable and likely to gain wide credence (cf. 1 Tim. 3.1–7; Tit. 2.1–15). They describe a safe, middle-of-the-road moral position, renouncing 'irreligion' and worldly passions, and endorsing sobriety, uprightness and godliness (Tit. 2.12).

As for authority, there is a high doctrine of the church in the Pastorals, involving an emphasis on church discipline and also on example. Office-bearers have a special role to play in these areas. The memory of Paul the apostle carries great weight. While he is seen, as Barrett puts it, through a haze of hero-worship (Barrett 1963: 30), he is invoked as a presence exerting discipline (1 Tim. 1.19–20) and commending scriptural teaching (2 Tim. 3.14–17). His authority springs from his special calling and, above all, from the quality of his ministry in the face of persecution and suffering (2 Tim. 3.10–13). Timothy and Titus are now the upholders of this ministry, with its evangelistic and teaching tasks. The 'faithful men' (2 Tim. 2.2) they train for work within the church communities must also set the same kind of example as Paul himself afforded. In this way, they will uphold his authority.[36]

The attitude to the world is complex. On the one hand, the world generates vices and wrong aims and promotes disorder, as well as representing an epoch that is soon to be superseded. On the other hand, it recognises virtue and has its own estimate of moral worth. Titus must show such qualities as a teacher that 'an opponent may be put to shame, having nothing evil to say of us' (Tit. 2.7–8). Among his other qualities, a 'bishop' must be well thought of by the non-Christian public, so that he may not give rise to scandal or be snared by the devil (1 Tim. 3.7). The Christian communities are now bidding for recognition as moral communities in the ancient world.

Moral procedures are fairly conventional. The Pastorals are, on the whole, paraenetic, exhortatory and moralistic in tone. Nevertheless, there is appreciation of the dialectic of faith and action, the Christian life being grounded in faith, not law, though law has a role in containing wrongdoing. There are teleological perspectives; there is a community ethos based on *agape*; there is emphasis on the importance of example or modelling; and ideas of virtue and vice, while in many respects shared by non-Christians, are related to the overall moral picture.

The ethos of the Johannine Epistles

Exaggerated pictures have been presented of the subordination of moral concern to the salvation motif in the Gospel of John in particular (cf. J. T. Sanders 1975: 100). Certainly, the combination of rejection by the synagogues as well as the wider world, alienation from some Christian groups and intense eschatological expectation led to a degree of introversion in community life. In the Johannine cosmic vision, the high christology of Sonship was asserted over against the denial of the messiahship of Jesus by 'the Jews' and the low christology of Jewish Christian groups (Smalley 1984: xxiii-iv) and emphasised the 'salvation' side of the Christian equation. God's love is seen in the sending of the Son to elicit 'belief' and thus rescue those who are otherwise 'perishing' (John 3.16).

Where does this strong mission statement leave moral teaching? In terms of community ethos, the Johannine communities turned in on themselves to a degree, expressing *agape* as *philadelphia* or community love as opposed to love for the other as outsider. 'Love seems almost like a huddling together for warmth and safety in the face of the world' (Houlden 1973: 39). Yet God's love, the source of this community's mission statement, is for the world. The Son who came to bring life is incarnate – born in the flesh (John 1.14, 18). Docetic tendencies are also severely checked. In washing the disciples' feet, Jesus memorably demonstrated the pattern of love as service to others and the reverse of status claims (John 13.1–17). Hence, in terms of moral procedures, we may see an element of modelling here. There is also a paradoxical awareness of commandment. The great commandment was now embedded in the relationship of Christ and the disciples as 'friends' of Jesus (John 15.11–17). Indeed, Jesus' teaching takes the form of a testamentary address, the bequest of the master to his disciples (Brown 1966: 498–600); and 'the Johannine commandments to "love one another" are at the very centre of the moral and spiritual legacy which is presented in the Farewell Discourses' (Furnish 1973: 135). In the epistles, not only is the ambiguity of the 'old' and 'new' commandment explored (1 John 2.7–11), but love is given a strongly relational orientation (1 John 4.7–12). It is bound up with 'abiding in God' and receiving the Spirit. John thus operates with a highly modified deontology.

As we have seen, alienation characterises the community's relationship to the world, and much healing is needed. But two factors prevent us from endorsing the caricatures of the unloving community as far as the world is concerned. One is that the world is the object of God's love (John 3.16). The other is that love abides in God; if we have the Spirit of God, we cannot hate people in the world, however much we deplore their conduct and hostility. Indifference to people may be consistent with a kind of gnosis, but not with the Johannine Gospel which seeks moral integrity in loving not in word or speech but in deed and action (1 John 3.18).[37]

CONCLUSION

Our exploration of the ethos of the early Christian communities may be rounded off with a number of brief conclusions, largely with the purposes of clarification, emphasis and caution in mind.

All the communities were profoundly affected by their context. Communities acknowledged boundaries of their own, but this fact does not put them into a sealed compartment. They belong to the sweep of the history of their times and relate to socio-religious dynamics of the period.

The formal arguments in the letters and documents tend to have specific foci or concerns, and thus do not always reflect the entire ethos of the faith communities. Paul's formal arguments – for example, about justification by faith – do not give prominence to thanksgiving, for he has particular polemical aims in view. His letters, however, do reflect the ethos of thanksgiving, praise and prayer which are the high points of the worshipping community. The form of the Lord's Supper he recommends begins on the note of *eucharisteia*. The ethos of the community is defined by what it is, rather than by specific arguments.

In the interplay of cosmic vision and community ethic, there is two-way traffic. The cosmic vision is shaped by the memory and experience of the community, and the community is shaped by the power of the cosmic vision.

The ethos is multi-cultural and diverse: Jews, Greeks, Scythians, men, women, freedmen and slaves, rich and poor, males and females. It is this very problematic diversity which prompts the emphasis on unity and divine impartiality. These features not only represent the indicative of baptism and grace, they also embody a call to Christians to capture in their own communities the unity of faith in the bond of peace.

The ethos of the communities is defined by their leading model, Christ, and those who reflect the pattern of his ministry. Various emphases emerge from this *imitatio Christi* or *imitatio dei*: faithfulness, love, truthfulness, steadfastness in trial and – for the vision of Christ has always an eschatological aspect – hope. The mutual support of the community is essential for preserving such an ethos and countering destructive trends.

Because the ethos is contextual and combative, much care is needed in drawing conclusions for ethics today. The central principles may possess an enduring validity, but they are organically related to the overarching cosmic vision and lose meaning if divorced from it. Again, all specific and concrete statements must be related to their contextual purpose, which is often controversial and combative. To indulge in non-contextual exegesis is to risk endorsing what would be, in the modern context, highly prejudicial views – whether related to issues such as anti-Semitism, sexual proclivity, gender differentiation, economic status or political authority. Some of these issues are discussed in the following chapters.

2

MORAL INTERPRETATION

The scriptural foundations
of Christian ethics

In the first chapter, the moral context of the early Christian communities was seen to be fundamental to the moral ethos which these communities developed. This ethos was explored through the use of a descriptive model designed to show the correlation of cosmic vision with personal and community ethics in particular, and to note the nature of the moral discourse involved. Underlying these developments was the use of the scriptures of Israel, particularly in their Greek form (the New Testament had not yet come into existence). In this second chapter, attention is focused more particularly on the question of the role of scriptural interpretation in the making of the Christian ethos. However, it must be recognised that morality is not simply a matter of instruction. The converts to the early Christian communities brought with them the habits and presuppositions of a lifetime, together with relationships and involvements with the life of society which could not always be abandoned totally. To be sure, conversion entailed transformation, but converts did not lose their identity or distinctive characteristics. What is involved is incorporation into the new communities and the nurture they offered. This certainly included engagement with patterns of Christian moral teaching which might confirm or transform previous attitudes and invited reinterpretation of previous moral assumptions.

If we were to ask on what Christian morality was based, the popular answer might well be 'the teaching of Jesus', or 'the ten commandments', or even 'the Bible'. While such answers contain truth, they are not entirely adequate. The teaching of Jesus is important (we will look at it more closely in the next chapter), but Jesus himself was an interpreter of scripture, pointing beyond himself to creation, covenant and prophets in Israel, and above all to the will and purpose of God. While the ten commandments formed an important part of the moral teaching of the Torah or Law of Moses, their context was that of the covenant with Israel and they required to be interpreted accordingly.

This hermeneutical dimension was far reaching. It involved much more than simply recognising the force of the commandments and the moral concern of Israel's religious tradition. To read the scriptures was to claim an identity with Israel as the people of God. It was to identify with the story of God's dealings with his creation through his people. It was to evoke the memory of covenant and promise, of salvation itself. For Christian communities, it was to follow the story through to the fulfilment of God's promises in Christ and thus discover a new way of understanding what God had accomplished. Here was the *eschaton* – the end-time, the time of salvation – appearing in the midst of history and providing a new focus for thought and devotion, new perspectives and new possibilities. Prominent among these was a new way of reading the scriptures, so that they testified to Christ, and Christ opened up new understandings of them.

In this chapter, we explore some of the 'necessary possibilities'[1] of these developments. We will be concerned with how the early Christians interpreted the totality of the tradition – the scriptures as a whole – and we will try to understand the implications of eschatology and related matters for moral thought and practice. In particular, we shall attempt to set the memory of Jesus' ministry in eschatological perspective and to appreciate the importance of christocentric perspectives on the scriptures for moral understanding in the early churches.

MEMORY, INTERPRETATION AND THE TOTALITY OF TRADITION

The variety, even the pluralism, of the early Christian Church should not obscure its essential coherence. Whatever their differences, the faith communities were united in the confession of Jesus as Lord and in their commitment to a way of life that was well pleasing to God, the creator and judge of all. This identification of Jesus with the ultimate purpose of God indicated that through his ministry, death and resurrection – what we shall call 'the Christ event' – the *eschaton* or final age had been brought close to them, so that its 'necessary possibilities' determined their worship, life-style and self-understanding. In this prophetic stance their moral outlook was characterised by a dialectic between the penultimate and the ultimate, between responsibility for present action and the claim of the future, between the situational issue and the categorical requirement, a dialectic which gives Christian ethics its special nature (cf. Rogerson 1995: 17–26). To live with the dialectic, however, required not only the strenuous guidance of apostles and teachers but also a sharing in the nature of the Christ event. The churches were therefore communities of memory and interpretation, whose identity and life were dependent on 'faithful remembering of God's care of his creation through the calling of Israel and the life of Jesus' (Hauerwas 1981: 53), although the Christ event is wider than the life of Jesus. Through such activity they came to share an active awareness not of 'battles long ago' nor even of the recent past but of the merging of past, present and future in the present claim of Christ. In a sense, therefore, they were in the process of recreating their tradition. As has been well observed, the presence of the prophetic factor in canon and church life 'means that it will always be possible to remould tradition as a source of life-giving power' (Blenkinsopp 1977: 152).

Intuitively the churches were feeling their way towards, or were being led into, an understanding of history and interpretation which, however paradoxically, anticipated aspects of modern debate (Cf. Clines 1995: 77–106). If they did not have the putative benefits of modern historical criticism, they were at least free of the distorting and inhibiting effects which form the less creative side of its bequest.[2] They had the sense of living in the flow of history, within which God was active. Hence they had a strong sense of living tradition, of continuity and discontinuity, as the thrust of history moved forward, demanding their own participation and action. They recognised that the story they remembered as their own demanded change – in themselves, their understanding of their world and their values. Their story did not simply endorse their established life-world, but demanded that they identify with what they were led to see as the purpose of God in history (cf. Auerbach 1968: 48).

Their remembrance of the past, while selective, was not subjective. It was controlled by scripture and tradition. The scripture was, of course, the sacred books of Israel, most often in Greek translation (the LXX) and embodying the formative traditions of Israel's faith. Theirs was primarily an oral tradition, in which the message was 'inscribed on the heart': that is, memorised and understood. The scriptures were read in public and in communities; they were expounded, taught, argued over and applied. They were searched for the means of identifying 'the signs of the times', the indications of the final events that would establish the new aeon. They were not written on tablets of stone, nor bound in a pocket-sized book for casual consultation. The 'Gutenberg galaxy'[3] was nowhere in evidence. Reading was a corporate event, a searching for and a sharing of meaning; and in the sharing the weaker were supported by the strong. Such shared meanings in time became traditions – like Pharisaic casuistry or Qumranic commentary and community rule, briefly discussed below. All such religious communities had their teachers and teachings. Induction into the community or movement involved learning its ways and ethos, and how its identity was established through the interpretation of scripture. The variety of genres in scripture itself – whether poetry or prophecy, sagas or saws – required imaginative handling. The dominant conviction was that scripture had great depths. To read it literally was to move at a superficial level, no more than the first intimation of divine mystery. To enter into that mystery one must seek the deeper truth, whether moral or mystical, metaphorical or practical.[4] The vocation of the interpretative community was to express in its own life the concern for justice, love and impartiality which was consonant with such perceived and revealed truth.

Of course it can be argued that the scriptural tradition of Israel is itself vulnerable on moral grounds. It was hopelessly one-sided; it adopted a monocular perspective; everything was told from the standpoint of the dominant culture – a limitation imposed by a lack of critical historical *nous* (cf. Carroll 1991). The perspective of the gifted Canaanite civilisation, for example, is nowhere in evidence, nor does anyone speak for the Egyptian army at the Sea of Reeds. The people of the land are silent. Israel hears what Israel has to hear! Such modern critiques are not without substance, and there is an ethics of interpretation which requires that new insights, however precious, must not be expressed in a manner prejudicial to others, and that justice is done to hidden or suppressed perspectives (cf. Fiorenza 1988: 15). Nevertheless, the scriptures are not an ancient history lesson, nor an encyclopaedic excursion into ancient civilisations. It remains a point of historical as well as religious importance that it was the religious tradition of Israel which mothered Judaism and Christianity – and arguably Islam as well. Therefore, to attend to the particular perspectives which Israel's scriptures offer is to begin a journey of deeply religious significance. To travel in the presence of Christ is already to have adopted critical openness to the outsider.

To know the scriptures was to know and identify with Israel's story, to recognise it as a true story and make it one's own story. True, it was not a uniformly narrative tradition – as we suggested above, it contains many genres – but its overall concern was to tell the story of God's people Israel and to ensure that Israel remained true to her vocation. To grasp the totality of the story required comprehensive symbols, such as 'Torah' or 'Moses'. The first five books of scripture can be summarily described by either term. Here is God's teaching (*torah*) of Israel, through his greatest prophet (Deut. 34.10–12). Here is the story of creation and fall, of covenants and commandments. The Torah was the hub of Jewish scripture, although the need for commentary was recognised by many. It was provided in various measures by the Prophets and Writings (although the Writings and to some extent the Prophets were open ended, and it was some time after the rise of the Christian churches before the canon was closed). For the Pharisees the oral tradition of interpretation was a *sine qua non*, not least for reasons already mentioned: the word of scripture had to be heard and acted on within the interpretative community. The Pharisaic ideal, which became normative in Judaism after the disasters of the Jewish Wars, was that every detail of life was to be controlled by Torah. This was achieved by the most detailed scrutiny of scripture and by casuistry or case law as changing circumstances required. As for the priestly community, the Torah prescribed their cultic duties, and there may well have been a priestly commentary to explain precise practice.[5] For the Qumran community, the commentary revealed the hidden eschatological message.[6] The Community Rule, a code of regulatory teaching, governed the life of their community. Generally, the understanding of ethics was 'deontological': moral teaching prescribed what must be done, and the exposition was in the hands of recognised teachers. Thus Israel's way was safeguarded and the community's identity preserved and enhanced. The faith of Jesus' followers shared in the expectation of imminent eschatological fulfilment. What is deeply significant about their faith, however, is not so much the details of the cosmic upheavals and the visions of the new world but the fact that the tradition was now being fed into a particular crystallisation which represented the totality of God's purpose at the crisis of the ages. Their resort to apocalypticism, for all its peculiarities, was not merely an opt-out clause in their nation's contract with history. It represented – again in a peculiar way, and under stress – memories of Israel's heritage, interpretations of its history and, above all, a longing for

God's purpose to reach 'fulfilment', or total expression, in the present.

ESCHATOLOGY AND MORAL AMBIGUITY

To attempt to present a neat account of the relationship of eschatology and ethics in the tradition of Israel is to risk an oversimplification of a highly complex subject.[7] The raw material of eschatology has been described as 'multivariate metaphors, images and figures, often inconsistent, contrary, and contradictory', the various books of scripture providing 'impressionistic and paradoxical elements lacking a unifying structure' (Carroll 1990: 200). Many factors contributed to this rich, if perplexing, tapestry. We may instance differences of perspective in the communities that comprised ancient Israel, varieties of contexts and situations which coloured their thinking, and the factor of cultural interchange subtly informing Israelite expectation.

The ideology of the kingdom is one area where foreign influence is readily detected, shaping a mythology which is reflected in eschatology and, even more, in apocalypticism, with its unveiling of future cosmic upheavals. Yet the notion of kingship comprehends the moral tradition of Israel. The reign of the Isaianic king will not only be filled with the joy of harvest and victory but will afford good government characterised by justice, righteousness and well-being, when implements of war will be converted to peaceful purposes (Isa. 9.2–7; 11.1–9). A similar scenario is presupposed in the pastoral picture of the smallholder enjoying life in peace, security and neighbourly fellowship under his own vine and fig tree (Zech. 3.10; cf. Mic. 4.4). But as Israel was overwhelmed by disaster after disaster and such longings appeared totally unrealisable, eschatological hope was couched more and more in apocalyptic and explicitly mythological terms, with the focus on the cosmic upheaval by which God would overthrow the bestial powers that hold the world in thrall and inaugurate through divine intervention the rule of the saints (cf. Dan. 7.1–14). Now the emphasis was on faithful endurance and on remaining loyal under stress.

Such sweeping scenarios often ignored implicit moral issues. For example, the final destiny of Jerusalem was a matter of great concern to Israel. According to one tradition, the city was to be a world focus of unity, the nations streaming to it to find divine instruction and share in peace under God (Isa. 2.2–4; Mic. 4.1–3;

Zech. 14.16). Here Zion was virtually the focus of a comprehensive world faith, even if it had a particular centre. Elsewhere, the thought was that when Jerusalem was renewed no strangers or foreigners would ever again violate its sanctity (Joel 3.17; cf. Isa. 52.1). The common factor in the differing pictures was the purity and inviolability of the Temple, which would never again be misused (cf. Zech. 14.21). The tension between openness and sectarianism was a powerful factor in Israel's tradition, reflecting the bitterness of experience but also involving moral failure. In these terms one can set Isaiah 40 and the so-called Suffering Servant passages, with Ruth, Jonah and Jeremiah, over against the determinedly exclusive Ezra and Ezekiel. Again, the book of Isaiah, which in its final form includes some of the most sublimely universal sentiments, closes with a remarkable juxtaposition of the new heavens and new earth, when 'all flesh shall come to worship before me', and the death and destruction of the rebellious (Isa. 66.22–24). The question of particularity, which is inherent in the notion of the chosen or holy people, presents an unresolved moral dilemma in Israel and a moral issue for all who claim to stand in its tradition. It is reflected in the New Testament in pictures of the Last Judgement where the fate of the elect is sharply contrasted with the destruction of the wicked. Paul faced the same problem when discussing the unity of Jews and Christians in the people of God – but the particular condition was belief in Jesus as the Christ (cf. Rom. 9–11 *passim*).[8]

Moral ambiguity is found to an acute degree in apocalypticism. Whether stemming in the main from prophetic or wisdom roots, apocalypticism addressed the present fears, confusions, contradictions and sufferings of the nation through a claim to unveil or reveal the hidden purpose of God. Within the ample scope of its creative imagination, it portrayed the coming of the transcendent new age, with cosmic upheavals, the appearance of the deliverer from heaven, the defeat of God's enemies (who were, of course, the enemies of Israel also) and the vindication of the elect. Defying rational assessment of events and common-sense views, it presents at times a deliberate parody or counterpoint to worldly power structures and points to fundamental realities, 'the way things really are'. It can be accused of taking the easy way out by projecting a dream world in face of despair. It is open to dangerous manipulation by the fanatical and the obsessed. Yet, for all the moral ambiguity of the medium, it is basically on the side of the angels. Its metaphorical coding enabled it to give voice to the claims of the oppressed, the persecuted and the hopeless which would otherwise have had to remain unexpressed (cf. Rowland 1982: 1988). Indeed, it is this moral strain which in large measure provides its validation as an expression of the tradition of God's people, Israel.

In New Testament studies, much has been written about the relation of eschatology to ethics since the revolution in interpretation effected by Weiss and Schweitzer and, more specifically, the pioneering work of Amos Wilder (cf. McDonald 1993: 65–95). In reaction to liberal influence, with its assumption of eternal (moral) truths, many studies of 'New Testament ethics' have emphasised the limiting, even undermining, role of eschatology in relation to moral thinking (e.g., J. T. Sanders 1975: 1–11; Houlden 1973: 9–13). More recently, a corrective to such extremes has become apparent; eschatology can reinforce ethics (Hays 1997: 20–7).

An important aspect, relatively neglected in the discussion, has been the relation of creation and eschatology. Creation is, of course, implicit in the theology of the kingdom in Israel's symbolic world. Yahweh, King of Israel, is creator and sustainer, the victor in the struggle with the chaos monster. From him humankind derives its 'dominion' of the created order (Gen. 1.26–28) – a stewardship, not an absolute dominion, for the creator is also King (cf. Gibson 1981: 80–2). The enthronement psalms reaffirm the sovereignty of the creator, who will also judge the world with justice and faithfulness (cf. Ps. 96). Creation, eschatology and moral order thus interact. In short,

> the creation strand provides a critical balance to the more limited 'Israelite' theology and preserves the idea of divine sovereignty over the entire cosmos. Later, it is evident in apocalypticism, which is really the old creation/chaos conflict transferred into the future. It is explicit in the devotions of Judaism. Indeed, it is the element which enabled Judaism to survive the collapse of apocalyptic hopes and praise 'the King of the universe who bringeth forth good from the earth'. It is represented in much of the Kingdom language in the Gospels and in Revelation.
>
> (Chilton and McDonald 1987: 50)

The Qumran community testifies to the positive relation between creation, eschatology/apocalypticism and ethics. In protest against the corrupt ways of the Temple authorities, this community of intense piety awaited the cosmic upheaval which would purge

Israel of pollution and restore the true Temple. Every study, every act of devotion was directed to this end. There was even an elaborate plan of action for the final conflict or Armageddon, in which the saints would be victorious and the enemies of Yahweh utterly destroyed.[9] Meanwhile, the community, freed from pollution by baptismal washings, maintained its purity through moral action. The Community Rule set out in detail the required code of conduct, possibly for the guidance of teachers or guardians. True to apocalyptic perspectives, there was a complete dualism between truth and falsehood, right and wrong; there were no shades of grey. There were detailed instructions for the initiates and rules for its common life and discipline. It was, as we have noted already, thoroughly rules-based or deontological, prescribing duties which must be carried out. Fear of the laws of God had to be instilled in the heart. But it also had, perforce, a concern for personal character and qualities, which contributed to and sustained community life: humility, patience, charity in abundance, unending goodness, understanding and intelligence. Clearly at Qumran, creation, eschatology and ethics cohered; moral ambiguity was overwhelmed by the righteous wrath of the Holy God.[10]

For the early Christian faith communities, the Christ event stood as the focus of the cosmic drama of salvation, related as it was to Jewish and messianic eschatological world views. Moral ambiguity was by no means absent from the picture – particularly in the judgemental strain of apocalypticism, represented above all in the Apocalypse of John. Yet the churches were intrinsically moral communities, dedicated to knowing and doing the will of God. Visionary extravagance was more than balanced by the recollection of the historical ministry and mission of Jesus. Even in the early 'Q' tradition (Matt. 11.25–27/Luke 10.21–22), Jesus was seen as the envoy of divine Wisdom (Tuckett 1996: 279–80), while in the Johannine tradition he was interpreted as incarnating the Logos or divine Word (John 1.14, 18). Hence the Christians interpreted scripture in the light of the Christ event, and interpreted the Christ event in the light of scripture. The result was that the moral element was always kept in the foreground of their common life. Although the tradition will be discussed more fully in the next chapter, something requires to be said here about these fundamental matters.

ESCHATOLOGY, ETHICS AND THE
MEMORY OF JESUS' MINISTRY

The eschatological age of fulfilment, centred in Christian terms on Jesus, was remembered as a sequence of events that began with the Baptist's ministry. Indeed, it was the Christians, rather than Baptist sectarians, who preserved the record of John's ministry, although it was a public event as Josephus' account confirms (*Antiquitates Judaicae* 18.5.2). The early strands of the New Testament emphasised his eschatological significance. John called Israel to repentance and baptism, apparently as the first stage of the messianic action, to be completed by 'one greater than I'. There is no sign here of Armageddon, but much emphasis on the radical nature of the coming judgement. With this imminent eschatology John combined a strong ethical note. Repentance (*teshuvah*) was a turning to God, and to turn to God was to participate in his righteousness. This was the unconditional call. When the early churches and perhaps Jesus himself looked back on John the Baptist, they saw him standing at the threshold of the new age, the age of fulfilment (cf. Luke 16.16; Matt. 11.12; cf. Tuckett 1996: 137).

The ministry of Jesus was presented in the same framework of eschatology, extending (in the main) from his baptism to his ascension. The question of eschatology and ethics has been raised repeatedly in relation to his teaching. Its most celebrated form was the 'interim ethics' approach of Weiss and Schweitzer, associated with a 'consistent' or 'thoroughgoing' interpretation of eschatology. These views have been influential, but 'interim ethics' as the characterisation of Jesus' teaching is, at best, only a half-truth, although a significant milestone for critical scholarship (cf. McDonald 1993: 75–95). Subsequent scholarship has wrestled with other possibilities, such as realised or inaugurated eschatology. The danger of such views is that of reading into the material extraneous perspectives which come from the theological or philosophical world of the interpreter. As one critic has put it, 'the texts are inchoate and variable and so cannot be used to demonstrate a fully worked-out view of the future' (Carroll 1990: 202). What one can do, however, is examine characteristic features of Jesus' ministry for indications of inherent eschatological emphasis. One can certainly find evidence of eschatological urgency in, for example, Jesus' initial proclamation of the kingdom of God and the disciples' mission to Israel, implying an imminent eschatology. Certain texts – admittedly ambiguous but well attested *cruces* of New Testament interpretation – suggest that the kingdom was in some way present in and through Jesus' ministry. 'If I by the finger of God [or 'the Spirit of God'] cast out demons, then the kingdom of God has come upon you' (a 'Q' passage: Matt. 12.28/Luke 11.20). 'The kingdom of God is in your midst' [or 'within you' or 'among you'] (Luke 17.20). Such passages do not justify a theory of 'realised' or 'inaugurated' eschatology, both of which are twentieth-century constructs. They might be used to support the primacy of a charismatic, miracle-working ministry (cf. S. L. Davies: 1995). But the parables of Jesus take us back to the centrality of teaching in Jesus' ministry and to the interpretation of eschatological symbols such as the kingdom of God. When a gifted teacher is confronted with a symbolic world which is complex, confusing and contradictory (and who can deny that the eschatological and apocalyptic tradition in Jesus' day was precisely that?), a possible strategy is to select leading symbols and explore them in such a way that meaning is created for and with the audience and the reality of what is signified is encountered as a presence, a living truth. The parabolic ministry of Jesus would seem to be precisely of this kind (cf. Shillington 1997). Hence it is at least reasonable to conclude that Jesus' ministry was in its entirety an enactment of ultimate concern in the particular circumstances of his day. If we may coin a phrase, it is a 'performative' approach to eschatology. Cosmic meaning – including cosmic conflict – is played out in the theatre of his ministry. When that ministry takes him to death on a cross, that too is seen in the same eschatological context (cf. Chilton and McDonald 1987: 31–43).[11]

The fact that John and Jesus were interpreted in terms of earlier figures (Elijah, a greater than Elijah or Jonah, son of David) indicates that they were seen to encapsulate in their ministries the spirit and purpose of Israel's tradition and to give it new direction. In this sense they 'fulfilled' scripture – not in the literal sense of word for word correspondence (as ever, the literal distorts the point) but in the sense of crystallising the tradition in its totality at a critical moment in the history of Judaism and so opening up new possibilities for it. The potentiality of the end-time, the time of fulfilment, was thus made real in their life and death. To confess that Jesus is risen and seated at the right hand of God was to say that a new transaction had taken place between God and creation, and entirely by divine initiative. All that had gone before and all that was yet to come could now be reread in the light of his story. The tradition had been effectively re-centred and had acquired a new spirit.

Such a re-centring offers a powerful hermeneutical tool. The scriptures of Israel, the testimony to its faith and life, could be read in the light of Christ, and Christ could be read in the light of scripture. The life of the churches was bound up with such activity, and they did not find the task free of difficulty. A re-centring brought obsolescence to some aspects of scripture, not only circumcision and sabbaths (the prophets had sought a partial reorientation along similar lines) but also moral and legal aspects, such as some expressions of the *lex talionis*, or principle of retribution. It also revitalised others – covenant, freedom, reconciliation and forgiveness, for instance. A new spirit was engendered in the churches, cohering with the Spirit of Christ. Hence to remember Jesus and his work was to know his presence and benefits. Past and present merged. The remembered Jesus was a power in the midst of the community and in the believer's experience. A new age had dawned, and with it a new morality was affirmed, based on the community of faith, the people of God, but cohering with the 'totality' of God's purpose for his creation.

SCRIPTURE, CHRISTOCENTRIC INTERPRETATION AND ETHICS

The Christian faith communities absorbed scriptural meaning into their very being. Divine teaching had, after all, to be 'remembered and taken to heart' (Deut. 6.6 REB). It was to inform the whole of life, so that the believer was to be engrossed in its possibilities and requirements. The churches worked mainly with the Greek translation (the LXX), exploring meaning in the light of the tradition of Jesus' teaching, itself carried in the mind, and in the light of the Christ event. The outcome of interpretation was the strengthening of faith through deeper understanding of God's ways and the reinforcing of moral practice. To know God's will is to understand what one must do.

The scriptural foundations of their moral practice can be illustrated briefly from selected themes of church faith and practice.

Justification

James and Paul appear to come down on opposite sides in the dispute about justification by faith or works. The pitch has been queered by the history of the debate since Reformation times, and the ancient disputes still affect modern interpretation (cf. Marxsen

1993: 18, 260–3). Tradition, however, is open to correction and renewal, and it is well to make a fresh start in properly contextual vein. Here, the focal concept is that of the *Aqedah*, the story of Abraham's offering of his son Isaac in Genesis 22.1–14 (cf. Vermes 1961: 193–227).

While James appeals to the Aqedah, he readily uses the term 'justified by works', but his reading of the story was that 'faith was active along with his works, and faith was completed by works' (James 2. 21–22). Faith alone is not enough; faith must be expressed in action. This is what it means to be counted as righteous by God (2.23–24; cf. Gen. 15.6) and to be the friend of God (Isa. 41.8; 2 Chron. 20.7). The writer's mind then jumps to the story of Rahab the harlot to reinforce the importance of what one does (Jas. 2.25; Josh. 2.1–21). The argument may well have been directed against views which emphasised the primacy of faith while denying the importance of loving action in the world. Such views might be found in certain charismatic or apocalyptic groups, as well as in some which reflected 'a kind of gnosis'. Paul was as exercised about them as James, for their presence was felt across the entire range of Christian communities. The wider context of James' passage, however, concerns the honour paid to the wealthy in the churches, to the neglect of the poor (2.1–7; cf. 1.10–11). His intended target is therefore the richer Christians – the new Christian bourgeoisie – emerging in Asia Minor and the city churches of the Gentile world. Negative consequences of their dominance included the involvement of church members in litigation (2.6) as well as the sin of 'partiality' (2.4). It is with this kind of situation in mind that James cites 'the royal law' of love (2.8) and underlines the necessity of expressing the will of God in one's actions.

Interestingly, the writer to the Hebrews also cites the Aqedah (Heb. 11.17–20). Here it is suggested that it was through his faith that Abraham was ready to offer Isaac, trusting to God to raise him from the dead (as, in a sense, he did). Indeed, in some rabbinic circles, the Aqedah became a symbol of resurrection. However, the writer also cites other parts of the Abraham tradition, such as his journeyings and goal (not to speak of Sarah's conceiving of a child in advanced years), all of which emphasise basic trust in God.

In his underpinning of the Gentile mission, Paul did not explicitly cite the Aqedah, but it is implicit in his thought, for the promise to Abraham (of which Paul makes much) is associated with the Aqedah as well as other parts of the Abraham tradition (cf. Gen.

12.15–18). His intertextual use of the scriptures affirmed faithfulness to God as the condition of 'life' (cf. Hab. 2.4). This notion of faith or faithfulness had a strong moral quality. The reckless, conceited and arrogant, like the oppressive rich, represented the denial of faithfulness (Hab. 2.4–11). To be faithful to the God of righteousness meant to live righteously. Here is common ground with James. When Paul invoked the image of Abraham as one who 'lived by faith', this did not exclude the fact that Abraham acted righteously. To allege outright opposition between Paul and James in this matter is to misrepresent the issue. In his conflict with the 'Judaisers', Paul's antagonism to 'justification by works' may well relate to the interpretation of the Aqedah as showing that Abraham gained merit with God through his obedient action and even built up a treasury of merit for his descendants (cf. Matt. 3.9/Luke 3.8: a 'Q' saying). His emphasis on 'justification by grace through faith' arises from the perception that, if faithfulness and righteousness are linked and Abraham is taken as the type of the faithful, then the image has fundamental implications. It is those who have such faith who are Abraham's children (Gal. 3.6). Faith or faithfulness is the criterion of belonging to God's people, the boundary of the true Israel. Thus the new community is not bound by the old markers, such as race or nationality. Paul's reading of the scriptures establishes, on the one hand, that 'God shows no partiality' (Deut. 10.17; 2 Chron. 19.7), while on the other, the physically circumcised may be 'uncircumcised in heart' (cf. Jer. 9.25–26). The 'real Jew' is therefore one who is truly faithful to God – inwardly and spiritually circumcised (Rom. 2.25–29). In one respect the Jews were indeed better off in that they were 'entrusted with the oracles of God' (Rom. 3.2; cf. Ps. 147.19), but at the same time they were no better off, for 'no living being is innocent' before God (Ps. 143.2; cf. Rom. 3.20: Paul's case draws heavily on the insights of the Psalmist here). Hope is to be found in God's promise to Abraham, the father of the faithful (Rom. 4.16–17), for the promise made to him was made by the God 'who gives life to the dead and calls into being things that do not exist' – another of the themes of the Aqedah tradition. Abraham's weakness of body emphasised the fact that the power to fulfil the promise came from God alone. Within the faithful there are always disabling factors, including defensive literalism and self-assertion. The ultimate disability of humankind was expressed negatively on the cross of Christ but was overcome by the resurrection (Rom. 4.25). Faithfulness brings peace with God, and God's love ensures that, in the words of the Psalmist, our hope is not disappointed (Ps. 119.116). Faithfulness makes the promise to Abraham a vital reality for the believers of all nations (Gal. 3.6–9; cf. Gen. 12.3; 18.18). In the unity of the baptised community, it may be said that 'if you are Christ's, then you are Abraham's offspring, heirs according to promise' (Gal. 3.29).

Vermes has no doubt that Paul's doctrine of redemption is a Christian version of the Aqedah. 'Paul may, in addition, even be dispensed from the initiative of associating the self-offering of Isaac with the figure of the Suffering Servant and the Passover, since, in the first century AD, this association was already firmly established in Jewish theological circles.' (Vermes 1961: 219) Indeed, the Aqedah (and the figure of Abraham) became a remarkable focus of rabbinic interpretation. Isaac became a proto-martyr, symbolising perfect self-oblation, while the Aqedah became the focus of a theology of sacrifice, being seen also as a treasury of merits and a symbol of resurrection. Nor are its consequences for Christian faith exhausted by its exemplification of faithfulness and costly obedience. It is clearly relevant to the question of atonement and the death of Jesus. James and the writer to the Hebrews explicitly cite the Aqedah. Paul's teaching on justification by grace through faith, while related to a wider perspective on Abraham and to prophetic texts and texts from the Psalms, is consistent with the Aqedah motif and is beyond doubt generated through scriptural interpretation. Thus Paul's rationale of the Gentile mission – which is not to be confused with mere rationalisation – rests on a characteristic hermeneutic which has much to do with memory and interpretation: the memory of God's faithfulness to Abraham and his children; the promise to Abraham and the spiritual pilgrimage of his people, with its successes and failures; the ministry of Christ, the faithful son of Abraham through whom the full dimensions of the promise were brought to light; and the experience of God's love, hope and peace in a faithful community drawn from all nations. The memory is largely Hebraic; the catalyst of his interpretation is Christ; the context in which it is activated is that of the Gentile churches.

Holy community

The question of identity is important for the formation of a moral community (Birch 1995: 133). In 1 Peter and in Paul's writings, the faithful are encouraged to think of themselves as the holy people of God. In 1 Peter, this reconstituted community of faith is informed by a special story and memory which it cherishes in its exile in an alien world. Central to it is the Christ event, the key to its future hope and present task (cf. 1 Pet. 1.3–9, 17–21). Scriptural interpretation, geared to them as participants in the eschatological drama (cf. 1. 10–12, 24–25), elucidates the revolutionary nature of God's work. The images of the cornerstone and stumbling-block, derived from Psalm 118.22, Isaiah 28.16 and Isaiah 8.14, are reinterpreted in terms of the story of Christ. He is indeed the cornerstone of the new edifice of God's people, rejected by those who thought they were building that very edifice but affirmed by God. He is no inert stone, though, nor are the members of God's spiritual house or sanctuary. Rather, he is the power that recreates the people of God's choice, the people of the covenant (cf. Exod. 19.5–6), the holy community which in its life, faith and worship offers the only sacrifice acceptable to God (2.9). Brought from nothing by God's grace (2.10; cf. Hos. 2.23), it has indeed 'tasted the kindness of the Lord' (2.3; cf. Ps. 34.8). The faithful live in hope of the blessings of which the prophets spoke, for complete fulfilment – 'the grace that is coming to you at the revelation of Jesus Christ' – still lies in the future (1. 10–14). Hence the community is called to holy obedience, to the covenantal responsibility of the holy people of God (1.16; cf. Lev. 11.44–45).

Whatever else, holiness involved dedication and obedience to God, and separation from 'uncleanness', now understood primarily in moral terms. Holiness thus carries the sense of separation, of moral differentiation, from the impurity of the world. The community has to distance itself from 'the passions of your former ignorance' and 'be holy in all your conduct' (1.14–15). Distance from the world means living in it as 'aliens and exiles' (2.11), abstaining from indulging the passions in pagan style while maintaining a witness to the Gentiles through good conduct (2.11–12; 4.1–6). This has repercussions for their attitude to the civil authorities, for the way they run their households, and for relationships within the family (2.11–3.7). The moral quality of relationships arising from the nature of the faith community is also important. Baptism, carrying as it does the connotation of purification, is not simply the washing away of physical impurity but an 'appeal to God from a clear conscience' (3.21); it involves learning 'obedience to the truth' until self-centred individualism is overcome and new members attain to genuine philadelphia. This is the basis on which they can wholeheartedly love one another (1.22). We may well detect echoes of baptismal catechesis. We may also conclude that the way of holiness that is commended, while interpreted in the light of Christ, is fundamentally indebted to the way of God's people Israel, as depicted in the scriptures (cf. Birch 1995: 119–35).

Paul's startling image of the faith community as the holy temple of God where the Spirit of God dwells (1 Cor. 3.16–17) is directly related to the quality of its moral life. The passions that have to be put aside as unspiritual are jealousy and strife (1 Cor. 3.3), as well as pride (3.18) – divisive qualities which destroy community. The image of the holy temple can be applied also to the body, not only in relation to inner purity but also to relationships with others (the interactive understanding of the person is discussed below in Chapter 4). The holiness of the body is thus defiled by prostitution and enhanced by spiritual union with the Lord through whom we were redeemed (1 Cor. 6.12–20). Separation from idolatry and 'from all that can defile flesh or spirit' is mandatory for those who consti-tute 'the temple of the living God' (2 Cor. 6.14–7.1). Aliens the faithful may be in a pagan environment but in God's eyes they are fellow citizens of God's people, a community which, with apostles and prophets as its foundation and Christ as its cornerstone, is being bonded together as a holy temple in the Lord (Eph. 2.19–22) and must therefore be worthy of its calling (Eph. 4.1). The temple as the dwelling place of God is now expressly identified with the faith community.

Fulfilling the law

Paul's concerns about the law evinced a certain polarity. On the one hand, obedience to law should not replace the freedom given in Christ (Gal. 5.1). This emphasis on freedom was partly provoked by the Judaisers or circumcision party, who were urging on Paul's churches a kind of legalism which led to subservience or slavery to external standards. It was also, however, true to the Gospel of Christ, with its relational character and its emphasis on inner trans-formation. On the other hand, Paul had to show that the way of freedom he was commending – 'faith working through love' (Gal. 5.6) – was not an invitation to licence but was the best way, the truthful way, to fulfil the moral law (cf. Gal. 5.14; Rom. 13.8–10). This kind of polarity is the essence of moral discourse. Paul has, in fact, 'deconstructed' the law by positing the binary opposition of law and freedom, exposing the faults in the differentiation and defi-nition of these terms in common discourse and showing that in certain ways the one implies the other (cf. Clines 1995: 78). Paul 'problematises' the law, opening up the question of doing God's will to the faith community and its members and promoting moral responsibility (Clines 1995: 105). Thus, born to freedom, like Isaac (Gal. 4.28–31), the faithful bring forth the harvest of the Spirit in their lives and so fulfil the law of Christ (cf. Gal. 5.22–23).

In James, the 'royal law' (that is, the supreme law as given by a king, namely God (Martin 1988: 67) is expressly loving your neighbour (Lev. 19.18). Here the moral issue is about keeping 'the whole law' (2.10; cf. Matt. 5.18–19). Is it about keeping to the last detail of written law (to the last 'jot or tittle') or is there a genuinely holistic way of viewing the issue? Appeal is made to the 'royal law'. If one fails to love one's neighbour, and particularly if one has shown partiality (Lev. 19.15), one has omitted a major part of one's obligation under God. Hence there can be no valid claim for faith apart from works: one has to honour the full range of one's moral obligations. To keep the whole law is neither to be immersed in the multiplicity of laws nor to engage in excessive religiosity but to take the supreme law as the guide to fulfilling the divine requirement in its entirety. Whether one thinks of a self-absorbed piety or of bondage to legalism (and to base an ethic on the multiplicity of laws would seem to require such a description), James' discourse emphasises the liberation effected by the law of love (1.25; 2.12). Indeed, any attempt to fulfil God's law other than through loving action will incur divine wrath; it is for 'mercy' that God looks in judgement (2.13).

Neither Paul nor James explicitly cite the 'great commandment' as Jesus taught it, a fact which might occasion surprise. Both relate, as Jesus did, to Lev. 19.18.

> To love your neighbour means not taking vengeance nor bearing grudges 'against the sons of your own people' – not hating but reasoning with your neighbour (19.17). It means making provision for the poor and the sojourner (19.10), dealing honourably with your employees (19.13), acting positively towards the disabled (19.14), safeguarding justice in the community (19.15), and refusing to discriminate against the stranger in your midst. 'The stranger who sojourns with you shall be to you as the native among you, and you shall love him as yourself' (19.34).
>
> (McDonald 1993: 219)

The 'deconstruction' now centres on the polarity between the terms 'neighbour' and 'stranger' and their problematical reference. In the Pauline thought-world, the 'stranger' was the Gentile, alienated from God's people, but now Christ has effected a unity, bringing the hostility to an end (Eph. 2.11–22). His reconciling work has swept away 'the law of commandments and ordinances' (2.15) which reinforced the gulf between them and afforded them access to the household of faith and the Spirit of God (2.19–22). Thus, with the overcoming of 'partiality', the deeper moral purpose of the law is fulfilled. James holds more conservatively to the tradition, which has its own in-built 'deconstruction' of the obligation to neighbour. Loving one's neighbour has to do with caring for the poor and needy, countering oppression and overcoming class distinction (cf. 2.1–17). Without this, obedience to the law is incomplete.

That all this follows the spirit of Jesus' interpretation is beyond dispute. 'The New Testament writings consider the commandment to love to have central meaning for the ethical orientation of the church' (Lohse 1995). This does not mean that the principle of agape or the command to love provides an automatic answer to all the dilemmas of Christian ethics. 'All you need is love' would be a tendentious and misleading summary of Paul's moral position. At times, Paul appeals to a more specific command of the Lord (for example, 1 Cor. 7.10–11) but even then uses it with imaginative freedom according to the demands of the situation (cf. Schrage 1960: 207–33; English translation in Rosner 1995: 301–35). In this connection it has been observed with emphasis that *it is precisely when one examines Paul's explicit use of the sayings of the Lord that one most clearly perceives how indirectly and allusively he depends upon them* (Dungan 1971: 147, his italics). This is not to take dominical commands lightly – Paul carefully distinguishes his own require-ments from the dominical tradition, although his own rulings have no less force. What it suggests is an interpretative tradition of which Jesus is the fountain-head, and in which scripture is basic, but where the situation or context addressed puts the questions. Paul has therefore to use a variety of moral arguments and proce-dures: deontological ('this is the rule I give in all the churches': 1 Cor. 7.17), teleological ('make love your aim': 1 Cor. 14.1) or conse-quential ('my conduct must not result in harm to my fellow Christian': 1 Cor. 8.13). These strategies can be seen to effect loving action in specific cases. One must therefore not drive a wedge between the principle or command of *agape* and situational strategies.

The study of Christian morality has thus a close relation to hermeneutics. To put it another way, Jesus' teaching, work and interpretation are part of the active memory of the interpreters as they interpret scripture in relation to their contemporary scene. They are fellow interpreters with Christ of the will of God through the scriptures. Hence Paul's knowledge of Jesus' teaching may be considerably greater than the number of times he actually cites commands of the Lord. In relation to the command to love one's neighbour, it is almost certain that he was aware of Jesus' treatment of Lev. 19.18 (cf. Thomson 1990: 131–42). James also rarely cites Jesus' words directly. The nearest he comes to doing so is at 5.12 ('swear not at all'), which relates to the tradition recorded in Matt. 5.37. There are in his work many echoes of traditions which came to be included in the Gospels of Matthew and Luke. Martin suggests twenty-three allusions from Matthew in the letter (Martin 1988: lxxiv-lxxv). Imprecise as they appear, the writer reflects a tradition of moral understanding rooted in the scriptures and reinforced or clarified by Jesus' teaching. It is a memory, indeed a presence, with the writer and his addressees as they engage with the total meaning of the scriptural teaching. It constitutes a hermeneutical tradition by which the word of God in scripture can be heard and acted upon.[12]

The *Didache* places the double commandment of love and the golden rule in the context of the 'two ways' pattern of moral instruction as the leading expression of 'the Lord's teaching to the nations'. Here, dominical and scriptural traditions combine. In the *Didache* the two ways are 'life' and 'death', and it expands on 'the way of life' by citing Gospel or pre-Gospel tradition – loving one's enemies and praying for persecutors, as well as non-retaliation (with Lucan overtones). Abstaining from fleshly passions recalls 1 Peter 2.11, and commends sharing rather than acquisitiveness. The second commandment is enlarged upon by a series of prohibitions relating to offensive action against one's neighbour, mostly (but not all) from scriptural sources. The scriptural commandments are emphasised but are expounded in a fatherly way that recalls the wisdom tradition. Koester described the *Didache*'s procedures as a momentous step, for the interpretation of the sayings of Jesus was now tied to a developing Christian catechism (Koester 1982: 158), thereby thwarting the attempt by eschatological and Gnostic enthusiasts to take over this material. Our interest is rather in the consequences for moral understanding. Jewish patterns of moral education were now subject to revision in the light of Jesus' teaching. In this connection, reference should also be made to the *Epistle of Barnabas*, in which the 'two ways' motif appears as 'light' and 'darkness'. The 'way of light' is described in a long list of commandments. Both the *Didache* and *Barnabas* cite extensive lists of vices in their description of the way of death or darkness. It would appear that the 'two ways' motif represents a Jewish catechism, to which *Barnabas* relates more directly. The two documents confirm that the basic parameters of Christian conduct were derived from Judaism but set in the context of Christian interpretation and expectation. They rely on precepts and commandments to a greater extent than Paul, although as we have noted the *Didache* develops the 'way of life' with particular reference to (pre-)Gospel tradition. *Barnabas* is no less concerned with 'the way of the law of the Lord, which is in Christ Jesus' (*Barnabas* 1), and is concerned to perfect scriptural knowledge, particularly in relation to the death of Jesus and the expectation of the 'Parousia' or final coming.

A brief comparison may be made with the rabbinic tradition, which was divided over the advisability of summarising the law. Shammai rejected any kind of reduction of the Torah to a single principle, no matter who the enquirer was. Hillel was more sympathetic to the Gentile enquirer who required such a guideline, and offered the 'golden rule', adding 'the rest is commentary; go and learn it' (cf. McDonald 1993: 214–15). It is sometimes assumed that the Christian position accepted the 'great commandment' *tout court*, without commentary, but the above study indicates that this was far from being the case. The 'great commandment', and moral teaching in general, required to be contextualised in the story of the ministry of Jesus as well as in the world of the interpreter. This was the Christian commentary, the community memory which new members internalised and made their own. It was the hermeneutical guide to the reading of the scriptures, which – in Paul as in James – was the root of the Christian moral tradition.

Community ethics

Selected examples from Paul's writings will further illustrate the relationship between scripture, christocentric exegesis and moral practice in the Christian communities.

Community ethics in Romans 12

The 'mercies of God' in Romans 12.1 is a summary phrase for the working of God in Israel, as outlined in the previous chapters of Romans. Three themes present the dynamics of the Christian way. The first relates the mercy of God to worship and moral behaviour – the offering of oneself, one's life in its totality, ('your bodies') as a sacrifice to God in response to his mercies (12.1). Worship is a key indicator of the transcendent horizon of ethics, while the idea of sacrifice has scriptural roots (cf. Ps. 51.17; Barrett 1991: 213). The second theme is that of the transformation and renewal of one's outlook, without which the will of God cannot be discerned and acted upon; the obverse is conformity to the world's standards (Rom. 12.2). This is the corollary of responding to the mercy of God. The third theme is the morality of interactive community (12.3–8), recognising interdependence and the pooling of gifts. It underlines the notion of the people of God as a community and reveals the underlying dynamics of the 'body of Christ' metaphor developed in 1 Cor. 12. and Eph. 4. There is a Christian communitarian spirit, closely related to the humility of self-appraisal in relation to what each can offer the community (Rom. 12.3). Undergirded by agape and philadelphia, it gives community expression to the age-old principle that one should avoid evil and hold fast to good (e.g., Amos 5.14). It also gives expression to spiritual ardour and provides resources for meeting trouble. Mutual support and the traditional virtue of hospitality are set pieces in the pattern (12.9–13).

The radical edge of the community ethic is more revealing. 'Bless those who persecute you' (12.14) recalls a 'Q' passage in Gospel tradition (Matt. 5.44/Luke 6.28). Yet even here the scriptural tradition is strong (see below, 'Response to Unjust Treatment'). There are further examples of biblical interpretation with a moral emphasis. 'Don't be wise in your own eyes' (12.16) echoes Prov. 3.7 and 26.12. 'Repay no one evil for evil' (12.17) echoes Prov. 20.22; one should do what is honourable in the sight of God and humankind (2 Cor. 8.21; 1 Thess. 5.15). The form in which the prohibition of vengeance is given (12.19) combines the royal law of Lev. 19.18 with Deut. 32.35 ('vengeance is mine'). Care for enemies (12.20) reflects Prov. 25.21–22, although one might have expected stronger echoes of the tradition of Jesus' teaching ('Q': Matt. 5.44/Luke 6.27). The general tenor of the passage suggests church paraenesis: the prohibition on returning evil for evil, for example, also occurs in 1 Peter 3.9. If so, such paraenesis stood in the tradition of popular wisdom teaching, echoing Proverbs in particular, and is designed to reinforce Christian ethos and praxis. The overtones of Gospel tradition are not made explicit even in areas which seem positively to invite it. Paul's moral teaching draws heavily on the scriptures.

Problems at Corinth

Paul's advice on moral matters to the Corinthian Christians also reveals the roots of his ethics. While the reported case of immorality – a man living with his father's wife (1 Cor. 5.1) – is shocking even to Gentile sentiment, it is seen as wrong by Paul because such sexual impurity was an explicit contravention of holy law: 'A man shall not take his father's wife, nor shall he uncover her who is his father's' (Deut. 22.30, cf. 27.20; Lev. 18.8). As the Levitical priest formally pronounced the curse on the unholy, Paul the apostle pronounced judgement on the perpetrator of this act 'in the name of the Lord Jesus'. The seriousness with which Paul takes this case suggests that the attitude of the church community has compounded the offence. It has been excessively permissive and thus shares in the deviance (Harris 1991: 1–21) – it has shown confusion about the application of agape in such a case. For Paul, the man is to be excluded for his own good so that he may be saved 'in the day of the Lord' (1 Cor. 5.3–5), a punitive but ultimately loving stance. Jesus is taken to reinforce the moral stance of the Torah. Furthermore, Christ is our paschal lamb (1 Cor. 5.7), and therefore, when the church met in celebration, the Jewish custom of purging the house of leaven (cf. Exod. 19.12; 13.7; Deut. 16.3) was to be reinterpreted metaphorically in moral terms (1 Cor. 5.6–8). Malice and evil are out; sincerity and truth in. The frame of reference is scriptural as well as liturgical, and the Corinthian Christians are expected to understand it.

Paul's insistence on the settling of disputes within the community rather than having recourse to the Gentile courts of law became part of early Christian practice and procedure (cf. Matt. 18.15–17). Several considerations were involved. One was the litigious nature of Graeco-Roman society, with its power play, corruption and enmities (Winter 1991: 559–72). The Jewish tradition of jurisprudence was relatively advanced. On the advice of Jethro, Moses appointed able men from the community to administer justice (Exod. 18.13–26; Deut. 1.9–17). They were charged to hear impartially 'the cases between your brethren', and to 'judge righteously between a man and his brother or the alien that is with him' (Deut. 1.16). Why then turn for judgement now to 'those who are least esteemed by the church' (1 Cor. 6.4 – probably a reference to outsiders who deserve little respect, rather than an ironic reference to Paul himself, contra Winter 1991)? To be sure, times had moved on. The faith community rather than a nation now represented God's people, as later Jewish writings recognised. Thus in Daniel judgement was entrusted to the saints of the most High (Dan. 7.22), and the righteous will govern nations and rule over people (Wisd. Sol. 3.8). Was there no one in the church wise enough to undertake this role (1 Cor. 6.5: here a degree of irony is certainly evident, cf. 1 Cor. 1.20, 26; 3.18)? Besides, instead of being litigious and thus bringing defeat on the church, why not absorb the wrong done to oneself and so fulfil the Gospel (6.7–8)? Once again, the social context provides the real issue, and both Paul and early Gospel tradition interpret the spirit of scripture (cf. Matt. 5.39–40; Luke 6.29), but scripture provides the bedrock.

As already indicated, Paul cites the Lord's charge in relation to the inviolability of marriage (1 Cor. 7.10–11). The traditions that came to be recorded in the Gospels (Matt. 19.1–12; Mark 10.1–12) testify not only to controversy on the matter of marriage and divorce but specifically to the problem of interpreting scripture on the matter. As we shall see in the next chapter, Jesus found the centre of the tradition in the creation story (Gen. 1.27; 2.24), while Deuteronomy 24.1–4 was a 'lighter' commandment relating to human 'hardness of heart' (Matt. 19.8; Mark 10.5).[13] Jesus therefore gave hermeneutical direction to the interpreting community. There is some evidence that, by the time the Gospels were published, this 'hard saying' was hardening into law (cf. Matt. 5.32; 19.9; Mark 10.11–12; Luke 16.18). At the earlier stage, Paul accepted the dominical directive regarding separation but gave consideration to the correct policy if separation occurred, ruling out remarriage (1 Cor. 7.10). Paul appears to recognise the limitations of a 'bare command', even one with dominical authority. One cannot proscribe separation when mixed marriages are breaking down in front of one's eyes (cf. 7.12–16). The casuistry in which Paul was involved is part of the continuing process of interpretation. Paul also located marriage in the order of creation, as he showed when discussing the inadmissibility of having sex with a prostitute (6.16). His interpretation was informed both by the scriptural tradition as he read it and the teaching of Jesus, but the catalyst was actually the situation in which he and the Corinthian Christians found themselves. There was a tradition of godly behaviour. It involved shunning immorality (6.18) as well as recognising marriage as a divine vocation. Within the reciprocity of marriage conjugal rights should be respected (7.1–14) – unless one invoked the tradition of temporary abstention for reasons of piety or holiness (cf. Exod. 19.15). In the prevailing circumstances it was better, but not at all mandatory, to remain unmarried (7.25–40). In general, people should remain as they were when called by God (7.17–24).[14]

Response to unjust treatment

Persecution or rejection, and the suffering occasioned thereby, is a recurring biblical theme. 'The prophets often suffered persecution for their stand, and in the concept of a righteous remnant we have a glimpse of a small minority who were prepared to stand against the inhumanity of the larger society' (Rogerson 1995: 26). The *locus classicus* is Hebrews 12. The previous chapter was devoted to examples of faith from the scriptures and history of Israel – indeed, of faithfulness through times of great hardship, almost luridly described in a final rhetorical flourish (Heb. 11 *passim*, esp. 11.32–38). Yet none of those cited had seen the vision now set before the faithful by the Christ who was faithful to death and is now seated at God's right hand (11.39–12.2; cf. Ps. 110.1). The Christian way gains inspiration from the 'cloud of witnesses' but above all from Jesus, with whom faith now begins and ends (12.2). Several features of the Christian way are indicated at this stage. It is characterised as a race; sin must be put aside as a weight that impedes; the leading quality required is perseverance (*hypomene*), and the goal or finishing-post is the heavenly vision (12.2). Jesus is an inspiration not simply because he is exalted to heaven but because his journey there was accomplished in the face of hostility that cost him his life (13.3–4). Those struggling to remain faithful in the face of difficulties should therefore not lose heart. The note of discipline, characteristic of a wise and loving father and cohering with God's love for his sons (11.6–10), is introduced from Proverbs 3.11–12. Painful at the moment, it is a training in the peaceful and upright life. Therefore do not yield to the stresses! Aim at peace with everyone and a holy life (11.11–14), for it is the pure in heart that will see God. There is a similarity here with Matthew's beatitudes (cf. Matt. 5.8–10). The community itself should exert a matching discipline over its members (11.15–17).

In fact, the theme of patience and long-suffering in the face of difficulties and trials is common to all the early Christian missions. Paul treats it as part of a learning curve in Romans 5.3–5, not least his own (2 Cor. 6.4–10). He offers prayers for strength to endure in Colossians 1.11, and connects perseverance with hope in 1 Thessalonians 1.3. He links discipline with the training of the young in Ephesians 6.4 and uses the image of the race in 1 Cor. 9.24–27 and Phil. 3.14. The theme of patience and endurance also occurs in the Pastorals (1 Tim. 6.11; 2 Tim. 3.10; Titus 2.2). James looks positively on the testing of one's faith for it engenders the strength to endure and contributes to the completing of one's faith (Jas. 1.2–4). The example of the prophets' patience under ill-treatment is cited in 5.10. 'We count those happy who stand firm' (5.11).

1 Peter addresses the question of the unjust suffering which the servant of the oppressive master undergoes, as do the faithful in their encounters with the world (cf. 1 Pet. 4.14). The appropriate moral maxim is to do right, whatever the cost; that is the way that has God's approval and blessing (2.18–20; 3.14–15). Here the example of Christ's suffering provides the immediate model (2.21). The Passion story has moral and existential significance for believers, brought out by reference to the so-called 'suffering servant' passages in Isaiah 53. Though under severe pressure, the servant did not sin through violent action or deceitful word (2.22–23; cf. Isa. 53.9). He was wounded for the transgressions of others and is the shepherd and guardian of his straying flock.[15] Suffering for righteousness' sake rather than fulfilling the expectations of society is a scriptural injunction (Isa. 8.12–13). It is also a prominent part of early Christian tradition, as in Luke 6.22–33 and the beatitude ascribed to Jesus (cf. Matt. 5.10). It is always important for members of the faith community to be seen to act rightly (1 Pet. 2.12; cf. Matt. 5.16). Notions such as acting rightly whatever the cost are linked to the theme of love for enemies, both in the tradition of Jesus' teaching and in 1 Peter. Overtones of Luke 6.27–28, 33 are found in 1 Pet. 2.11–4.11. While the writer does not cite 'Love your enemies', he attempts to do justice to it by emphasising 'humility, gentleness and non-retaliation as the proper responses toward those who slander and oppress the Christian community' (Michaels 1988: lxxiv). Thus knowledge of several areas of Gospel tradition, from Luke especially but also Matthew, is evident in the letter, although the author may not have known the Gospels in their entirety (Best 1969: 112).[16]

Finally, it is to be noted that when the Gospels came to record the Passion of Jesus, they preserved its existential significance for the disciple: 'let him deny himself, take up his cross and follow me' (Mark 8.34, Matt. 16.24, Luke 9.23; 'Q'+Mark). The metaphor has given rise to much discussion, probably being designed 'to impress upon the audience the hardness of the Christian calling' (Tuckett 1996: 321). In his Passion story, Mark dealt with the redemptive significance of Jesus' death (cf. 10.45), but in so far as 'Q' dealt with the death of Jesus, 'the final messenger of Wisdom' (Tuckett 1996: 218–21), it was to relate it to the violent fate of the prophets and to emphasise its significance for the ethics of discipleship. There is therefore some kind of correlation between 'taking up one's cross' and 'dying and rising with Christ'. The Passion story, when it came to be written, preserved the 'example' of Jesus' suffering and self-denial for those who followed him.

Moral qualities

From the time of Seeberg (1903), many have canvassed the influence of the ten commandments on Christian moral instruction.[17] Hartman (1987: 237–47) drew attention to the Decalogue as the structuring factor in several lists, including Mark 7.21–22 and 1 Timothy 1.8–10, as well as Jewish texts such as the Fourth Sibylline Oracle (4.24–39) and Pseudo-Phocylides (3–21). Synagogue teaching and worship were possibly a mediating factor. Hartman then argued that the two vice catalogues in Colossians 3.5 and 3.8–9 reflected six of the ten commandments. These set the parameters of Christian behaviour. The listed virtues were not the direct corollaries of the vices cited but reflected an interpretation of the conduct that becomes 'God's chosen and beloved people' (3.12): compassion, kindness, humility, gentleness, patience, tolerance and forgiveness, love, peace and thankfulness (3.12–15). These are not merely moral precepts but are qualities engendered by the Gospel of Christ and Christian worship and fellowship (3.11, 15–17).

If we take Galatians as a test case, two observations may be made about the catalogues of vices and virtues it contains. One is that they are part of the whole thrust of the letter and suggest a call to the Galatians to fulfil their vocation not through uncontrolled freedom but through mutual service in love (5.13–14) – a calling dishonoured through infighting. The second is the perceived tension between the promptings of the Spirit and the desires of one's unspiritual nature (Gal. 5.16–18). There is a civil war in the soul, and the believer is urged to 'walk by the Spirit'. What does this involve? Although law is not the basis of moral endeavour for the Christian, anyone can see that certain types of behaviour are 'unspiritual'. Here Paul gives three examples of sensual passions ('fornication, uncleanness, licentiousness') which would certainly breach the fifth commandment but also, and more directly, the law of holiness, the divine teaching which expressly separated the people of God from the surrounding cultures (cf. Lev. 18.1–5). He then proscribes idolatry and witchcraft, reflecting the second commandment and also the law of holiness (cf. Lev. 19.4, 31), and sins that disrupt community – 'enmity, strife, envy . . . party intrigues and jealousies', the antithesis of the organic unity and freedom from party spirit for which Paul was always pleading. Here, the prohibitions seem to proceed as much from Christian community experience as from scriptural sources. Finally, there are excesses such as drunkenness and carousing which not only incur the censure of prophets and wisdom teachers but also destroy the worshipping community (cf. 1 Cor. 11.21).

The Spirit, mediating the present lordship of Christ, is a divine dynamic in life, contending against 'the desires of the flesh' and specifically producing the harvest of love, joy and peace, the realisation of the eschatological virtues (cf. Micah 6.4). The Spirit also engenders community virtues – long-suffering or patient endurance (virtually 'moral courage'), kindness and goodness (or benevolence) – together with the qualities of Christian character – fidelity, gentleness (or 'meekness') and self-control. Unlike law, which restrains, the Spirit is creative. The basis of it all is love of one's neighbour (5.13–14), itself the heart of the holiness ethic (cf. Lev. 19.18–37). While the Decalogue was undoubtedly influential, a reasonable conclusion from Galatians is that the 'two ways' pattern sets out, negatively and positively, the morality that befits 'God's chosen and beloved people' (Col. 3.12), and in the process effects a merging of the horizons of the chosen and holy people in Leviticus and the church as the chosen and holy people in Christ.

A comment may be added about the special nature of one of the Christian virtues, represented as humility (*tapeinophrosyne*) or meekness (*praotes*). 'Humility before the Lord' characterises the appropriate attitude of the creature in the presence of the creator, and of Israel before Yahweh (cf. Micah 6.8). It is in accord with the recognition of the greatness, the transcendence of God, which puts human achievement in perspective. It is therefore intrinsic to Christian worship (Fairweather and McDonald 1984: 110). In the

Torah, Moses was described as 'very meek' (Num. 12.3). In the Prophets, God's presence dwells 'with him who is of a contrite and humble spirit' (Isa. 57.15). Furthermore, God does not forget the cry of the 'afflicted' (or 'humble poor': Ps. 9.12), and the wisdom teacher urges that 'it is better to be of a lowly spirit with the poor than to divide the spoil with the proud' (Prov. 16.19). The rabbis also emphasised the virtue of humility.[18] New Testament writers embrace this tradition in their community ethics. Rebuking the contentious – not least the contentious teachers – James urges them to show 'the meekness of wisdom' (James 3.13); and quoting Proverbs 3.34 ('toward the scorners he is scornful, but to the humble he shows favour'), he bids them submit to God so that God may truly exalt them (cf. 4.7–10). 1 Peter urges a similar message based on the same passage. 'Clothe yourselves, all of you, with humility toward one another' (1 Pet. 5.5). Paul's version of the *imitatio Christi* in Philippians 2.5–11 concentrates on the humble obedience of Christ as the model for community ethics (cf. 2.1–4). True humility of mind is a virtue (Col. 3.12), but self-abasement can be abused and misinterpreted (Col. 2.18, 23). As in the Jewish tradition, meekness or gentleness is not to be associated with weakness; the way of the faithful requires inner strength (cf. Eph. 3.16; 1 Pet. 5.10). Nor is it to be associated with being put to shame; Paul fears that he may be humbled as an apostle when confronted by the moral failures in the Corinthian community, over whom he may have to mourn (2 Cor. 12.21). This whole realm of discourse provides an interesting commentary on three of the beatitudes in the Matthean tradition (Matt. 5.3–5). Its opposite, boasting, is also an ambivalent activity and at worst reprehensible (2 Cor. 10.7, 13; 12.1; cf. 1 Clem. 13.1).

POSTSCRIPT

The moral practice of the early Christian communities was grounded in the scriptures and moral tradition of Israel. However, much reinterpretation was called for – in the new faith communities as in those of Judaism which, though centred in Torah, evinced a variety of emphases. Eschatology was an important factor in this diversification. For example, in the Christian community eschatology related to the fulfilment of scripture, the sense of living in 'the last hour', the manifestations of the Spirit and charismatic activity. It therefore intersected and intensified the moral dimension.

Put another way, the question was how far salvific knowledge (the Christ event) should transform control language (the moral ethos of the community). It was all too easy for the community to lapse into charismatic excess (cf. 1 Cor. 14) or disabling otherworldliness (as in some cases at Thessalonica). Moral control had to be asserted, in the Pauline churches as elsewhere. There must be order, not chaos; people must act for the good of the community, not for self-satisfaction; the commandments are to be affirmed and summated in the love command. The Jewish moral bequest, underlying a wide spectrum of early Christian community life, continued to be explicit in the catechetics of *Barnabas*, where the transformational aspects of Christian understanding were focused on the salvific dimension, while control language remained in the area of divine (scriptural) command. The *Didache* represents a distinct move within this tradition to 'Christianise' moral controls and relate them more directly to dominical and apostolic tradition.

In Paul, transformation language is applied both to knowledge of salvation and to moral practice. If the hub of the faith is now the love of God manifested in Christ, the Christian life is an identification with Christ in his death and resurrection. This re-centring of tradition in Christ occasions discontinuity (for example, with the law as the ground of salvation), but it also reaffirms continuity and strengthens moral resolve. The new dynamic of the Spirit produces an even richer harvest of character-forming virtues. Paul could speak freely of the law, the *nomos*, of Christ. Yet here was no sectarian movement, with eccentricities of belief and practice. Nor does it represent a totalitarian ethic requiring unthinking obedience. The Spirit engendered freedom, responsibility for moral action and genuine community and personal growth, while affirming the groundwork of tradition and of orderly creation. In John, memory and interpretation, under the guidance of the truth-giving Spirit, bring the community into the presence of Christ; the presence of Christ, in the Spirit, creates a community of friends (15.14–17), pledged to self-giving and obedience to him who in his ministry provided a memorable example of service in community (13.1–11) and in his death showed unsurpassable love (15.13). The paradox of the old and new sources of moral authority – distinguishable but also identical – is brought out in 1 John. If Christ is indeed the expiation for the sins of the whole world, we ought to keep his commandments and walk as he walked (1 John 2.1–6). This is, in a sense, no new commandment, for the way that is commanded is the same as that set out from the beginning; yet at the same time it is a new commandment in that the darkness is passing away and the true light is already shining in a manner that was not so before (2.7–8). Here is the paradox of old and new, of the end and the beginning. The moral tradition of Israel is affirmed, but it is re-centred and brought to a new crystallisation.

Perhaps the position may be restated in the following way. The Jewish tradition of moral practice gave stability to the early Christian communities, particularly in their encounter with the *mores* of the Graeco-Roman world. To be sure, there were extremists – whether Jews or others – who were prepared to insist on a legalistic core of practice which, in Paul's view, was inconsistent with a Christian view of salvation. More typically, the movement was in the other direction. Since the Christ event was absorbed into salvific knowledge, moral controls could not continue to be unaffected by it. The tradition of Jesus' life and teaching, as well as his death and resurrection, provided new motifs for moral practice. This involved an element of discovery. One can hear Paul rethinking, say, the issue of meat offered to idols in 1 Corinthians 8 – carefully teasing out the moral issues, establishing the basic principle in the light of the atonement, and ending up with a considered solution which, on the one hand, established the priority of agape over gnosis, but on the other hand seemed at least to qualify the simple catechetical maxim that one should have nothing to do with idols! At the very least, this last requirement is substantially reinterpreted.

A factor which should not be overlooked is that the development of Christian moral understanding took place amid the welter of disputation and controversy. Reference has been made to Paul's 'Judaisers'. The pressure of pagan ways was ever present. The emergence of 'a kind of *gnosis*' – the first steps on the way to full-blown Gnosticism – brought another form of threatened distortion, all the more menacing in that it seems to have been nurtured within some circles in Judaism and resonated with influential strands of Greek culture. The main battles with it lay ahead, but one can see the battle-lines being drawn up in the New Testament and the immediately succeeding period. Paul treated it largely in moral fashion: agape takes priority over gnosis. John focused on the example and command of Jesus, as well as on the incarnation of the divine *logos* in the Son. The Pastorals and Irenaeus emphasised apostolic authority and church order as ensuring the true gnosis. The Jewish Christianity of *Barnabas*, with its emphasis on scriptural interpretation and moral practice, also reinforced the notion of true gnosis. What was at stake was the connection between knowledge of salvation and moral control. Apart from the key question of the nature of divine knowledge, the Gnostic put all the eggs in the first basket – gnosis was everything. Here indeed was a crisis for Christian morality.

Could the answer be found in the tradition of Jesus' teaching? That is the subject of the next chapter.

3

MORAL TRADITION

The 'sound words of the Lord' in early Christian recollection

As we have seen, early Christian teachers such as Paul and the writers of 1 Peter and James were aware of a tradition of dominical teaching at the heart of Christian moral instruction. 'If anyone . . . does not agree with the sound words of our Lord Jesus Christ and the teaching which accords with godliness, he is puffed up with deceit, he knows nothing' (1 Tim. 6.3–4). Yet often they do not quote a 'word of the Lord' when we might expect them to do so. Often the dominical tradition seems glossed rather than cited directly. Is there a reason for this, other than the lateness of the written Gospels? There is, after all, considerable evidence of an early collection, or collections, of Jesus' teaching. Were these sayings collections less than adequate to express the 'sound words of the Lord'? Is the 'word of the Lord' more than mere sayings? If so, how are we to estimate the value of Jesus' moral teaching? These are some of the questions we must attend to in this chapter.[1]

ESCHATOLOGY AND THE TEACHING TRADITION

As we have already seen, eschatology and apocalypticism were important factors in the life of the early faith communities, not least because they gave rise to differences of interpretation and posed something of a dilemma for moral teaching. Apocalyptic was particularly prominent at the time of Jesus. It stemmed in the main from the wisdom tradition, with its international links and a world view in which good and evil were in ultimate opposition. This inherent dualism is often referred to Babylonian-Iranian syncretism, coming from a period much earlier than Hellenistic times (Otzen 1990: 233; Cohn 1993: 195). Yet if apocalyptic was not a Hellenistic phenomenon, the terrible times of the confrontation with Antiochus Epiphanes brought forth a rash of apocalypses, dedicated to assuring the faithful that God's plan was still in place, that the divinely determined cosmic order could not be shattered, and that in the end (foreordained and predictable) good would prevail. The Book of Daniel comprised an apocalypse full of eschatological motifs which came late into apocalypticism (von Rad 1968: 330) and gave special point in the Jewish struggle for survival against the Seleucids.

That such a cosmic vision sponsored an ethic of obedience to the law is well illustrated in the books of the Maccabees as well as in the Qumranic scrolls. A penitential ethos, embodying a call to repentance, was also prominent, on the grounds that the present crisis resulted from the sin of the people.

> Lord, the shame falls on us, on our kings, our princes and our forefathers. We have sinned against you. Compassion and forgiveness belong to the Lord our God, because we have rebelled against him. We have not obeyed the Lord our God, in that we have not conformed to the laws which he laid down for our guidance through his servants the prophets.
>
> (Dan. 9.8–10)

The community of the pious would provide an instructed élite (1 Enoch 93.10), 'wise leaders of the people' (the *hakamim*) who 'will give guidance to the people at large', although for a while they 'will fall victims to sword and fire, to captivity and pillage' (Dan. 11.33). Their ethic could take the form of non-violent resistance, or could be inflamed into active resistance and self-sacrifice for the divine cause. In the time of John the Baptist and Jesus, it was a potent factor in Jewish society.

Since eschatological perspectives were so prominent in the period, the question of their interpretation or reinterpretation was a primary factor in the tradition of teaching stemming from John the Baptist and Jesus – and the process was continued in the early churches. As we have already noted, the watershed was the death and resurrection of Jesus. God's decisive act had taken place in the midst of history, giving to Christian moral teaching a basis in the new age of the Spirit. It was not simply a matter of obeying the precepts of some kind of guru. Yet past teaching offered continuity as well as discontinuity. The early Christians acknowledged 'traditions of the Lord', which they could read and hear not simply as a message from a past age but as a vital message for the present, based on messianic authority and the revelation of God's will. This kind of consideration doubtless lay behind its collection and careful preservation in the churches.

Nevertheless, the link between the teaching of Jesus and John and its reception by the early Christians was not a simple one. Something of its complexity will emerge in the following discussion.

THE REMEMBERED MISSIONS OF JOHN AND JESUS

Our access to the moral teaching of John the Baptist and Jesus is through the memories, stories and traditions of the first Christian communities. Neither John nor Jesus wrote down their teaching, although their followers cherished and interpreted their words. It is true that we have some relatively independent testimony to their ministries, especially in the case of John the Baptist. For reasons of his own, the ancient Jewish historian Josephus gives an account of John's appeal to 'the Jews who practised virtue and exercised righteousness toward each other and piety toward God, to come together for baptism' – Josephus considered baptism a purification of the body while the soul was cleansed by righteous conduct – and goes on to testify to John's popular appeal and potential threat to Herod, who had him imprisoned in his fortress at Machaerus and subsequently killed (*Antiquitates Judaicae* 18.5.2). The authenticity of Josephus' account and highly Hellenised interpretation has been widely discussed (cf. Scobie 1964: 17–22). Even if we grant its substantial validity, it remains the case that our understanding of John – and not least his importance as a moral teacher – comes from the Christians' memory of him and their assessment of his importance. This memory may be presumed to have been well informed, for some of the Christian leaders seem to have come to Jesus through the influence of John (cf. John 1.37, 40–42). What we find in the Gospels is not an autobiographical sketch of either John or Jesus but an interpretation of their moral and religious importance.[2]

The nature of the evidence presents difficulties for the modern interpreters, especially if they have an overriding historical concern. Some writers on the 'ethics of the New Testament' have taken as their starting-point 'Jesus' moral demands' (Schnackenburg 1962: 15–89), or 'the ethic of Jesus' (Verhey 1984: 6–33), or 'Jesus' eschatological ethics' (Schrage 1988: 13–40).[3] Certainly, a study of the immediate origins of Christian ethics takes one into the eschatological world of Jesus and John the Baptist, but questions arise about how far the approaches of John and Jesus endorse accepted eschatology and how far they modify or depart from it. As E. P. Sanders has put it, 'we must be careful to enter the circle at the right point' (Sanders 1985: 10). The question of the possible distortions that memory can create has to be taken seriously. If the Christian communities emphasised teaching, did they recreate John and Jesus as ideal teachers of righteousness? Were John and Jesus actually moral teachers, or was this a role subsequently foisted on them? The latter extreme view has its advocates (cf. S. L. Davies 1995), who question the broad consensus of scholarship that Jesus was an outstanding teacher. After all, Paul cited very little of Jesus' teaching; sayings collections such as 'Q' and *Thomas* have very different perspectives on it; and Mark, for example, suggests that Jesus' parables were incomprehensible to his hearers. M. Smith found Jesus to have a much higher profile as miracle-worker than as teacher (Smith 1978).

The case is worth further reflection. In terms of environmental context, Jesus belonged to ancient rural Galilee rather than to modern academe (cf. Freyne 1980) and may well be described as 'a genuine charismatic, the true heir of an age-old prophetic religious line' (Vermes 1973: 69). Yet if he is depicted as a mere charismatic (that is, a charismatic devoid of teaching output), one may question whether his name would not now be at least as obscure as that of Honi the Circle-Drawer, and whether an heir to Israel's prophetic religious line would not *ipso facto* be an outstanding 'teacher of righteousness'. Indeed the Jewish scholar Geza Vermes, who drew attention to Jesus' affinities with *hasid* tradition, concluded magnanimously that, as regards teaching, 'no objective and enlightened student of the Gospels can help but be struck by the incomparable superiority of Jesus' (Vermes 1973: 224). Moreover, the statement that Jesus was a teacher can tell us much about the kind of person Jesus was and about the aims of his ministry. This does not mean, however, that his teaching was not subjected to the process of collation, exposition and interpretation at the hands of his followers in their anxiety to transmit, apply and explain. That activity is evident even in the earliest sources available to us.

An investigation of the moral teaching in the Synoptic Gospels thus presupposes a critical approach to the material. Fortunately, critical tools have been refined over a long period, although the process is continuous rather than complete. The recognition of Mark as the earliest of the Synoptic Gospels and an important source for the other two, together with the identification of a sayings source shared by Matthew and Luke in particular, was the great achievement of source criticism, which finally produced the 'four document' theory (Mark, Q, M and L). However, by the time Streeter (1924) presented his exhaustive study of the possibilities of this theory, other avenues of research were being pursued. *Formgeschichte* ('form criticism' is the usual translation) sought the history and development of the forms of tradition found in the Gospels. *Redaktionsgeschichte* ('redaction history' or 'composition history') studied the perspectives of the evangelists as editors. Other studies came to deal with literary, structural and hermeneutical questions, and renewed attention was given to the socio-historical context of the Gospels. It is worth noting, however, that Mark and the Q hypothesis have retained their importance for the study of Gospel sources, in spite of powerful challenges and alternative explanations (Tuckett 1996: 1–39). The interpretation of Mark has become a vigorous pursuit (Telford 1995: 1–61), while in relation to Q new synopses and reconstructions have been attempted, most recently by Neirynck (1988) and Kloppenborg (1988). Theissen's explorations of the social and political history of the Synoptic tradition attempted to ground the Q hypothesis in the religious and political life of Palestine in the 40s of the first century CE (Theissen 1992: 203–33), although others are more cautious (Tuckett 1996: 101–2). That there were several strands of it, eventually including a literary strand, is held to be probable, although detailed questions relating to its redaction remain problematic (Kloppenborg 1984: 34–62; Tuckett 1996: 41–82). Its significance for the present study is that it gives access to an early strand of Christian moral teaching which sought to preserve the teaching of John and Jesus as received tradition, to be given expression in community action. It not only articulates the views of the community but also speaks to the community (Tuckett 1996: 82).

Generally speaking, new models of moral teaching arise as a result of charismatic leadership and new movements or initiatives which serve as catalysts for change, reorientation and redefinition (Kee 1980: 54–98). The seismic consequences of such developments prompt fresh understandings of eschatology, religious identity and tradition, to all of which there are important moral dimensions. Thus there occurs a sharpening of the 'cosmic vision' in which ethical models are grounded.

Both Mark and Q appear to have used Baptist material to present important aspects of their cosmic vision. In doing so, they were reflecting and systematising the recollections, interpretations and cherished stories of early Christian communities, among whom moral teaching, like the story of Jesus, was seen in eschatological and christological perspective. Whatever links may be established with the wider Gentile world, the Synoptic Gospels were launched to the Jewish strains of messianic expectation and divine judgement.

THE RECOLLECTED MORAL TEACHING OF JOHN THE BAPTIST

The accounts in the Gospels, together with that in Josephus, provide an outline of the ministry of the Baptist. Common factors include his piety, moral concern, baptism, purification, political significance, imprisonment and death. The main, and very significant, difference of emphasis is found in the weight the Gospels place on John's eschatological role, which Josephus ignores completely. As a historian, Josephus was concerned with Herod's ruthless removal of a religious figure whose influence with the crowds represented a political threat. All the Gospel accounts were concerned to focus on the messianic significance of John's radical message to Israel. Tuckett observes, 'One of the more surprising features of Q is the amount of space devoted to John the Baptist', and he reflects on possible reasons for it, such as the complexity of the prehistory of the material and the need to place John's work in the context of Jesus' messianic ministry rather than allow it to represent some kind of rival tradition (Tuckett 1996: 108–9). In fact, the Christians saw John's mission as part of their own cosmic vision, inaugurating a new age in which Jesus was the central figure.

Cosmic vision

To enter the world of John the Baptist as the Gospels portray him is to engage with the heightened eschatology evident in some of the movements within Judaism in the Roman period, and particularly with the notion of pollution and purification that characterised all the beneficiaries of the Hasidic tradition. The present age was rushing to its close. The Day of the Lord – the day of judgement and vindication – was at hand. To this end, John proclaimed his prophetic message of the imminence of the day and the supreme urgency of moral and spiritual purification. The rite he administered was 'a baptism of repentance for the remission of sins' (Mark 1.4, Luke 3.3, Matt. 3.6). Cleansing by water was a necessary preliminary to the messianic age, when the reality of divine judgement would be experienced in all its power (Matt. 3.12; Luke 3.16; cf. Mark 1.8). Perhaps those baptised by John will subsequently be baptised in the Spirit, and those who refuse baptism now will be destroyed by fire (so Tuckett 1996: 123, but the matter is admittedly complex). John's call was in principle to all Israel – hence Mark's observation that *all* the country of Judaea and *all* the people of Jerusalem went out to him (Mark 1.5) – although some of his stronger barbs may be directed to those resisting his call. As we saw above, the question of the identity of God's people was important. For John, Israel in its present condition would not form the restored people of God. Truly the axe was now laid to the root of the trees (Luke 3.9Q). To the riposte, 'We are already God's people, the children of Abraham', perhaps offered by those resisting baptism, John's reply was that if Israel was disobedient God could readily raise up a new people for himself. The time of radical test had come. The cosmic vision, however, was the purification rather than the destruction of Israel as a preparation for the day when the holiness of the Coming One would burn up pollution like chaff and a new people, purged of all pollution, would emerge in a transformed cosmos.

Moral and community concern

Since John's message was a challenge to Israel not to hinder the divine approach by its own lack of purity, it had moral implications. The movement his preaching evoked suggested the image of vipers fleeing in panic before a forest fire (Luke 3.7–9Q), perhaps with emphasis on the poison of the viper. Matthew thought it particularly appropriate to the Pharisees and Sadducees who came for baptism (Matt. 3.7). John's baptism was not in itself, however, an insurance against divine judgement and 'the wrath to come'. The criterion was the moral product, the fruits, of changed lives that testified to the genuineness of repentance. Only in this way could Israel prepare to meet its God (Tuckett 1996: 113). An alternative explanation is that the Jewish religious leaders (perhaps the Pharisees are mainly in view) came out merely to witness John's baptism rather than to participate in it, and the 'fruits' would then refer to, or at least include, baptism itself.[4]

Nevertheless, the intrinsic link between religion and morality can hardly be denied. John 'preaches a baptism of repentance' (Luke 3.3; Mark 1.4; cf. Matt. 3.2). To produce fruit worthy of repentance (Matt. 3.8; Luke 3.8) cannot be without moral implications: 'prove your repentance by the fruit you bear' (REB). Their *teshuva* ('repentance', 'turning to God') was inseparable from the actions which followed it. In line with Israel's tradition, to turn to God was to turn to God's righteousness, to live in accordance with God's law. Ritual avails nothing apart from amendment of life. Here was an attempt to recover a principal strain of the prophetic message and to reaffirm the moral basis of Israel's tradition. Far from signalling an abandonment of moral concern for life in the world, John's charismatic preaching and eschatological focus entailed an intensification of the moral demand. Moral and ritual purity went hand in hand in preparation for the dread day.

Whether the John tradition was preserved for christological, apologetic or even polemical reasons, the moral import of his 'interim ethics' was clearly recognised as having continuing validity. Since the early Christian communities had an abiding concern with the moral tensions of living in a world that faced imminent judgement, teaching traditions which threw light on this kind of situation were valuable. Thus in Luke (source L in source critical terms), John is shown to relate to the problem of what his message might mean in social terms and to people committed to worldly duties (Luke 3.10–14). To the tax collectors, John said 'Exact no more than the assessment' (Luke 3.13, REB). If this assessment included the collector's commission, then John was making a plea for truthfulness in fiscal matters and an affirmation that, in the interim, moral purity overrode the pollution that their work was thought to entail. If commission was excluded, then tax gatherers could not be members of Israel (the conventional view), for they would have no means of subsistence. His answer to those on military service, which directed that vicious practices such as bullying, blackmail and extortion must be eliminated, suggests that it was the moral performance of duty that was the crux of the matter (Luke 3.14). To the crowds – probably Luke's shorthand for the people of Israel – John advocated the communitarian practice of sharing clothing and food with the needy in place of an individualistic concern for moral scruples (Luke 3.11). In the context of movements towards individualism in the Hellenistic age, evident in the marked concern for personal immortality and happiness as well as worldly success, John's emphasis on community responsibility may have been designed to illustrate, at least in embryonic form, a social ethic which anticipated the new age. Even if this tradition is secondary (it is very like the teaching of Jesus in some respects), it indicates that eschatology was compatible with a strong moral and social emphasis. A more radical conclusion is that moral teaching was not only given in the context of eschatological expectation but was intrinsic to it (cf. Dan. 9.8–10).

Concern with worldly and political issues

The parameters of the new community did not coincide with conventional views. All sources agree that John was uncompromising in his moral stance in relation to Herod the tetrarch, whose public and domestic life were alike subject to the judgement of God (Luke 3. 19–20; Matt. 3–4; Mark 6.17–18). However, as far as can be deduced from our sources, John advocated an 'interim ethics' rather than a radical reappraisal of the structures of society, and this perspective seems to have retained its relevance for early Christian communities. After all, if creation was about to be overwhelmed by the fire of divine judgement, there was no point in readjusting the worldly order. But the Coming One would test moral performance; baptism must bear fruit in good actions, as befits those who have turned to God's righteousness. The Christians saw the Parousia in similar terms. Hence, in the interim, one must show compassion to others and integrity in doing one's duty.

Moral procedures

Much in John's preaching and life-style – wilderness locale, asceticism, community of goods, eschatological intensity, messianism, water baptism, contempt for conventional religiosity – suggests an affinity with Qumran,[5] though John betrays no connection with the Qumran community as such. Perhaps he was one of its camp-followers who felt called to proclaim the message of the imminence of messianic judgement to Israel. Indeed, prophecies cited to interpret his mission were also in use in the Qumran community. Thus his emphasis on the remission of sins is best understood, not in conventional Christian terms, but in terms of ridding Israel of the stains of its pollution and restoring the purity of the people of God. If one of the purposes of the Israelite cult was purification and expiation (de Vaux 1961: 272), then John's baptism was an eschato-logical rite of similar intent which recalled Israel to its salvation story and the moral obligations inherent in it.

The concept of repentance (*teshuvah*) requires careful handling, especially if its Greek rendering (*metanoia*) is interpreted in terms of subjective consciousness. Modern anthropological studies of spirit possession and exorcism employ analogy and the notion of psycho-logical causality to portray John as 'strikingly similar to contemporary revival preachers' in his requirement of psychological change, in his emphasis on sinfulness and damnation, and in his offer of a way out of this predicament (Davies 1995: 56–8). But while there may be some merit in such analogical approaches, their typological procedures require to be supplemented and controlled by contextual evidence if distortion is to be avoided. Whatever pneumatic phenomena accompanied John's preaching, *teshuvah* involves a reorientation to God and his law, thereby ensuring that John's 'revivalism' always had the moral content appropriate to membership in the people of God. Thus Philo, in his discussion of *metanoia*, spoke of Moses offering to the repentant 'the high rewards of membership in the best of commonwealths' (*De Virtutibus* 175). 'Where honour is rendered to the God who is, the whole company of other virtues must follow in its train as surely as in the sunshine the shadow follows the body' (*De Virtutibus* 181). Referring to the harmony of words, thoughts and actions, he observed, 'If one is not forgetful of this harmony, he will be well pleasing to God, thus becoming at once a lover of God and beloved of God' (*De Virtutibus* 184). Colson argued that the moral of Philo's *De Nobilitate* was the same as the Baptist's call to 'bring forth fruit worthy of repentance' (Philo, Loeb edn, VIII (1939), xvii).

John the Baptist and Christian tradition

To many of the first Christians, John possessed the intrinsic authority of a prophet, and his moral teaching was imbued with the same spirit.[6] His identification with Elijah (cf. Mark 9.11–13; Matt. 11.14) shows that he was seen as having an eschatological role in relation to the Christian story centred on Jesus. His story was thus absorbed into the Christian story. His place in early Christian memory suggests that he was regarded as belonging in spirit to the new age rather than to the 'law and prophets', even if his place is somewhat ambiguous (cf. Matt. 11.11). 'Within the context of Q, however, it would seem that John must definitely be included in the new era' (Tuckett 1996: 137). The problem is bound up with the controversial logion, Matthew 11.12/Luke 16.16. Both Matthew and Luke seem to have wrestled with the text in their own way and left their mark on it (Catchpole 1987: 95–6; Tuckett 1996: 136). Much debate has centred on whether John's proclamation of the kingdom inaugurated the violent struggles of the end-time (so Matthew, it would appear) or whether since John's time the preaching of the kingdom as good news has triggered a mighty struggle to be part of it (so Luke, apparently). Although the text is obscure,[7] it is nevertheless clear that John belonged to the 'beginning of the gospel' (Mark 1.1). There was much more to be learned. Thus, Apollos who 'knew only the baptism of John' had to have matters further explained to him (Acts 18.24–28), and Paul insisted on baptising about twelve of John's followers in the name of the Lord Jesus, so that they could receive the Holy Spirit (Acts 19.1–7).

THE RECOLLECTED MORAL TEACHING OF JESUS: THE SAYINGS SOURCE ('Q')

However one views the theories about 'Q' in modern scholarship, it cannot be denied that there was a growing concern in the churches to recollect the moral teaching of Jesus, and that it gave rise to an identifiable body of material. The assumption is often made that the process of recollection was advanced by awareness of traditions of 'the sayings of the wise' in the wisdom tradition of Israel, including the Hebrew Bible and the Hellenistic Jewish period (Robinson 1971; Kloppenborg 1987a). The danger is that the assumption is transferred to the nature of Jesus' utterances – they become represented as 'wise saws'. Here we give cautious assent to the 'Q' hypothesis without presuming to arbitrate between 'strong' and 'weak' versions of it (i.e., fixed or fluid) or to speculate about the precise stages of its development (cf. Mack 1993: 71–102), but we expressly deny the proposition that it leads back to a 'non-mythological' or 'non-eschatological' picture of Jesus, the teacher of wisdom. Indeed, it seems clear that, because of the eschatological significance attaching to John and Jesus, it was indeed (in the forms known to us) always more than a simple collection of wise sayings. We agree with Theissen that the collected material 'contains the plan for an active, ethical way of life that takes radical demands seriously' (Theissen 1992: 233), and that its importance for the shaping of Christian ethics is beyond question. Theissen argued that the

Christian community had learned through experience to focus on 'the realization of Jesus' commands as the authentic formulation of the will of God and the responsibility of human beings before their judge for the way they have lived their discipleship' (Theissen 1992: 233). The material thus contained an implicit cosmic vision which was finally articulated in narrative.

Cosmic vision

The framework of the 'Q' collection, which included the Baptist's ministry, served to supply the cosmic setting of Jesus' teaching. At Jesus' baptism there is a veritable cosmic vision. The heavens are split asunder, the Spirit descends upon Jesus like a dove, and the heavenly voice bears testimony to 'my beloved son' (Luke 3.21–22, Matt. 3.13–17; cf. Mark 1.9–10). A more dramatic introduction to a body of sayings could hardly be imagined. This is not the place to explore the mechanics of the vision. Contextual and structural features, rather than subsequent christological interpretation, highlight Jesus' identification with Israel in its turning to God, and his heaven-sent vocation to embody the true Israel as Son of God. Thus the figure who stands at the origin of the sayings tradition is no ordinary moral teacher. His role is bound up with the religious expectation of Israel, especially in Hellenistic times, and with the future of the people of God in a time of crisis. His sayings have the authority of the Son of God and therefore portray the way of life to which Israel is called.

The sustained correspondences between the Lucan and Matthean accounts of the temptations of Jesus indicate a common source, although a transposition has occurred in the order in which the temptations are recounted. The material is highly mythological or symbolic, as is to be expected when its subject relates so directly to cosmic vision. The form is that of a narrative of test or ordeal, examples of which occur in other wisdom collections (Kloppenborg 1987: 322–4) and represent interpretations of the source and quality of the teacher. With its repeated refrain, 'If you are the Son of God . . . ', the narrative explores the implications of Sonship (Luke 4.1–13; Matt. 4.1–11). Jesus rejects the temptations to re-enact Israel's reception of the manna amidst the rocks of the wilderness (Matt. 4.3; Luke 4.3) and the cruder forms of messianic expectation (Matt. 4.8–9; Luke 4.9) as formal 'signs' or 'proofs' of the authenticity of his vocation. Astonishing miracle stories or epiphanies in the Temple are thus not candidates for inclusion in this collection. The most revealing political temptation is that Jesus should gain 'all the kingdoms of the (inhabited) world' by prostrating himself before the devil (Matt. 4.8–10; Luke 4.5–8). Luke's reference to the inhabited world (*oikoumene*) can hardly be other than to the Roman empire. Both versions speak of the 'glory' on offer, and it is made clear that it is within the scope of the devil's remit to confer the *exousia* or authority in question. The basic image which the narrative conjures up is that of satellite kings prostrating themselves before an oriental monarch. This act of *proskynesis*, with its implied claim to divinity, had been generally avoided at Rome, although isolated instances occurred, but the Emperor Caligula required it, as did some of the later emperors (Theissen 1992: 206–12). Philo clearly regarded it as a delicate issue in his account of his embassy to Caligula (*Legatio ad Gaium* 116–17). The formation of the temptation narrative might arguably be ascribed to Caligula's reign or to some time soon after, although the evangelists could also have had later emperors such as Nero or Domitian in mind. The point of the narrative, however, is not so much to demonise the Roman empire as to indicate Jesus' decisive rejection of imperialism as the means or goal of his mission and his significant transvaluation of power and glory. The issues, however, were of such moment as to present a real test – a trial to which Jesus had been led by the Holy Spirit (Luke 4.1; Matt. 4.1; cf. Mark 1.12) – and to occasion a battle of wills in which Jesus' superior strength, wisdom and truthfulness were demonstrated. A hermeneutical dimension is implicit. The basic text appears to have been Deuteronomy 6 (6.13 and 16, together with 8.3 and Ps. 90.11–12, are explicit), and fundamental to it is the Shema and the first commandment (Deut. 6.4–5), expressing Israel's primary creed and obligation which Jesus constantly 'remembers' (Gerhardsson 1996: 23, 221). The collected teaching thus rests on Jesus' moral authority and summons his followers to his clear-sighted vision.

A further assertion of the nature of Jesus' authority occurs in the midst of the collected teaching. In an astonishing little epiphany, the sayings source identifies Jesus as acknowledging in prayer the revelation of God's will to 'babes' (the opposite of the wise and learned) and to himself. 'No one knows who the Son is except the Father, or who the Father is except the Son or anyone to whom the Son wishes to reveal him' (Luke 10.22Q). This indeed is the high point in the story of salvation (Luke 10.23b–24), and the teaching is invested with the authority of the Son of God.

Moral and community concern

The sayings source ('Q') has an overriding interest in discipleship, which must be presumed to be a leading concern for the redactor and his audience. We deduce that the members of the faith communities encountered difficulties in their situation, which this teaching addressed. The disciple community around Jesus thus emerges as a model for Christian emulation.

The praxis of the righteous community

Do followers of Jesus keep the law of Moses? The problem is one of reassessment in the light of eschatological faith. In 'Q', there is a strong assertion that not a dot can be subtracted from the law (Luke 16.17; Matt. 5.18). There are clear echoes of controversy here, with which the churches were concerned from the beginning. Perhaps 'Q' had taken a rallying call of Jewish Christians and allowed the rest of Jesus' teaching to present the definitive sense in which the law should be understood. At any rate, it would have been extremely dangerous to appear to countenance any suggestion that Christian teaching undermined the law – as Pharisaic opponents doubtless suggested. Jesus took it extremely seriously, and Christian mission was inspired by firm faith in the durability of divine *dikaiosyne*.

The divine righteousness was to be lived out in the disciple community. In a world where wealth was power, at least some of the disciples were poor, perhaps through economic and social sanctions, although some needed to be warned about accumulating wealth (Luke 12.33–34Q) and serving mammon (Luke 16.13Q) and were clearly not destitute (they could be targets for borrowers, if not thieves: Luke 6.30Q). The way of the world gave little sign of the coming *dikaiosyne*; there was often occasion for frustration and grief, and one could be ostracised and insulted for one's faith in the course of social and religious life (Luke 6.22–23). All the more reason, then, to recall Jesus' primary teaching (Matt. 5.1b; Luke 6.20a): 'Blessed are you who are poor, for yours is the kingdom . . . ' (the *Gospel of Thomas* has, 'blessed are the poor': see below). Such logia can be interpreted in terms of imminent or futurist eschatology (Tuckett 1996: 141–2), but there is also the implication that the reign of God is opening up for the hearers as a present praxis or way of life. It may well be that traditional scholarly analysis has tended to impose its categorical presuppositions on this material, insisting that it must have either future or present reference, or that it must be either consistent or realised or at least 'inaugurated' eschatology. However, if one thinks of the disciples' group as being inducted into the praxis of hope (which is also the praxis of the kingdom), then there are two horizons, present and future. And with hope there is joy. The poverty which the disciples had embraced – they had left everything (Luke 5.11) – was an occasion for joy, for it removed one of the world's great distractions and left them open to the new age. The hungry enjoy blessing now because they have the assurance that they will be sustained; their feast is even now commencing. Those who weep would appear to be the recipients of the world's hatred and rejection. Their compensation is the joy of the kingdom, which comes with hope. Other beatitudes recorded in Matthew – such as blessings on the meek (cf. Ps. 37.11), the merciful (Hos. 6.6; cf. Matt. 9.13; 12.7), the pure in heart (Ps. 24.4; 73.1) the peacemakers (Ps. 34.14) and those suffering persecution (cf. 2 Chron. 36.15–16) – underline the notion of praxis, which derives from the piety, the constancy and the distilled wisdom of Israel's past. The woes, which express the converse and underline the reversal, are probably a secondary interpretation, though no less important for that (Luke 6.24–26). When one relates these sayings to the audience to whom this collection was addressed, the pattern of praxis (with the cosmic vision it presupposed) is seen to be commended as a model to sustain hope and endurance.

The beatitude or blessing – a familiar enough form in prophetic and wisdom sayings, in popular piety and in the prayers of the synagogue – possesses multi-dimensional possibility. It can express powerful religious emotion; it can have a poetic or moral function; and it can be formalised, as in liturgy. Three dimensions can be deciphered in Gospel usage. First, there is the fundamental elevation of spirit in which the eschatological reality of the new creation is experienced. Here the beatitude celebrates the reality of the kingdom, where the worldly disadvantages of poverty, hunger and sorrow are overwhelmed by the resources and joys of heaven. Second, when the vision passes, spiritual exultation is translated into sober reality of spiritual and moral existence on earth. Thus the beatitudes in Luke and 'Q' speak directly to the empirical condition of the disciples' group, with its hopes and hardships. Such a tensive 'community of character' (cf. Hauerwas 1981: 128–52), with all its possibilities of growth, modelling, failure and degeneracy, characterised Jesus' solidarity with his disciples. Third, Matthew tends to generalise, spiritualise and expand (5.1–12). His version highlights the moral qualities of disciples, to be emulated and reproduced in

the communities the evangelist was addressing, a move in the direction of the language of virtue. Luke, who is generally held to
preserve the earlier form, focuses on people, on the community of
disciples.

Response to hostile situations

But how should one respond to those who occasioned the vexation
which the disciple community experienced? The note of trauma
connects with the love command which is central to the praxis of
the disciples' group, and to the theme of non-retaliation and not
delighting in an enemy's downfall. The double love command,
bringing together Deuteronomy 6.4 and Leviticus 19.18 in the
manner of Jewish exegesis – which had its own canons of intertextu-
ality – was adumbrated in the *Testaments of the Twelve Patriarchs* and
in rabbinic literature, although nowhere precisely in the manner we
find it in the Synoptic Gospels.[8] This disapproval of retaliatory
action (cf. Prov. 24.29) and exulting over an enemy's downfall has a
considerable pedigree in Jewish and Near Eastern culture. Proverbs
24.17–18 contains the admirable advice not to rejoice when your
enemy falls but spoils the effect by suggesting that if one does take
such action God may not sustain his anger against him! There is a
similar ambivalence in Proverbs 25.21–22, which is repeated in
Romans 12.20. Those who mock one who is plunged into calami-
tous poverty will not go unpunished (Prov. 17.5). A powerful
statement concerning non-retaliation is found in Proverbs 24.29, a
passage which reflects the Babylonian maxim in Amen-em-ope
about returning good for evil and treating your enemy with justice.
The saying about love of one's enemies is longer in Luke than in
Matthew and implies verbal rather than physical abuse (such as
ostracism, personal insults, jibes, jeering, polite ignoring: Tuckett
1996: 304; Catchpole 1993: 110–11), precisely the kinds of difficulties which the target audience of 'Q' might be presumed to know
well. In the Mishnah, slapping someone with the back of the hand,
like pulling off a person's cloak, was an insult requiring double
recompense (*Baba Kamma* 8.6). The sayings in Luke 6.30, relating
to begging and robbery or confiscation of property, seem to relate to
a different scenario. Matthew extends non-violent praxis to
responding to being press-ganged into compulsory service (Matt.
5.41). This is almost certainly later, having its context in the
disturbed times of the Jewish Revolt and its aftermath. By inserting
it among earlier examples, Matthew encourages a reinterpretation in

relation to structural violence and in so doing further complicates the narrative. At any rate, the disciples' response should be qualitatively different from that of worldly people (Luke 6.32–34). Right praxis combines the love of enemies with merciful action (Luke 6.35–36). The disciple should give freely, without seeking recompense. The accent is on neutralising feelings of resentment and building community; their calling is to be 'sons of the Most High; for he is kind to the ungrateful and the evil' (Luke 6.35b; cf. Matt. 5.45b). In short, they must be inspired by the outgoing generosity that characterises God's reign. A premium is therefore placed on the quality of personal interaction and reciprocity, transcending considerations of role and status; the Golden Rule fits this context well (Luke 6.31; Matt. 7.12). In this radical interpretation of morality, the ultimate standard is God himself. It is he who is 'complete' (*teleios*: Matt. 5.48), 'merciful' (*oiktirmon*: Luke 6.36). Accordingly, one must not assume prerogatives which properly fall to God, such as passing judgement on others. If one does, the interaction takes another form: one will be judged by the same yardstick (Luke 6.37a, 38b; Matt. 7.2; cf. Mark 4.24).

The teacher as authority

The disciple community centres on its teacher, the source of wisdom. A focal part of the sayings tradition is the narrative of the centurion's servant (Luke 7.1–10Q). This picture of the reverent Godfearer would resonate with the target audience in a number of ways. The key section, however, is the analogy the soldier draws between the effectiveness of military orders and the power of Jesus' word to accomplish its purpose (Luke 7.7–8Q). 'Say the word, and my servant will be healed.' This passage throws light on the relationship of disciple and teacher. One should not follow a teacher who is himself without vision. (Luke 6.39Q). Human perspectives are frequently defective (Luke 6.41Q). The disciple must learn to recognise the teacher of true vision and accept him as model (Luke 6.42Q). The test is the quality of his praxis, the moral excellence that is the product not only of his teaching but of his very being (Luke 6.43–45Q). Profession of faith is not enough in itself; disciple, like teacher, must express faith in action (Luke 6.46–49Q). The sayings collection thus focuses on Jesus' *exousia*. Although 'signs' are always ambivalent (cf. Luke 11.16, 29–32), a short section relating to John the Baptist takes them as indicative of Jesus' divine mission (cf. Luke 7.19Q). His ministry of healing and teaching fulfils scriptural expectation (Luke 7.22Q). This amounts to the claim that his ministry demonstrates messianic power and authority, and those who do not find Jesus' claims to be an obstacle to faith are truly blessed. (Luke 7.23Q). This kind of teaching is particularly disturbing to those who have invested in existing structures. Hence the disadvantaged, including tax-gatherers (Luke 7.29Q), sometimes responded positively to both John and Jesus while stake-holders in the existing religious and social order did not, in spite of the fact that the two ministries were dissimilar (Luke 7.31–35). A 'Q' saying provides commentary on this situation: in the end 'Wisdom is proved right' (Luke 7.35; cf. Matt. 11.19c).

Attitude to the world

In 'Q', the attitude to the world emerges largely through the disciples' mission and the world's reaction to it.

Disciples and mission

Mission – a demanding, urgent and difficult calling – was a major concern of the sayings collection and, by implication, its audience, although presumably members might relate to it in different ways (it is unlikely that all family ties were wholly abrogated or that the whole community was expected to adopt homelessness as a way of life). By comparison even with Mark's uncompromising picture (Mark 6.7–13), the version of discipleship found in 'Q' is 'very radical, extremely harsh and painted in very black-and-white terms' (Tuckett 1996: 359). Imminent eschatology provides the strongest impetus for mission. The call to discipleship means leaving behind worldly security and obligations (cf. Luke 12.22Q, 12.30f.), and some are not ready to pay the price (Luke 9.57–60Q). The harvest is large, the workers few (Luke 10.2Q). The disciples are sent out 'as lambs [sheep] among wolves' (Luke 10.3Q), with precise instructions as to their demeanour: 'Carry no purse, no knapsack, no sandals; and greet no one on the road' (Luke 10.4). They must break with all family ties and be prepared to sacrifice life itself for the cause (Luke 14.26–27Q). They bear peace and blessing, but their rejection will incur the judgement of God (Luke 10.5–16Q). Simply being open-minded but neutral towards Jesus is not enough (Luke 11.23Q). The clue to this eschatological activity is the vocation of Jesus himself. To him the revelation of his Sonship was given by the Father in prayer. It is imperative, therefore, that the disciples learn to pray (Luke 11.1c,?Q). The short Lucan version of the Lord's prayer probably belongs to the sayings source, focusing as it does on the reign of God. Disciples pray confidently (cf. Luke 11.9–13) for bread for the day and for forgiveness, yet forgiveness is not only something they ask of God but also something they express to others. And they pray not to be brought to the final test – as Jesus was (Luke 11.2–4). Exorcism was clearly controversial. In a sharp exchange with his critics, Jesus demonstrates the logical possibility that his work evidences the reign of God in their midst (Luke 11.20Q). The importance of seeing (discerning, interpreting) is underlined. Right perspective depends on one's spiritual condition (Luke 11.34–36Q).

The opposition which has been apparent in the sayings collection is now crystallised in the woes against the lawyers and Pharisees (Luke 11.39–52Q). What we find here is a collision between different types of religion and morality. The Pharisees are criticised for the value placed on status (Luke 11.43Q), on pedantry (11.52Q), legalism (11.42, 46, 52Q) and external observances to the neglect of inner condition (11.39b–41, 44, 47). In the coming denouement, all that is hidden will be revealed (Luke 12.2–3Q). Opponents or persecutors who can 'kill the body' are much less to be feared than the judgement of God, yet he cares infinitely for his children (Luke 12.4–7Q). Disciples should therefore not be afraid to acknowledge their master in public, and should never 'blaspheme' (Luke, Mark), 'speak against' (Matthew) the Holy Spirit (Luke 12.8–12Q). Nor should they be distracted by worldly cares about food or drink or clothing. That is the way of the world! Accept God's reign and everything else will fall into place (Luke 12.22–32Q). Be clear about what you really treasure (Luke 12.33–34Q).

The nature of the mission

Beyond the general characteristics outlined above, the question of the nature of the disciples' community and mission has given rise to much debate. Was it a peace movement, in opposition to the Zealots (Hoffmann: 1972)? Questions of dating suggest that this dimension did not lie at the source of the tradition, nor does it cohere with the general tendency of the sayings collection. Was it simply a peasant movement, finding hope and liberation through a religious faith which reversed worldly values (Schottroff and Stegemann 1978)? Yet 'Q' implies the renunciation of wealth and the adoption of a missionary life-style; it is not simply speaking of a poor peasant community. Were the 'Q' missionaries modelled on the wandering Cynic preachers? Theissen (1982: 27–67) points to the similarities in life-style while recognising differences. The debate becomes intense and complex. Is all of 'Q' Cynic-inspired, or only some strata of it (Kloppenborg, Vaage, Mack)? There would appear to be real difficulties in defending the idea of a Cynic 'Q' in terms of date, place and genre (Tuckett). Downing makes a brave and sustained effort to define Cynicism in a way adequate to the purpose (Downing 1992: 26–56), concluding that 'anyone behaving like a Cynic, engaging in Cynic *askesis*, would have seemed to be a Cynic, almost whatever his (or her) opinions' (1992: 9). Perhaps the most we can say is that the 'Q' missionaries were like Cynics in a number of respects. It would be unsurprising if world-renouncing religious preachers who represented quite discrete traditions evinced some striking similarities, but any attempt to represent the 'Q' missionaries as fundamentally and originally Cynic appears to encounter acute difficulties in a Galilean context. Tuckett usefully distinguishes between itinerancy (a missionary necessity) and homelessness, which occurs only when the missionaries are rejected. In other words, it is far from being an intrinsic good. Were they liberationists, proclaiming 'good news to the poor' in an eschatological framework (Robinson, Tuckett)? In other words, the poor, hungry and those in mourning are promised a reversal of their position in the coming *eschaton* (Isa. 61). Tuckett, however, also describes their life-style as 'part of a realised eschatology in Q' (1996: 391), displaying the way of life that is appropriate in the kingdom. Perhaps we might see the missionaries as originally messengers of the kingdom to Israel who became, in the context of the primitive church, messianic prophets and guardians of the deposit of teaching contained in 'Q'.

Moral procedures

Two features call for comment. One is the love command and its setting; the other is the effect of eschatology on moral teaching and action.

The love commandment

The traditional origin of the 'double commandment of love' is beyond question. Derived from the Torah, it had become recognised in some rabbinic circles as an introductory summary of the law's requirements. When interpreted, however, with an eschatological intensity bent on exploring the divine purpose, the safe parameters of casuistic debate and gnomic utterance are assaulted by ultimate possibility. Covenantal discourse works with God's generous and righteous love of Israel and Israel's grateful responsive love for God's righteousness. Hence, love for God and neighbour are seen as inter-related. In legal terms, law-breakers are subject to punishment, and this dimension is caught up theologically in the concept of God's judgement. But as the initiator of the covenant, God's nature is not simply to meet alienation with punishment but to overcome it and bring the alienated within the effective scope of his love. Such possibility gains expression in a variety of Israel's writings, including Ruth, Jonah and the nameless prophet of the Exile. Hence Jesus penetrates beyond the confines of love for God and neighbour to the affirmation of love for enemy. The triangle of mutuality (God, self and neighbour) has become a tetrad (or four-stranded structure) of interrelationships which affords space for overcoming hostility and insult and expressing acceptance and forbearance. Within the disciple community, Jesus could translate such insights into the praxis of non-violence, the teaching of the 'peaceable kingdom' (cf. Yoder 1994).

The distinctiveness of this new praxis is not to be underesti-mated. While Graeco-Roman moral teaching expressed the beauty and obligations of friendship, the general consensus was that one should hate (=not love) one's enemies. Even the Jewish tradition could take the form of love for 'the sons of light' and hatred for 'all the sons of darkness'. Covenantal language in itself need not be interpreted to include love for God's enemies. Jesus took faith praxis beyond such boundaries into awareness of the need to meet anger with understanding and violence with non-aggression, and thus to develop practical means of reintegrating the estranged.

Eschatological concern

The collection resumes an overt eschatological emphasis with the summons to be ready for the coming of the Son of Man (Luke 12.39–40, 12.42–46Q) and the consequent division (Luke 12.51–53Q). In the present crisis, it is important to interpret rightly what is happening (Luke 12.54–56Q). Hence it is important to agree with one's accuser (Luke 12.57–59Q), to make for the narrow entrance to the kingdom and avoid the complacency bred by familiarity (Luke 13.24, 26f.Q). The messianic feast will bring people from all directions, but some who counted themselves first among God's people will not be there (Luke 13.28–30Q). The parable of the great supper is on a similar theme (Luke 14.16–24Q). Hence Jesus' lament over Jerusalem (Luke 13.34–35Q).

The framework can be seen to be rounded off in a group of apocalyptic sayings, including the coming of the Son of Man (Luke 17.23, 26, 30) and the final judgement (Luke 22.28–30), with the twelve sitting on thrones judging the twelve tribes of Israel. It is not triumphalist, but a claim that truthfulness is ultimately acknowledged. To his disciples Jesus says, 'You are those who have stood by me in my trials' (Luke 22.28). Trials or *peirasmoi* were thus a recurring theme in eschatological discourse, to which the audience of 'Q' would respond. Jesus related it to his own ministry and that of the disciples. They will therefore have a part in the final scenario when right and truth prevail.

Thus in the course of his ministry, Jesus employed a model of moral teaching which represented a development beyond 'interim ethics' while remaining compatible with it. The coming of the kingdom was in God's hands. It will indeed mark a dramatic divine irruption into history, destroying and transforming. One must prepare for it, and Jesus and his disciples aim to increase the number of those who will share in it (cf. Cohn 1993: 197). Jesus thus employs on occasion a form of imminent futurist eschatology and its moral admonition to watchfulness. But his ministry dictated a development of this purely future view, while not abandoning it. We term this new view 'performative' – that is, in his words and actions Jesus enacted or gave reality to the imagined world of eschatology in such a way that his hearers encountered and began to participate in the new world of the future. They not only prepared for entry to the kingdom but experienced its reality. Such performative experiences of the divine presence and power are also evident in the piety of the Psalmist (cf. Chilton 1996: 23–44). The performative model is readily seen in accounts of Jesus' ministry as healer and exorcist. 'If I cast out demons by the finger [Luke; or 'the Spirit', as Matthew has it] of God, then the kingdom of God has come upon you' (Luke 11.20; Matt. 12.28). Such exorcisms entail 'the binding of the strong man' (the power of evil) and the creation of space for God to act for the salvation of Israel, as in the Exodus story. The performative model is explicit in Luke 17.20–21, where the kingdom, so far from being an external, observable phenomenon, is portrayed as being *entos hymon*. If this is translated 'within you', the reference is more likely to be to the shared reality of God's reign effected by Jesus within the community of disciples, rather than to an individual psychic experience which would be more akin to Gnostic discourse (see below). A third example may be found in Matt. 11.12/Luke 16.16, a text difficult to construe. It may mean that from the time the kingdom became a present reality in the world, it has been a storm centre, as in the wars of the sons of light and the sons of darkness in Qumran thinking – the violent birth-pangs of the new age. Alternatively, it may mean that the new age has come in power with the proclamation of the good news of its availability, and everyone now strives to get into it, to seize upon its availability (Chilton and McDonald 1987: 60; Chilton 1996: 94–7). In either case, John stands at the watershed. After him, a new model is required for the new age in which even the law and the prophets are in some sense superseded. In the time of fulfilment, however, God's righteousness is the model; there is no question of weakening the demands of the law (Luke 16.17; cf. Matt. 5.17–18).

Concluding comments

In spite of a few arguments to the contrary, there is no reasonable doubt that Jesus was an outstanding teacher and inspirer of his disciples, and that his teaching, while availing itself of gnomic material, is far more than the utterances of a sage. In the sayings source, as in Mark, there is abundant testimony to the visionary or mystical aspect of his experience in which the will of the sovereign God and the mystery of his reign were revealed to him in ways which also clarified for him his vocation as Son of God. Thus in 'Q', the temptation story and the epiphany in Luke 10.22Q cohere as indicating the ground of Jesus' authority. Yet the disciple can, in principle, be as the master, for what is presupposed by the revelation is that one should be receptive as a baby (Luke 10.22Q). His teaching is sublime wisdom, but he is more than a wisdom teacher.

Nevertheless, the theological reserve in Jesus' moral teaching is important. God alone represents complete moral competence and compassion, and divine judgement is reserved for him alone. This impinges on the constitution of human community as well as on the relative nature of all human justice. Just as moral persons, however, reach out towards the fullness of divine righteousness, so the human process of law is constrained by awareness of a higher justice and compassion, however expressed. What is denied in this under-standing of morality is any attempt to claim for oneself the prerogative of judgement that properly belongs to God. In this sense, the ethic of Jesus is always subject to divine qualification, and an intrinsic humility is properly affirmed of the human condition, for we can never be as gods.

MARK'S GOSPEL: MORAL DIALOGUE IN THE COMMUNITY OF THE NEW AGE[9]

Mark's Gospel is the twin pillar of source criticism, but it contains relatively little moral teaching.[10] Its emergence as a written document was of great importance for the Christian tradition, supplying as it did the narrative framework of Jesus' ministry which the sayings tradition presupposed. Many other points could be made. It 'tackled the problem of the right of the Jesus movement to exist independently of the synagogue' (Mack 1988: 318). It emphasised the question of Christian identity, including the missionary nature of the community Mark addressed, the gulf that separated it from worldly society, and eschatological and apocalyptic features in its outlook. The moral effect was to subvert rather than support the values of the world or certain other religious communities. Disciples of Jesus did not simply follow his teaching; rather, they 'took up the cross' and followed him. By travelling with Jesus, Christians would fulfil God's will. Mark's greatest achievement, however, was to provide the necessary contours of the ministry of Jesus which the sayings traditions and eschatological expectations alike required. He articulated and co-ordinated the diverse narrative traditions current in the churches and gave them an overall shape. Above all, he incorporated the story of the crucifixion – not without irony – and presented its implications for discipleship (cf. Mack 1988: 340–1).

Cosmic vision

John the Baptist played an important role in Mark's cosmic vision. With him lay 'the beginning of the gospel of Jesus Christ' (Mark 1.1). He was a voice crying in the wilderness, making ready the Lord's way (Isa. 40.3; cf. Matt. 3.3; Mark 1.2; Luke 3.4). For emphasis, Mark prefaced his citation of Isaiah 40.3, common to all the evangelists and given in extended form by Luke, with an unacknowledged quotation from Malachi 3.1: 'Behold, I send my messenger before your face, who will clear a way for you'. The

Malachi passage evoked the symbol of Elijah, who was expected to return 'before the great and terrible day of the Lord comes' (cf. Mal. 4.5). Like Elijah, John was spartan in dress and diet (Mark 1.6; Matt. 3.4), and his mission was the purification of Israel (cf. Mal. 3.24). He was thus seen as having an eschatological role in relation to the Christian story centred on Jesus and so became part of the Christian symbolic world. For this reason, his story was absorbed into the Christian story. In the description of the baptism of Jesus, however, the emphasis is upon the rending of the heavens, the descent of the Spirit and the heavenly acknowledgement of Jesus' Sonship (Mark 1.9–11). John is removed from the scene and Jesus is at centre stage (Mark 1.14).

Mark's cosmic vision is further unfolded in the proclamation of the kingdom as 'good news', with the summons to repentance and belief, marking the crisis of the ages (Mark 1.14). The subsequent narrative is punctuated by interpretative passages, suggesting that something decisively new is unfolding (cf. 2.18–22), that apparent loss and difficulty are followed by abundant harvest (4.1–12), that the Baptist's death presages the death of the messiah (6.14–8.38) but also his final transfiguration (9.1–8), and that these travails foreshadow the imminent eschatological event that seals the present age (cf. Mark 13). We may well ask how such a cosmic vision was linked to moral concern, particularly since Mark cites relatively little of Jesus' moral teaching.

Community ethics

The question of identity is paramount. As recent studies have made clear, the community Mark addressed had already moved considerably in its attitude to the law of circumcision and even the sabbath commandment since the time of the early Pauline mission and the battles faced by James (cf. Kee 1977). The absence of any controversy about circumcision – even any attack on the relaxing of any commandment, such as occurs in 'Q' – may perhaps be taken as an indication that it no longer served as a boundary marker for Christian groups as it did in Judaism (cf. Catchpole 1996: 70–1). If so, a particular kind of interpretation (like the rabbinic *halachah*) was operating, which related the law of circumcision to the Jewish *genos* but not to Gentile Christians – a necessary step for a mixed group of Jews and Christians, bonded together by a common faith in Christ. The question of sabbath practice is given prominence in Mark (Mark 2.23–3.6). Again, the process of interpretation involves an element of deconstruction by which Jesus shows the antithesis between extreme Pharisaic observance and the requirements of mercy. The keeping of the sabbath, understood in relation to the divine care for creation, is affirmed, but it is no longer a boundary marker. Jewish Christians might well observe it in the traditional manner (cf. Hooker 1991: 102), but Gentile Christians, whose mode of life may have precluded such practice, were free to fulfil its merciful purpose in other appropriate ways. A contextual element is always present in casuistry. In terms of halachic debate, the procedures involved the setting of the higher principle over against the lighter, the 'weightier things of the law' always having precedence (cf. Bockmuehl 1996: 267–70). For the Christian communities, the 'weightier things' were the love and mercy of God and the authority of Christ, whose lordship (as 'Son of Man') extends even over the sabbath.

If circumcision and sabbaths were not boundary markers for the new communities, neither were the Jewish dietary laws (cf. Mark 7.1–23; Catchpole 1996: 73–4). Mark finds it necessary to explain Jewish practice to his audience (7.3–4) to illuminate the challenge of the Pharisees to the ways of Jesus' disciple group on the grounds of their ignoring the purity laws when 'eating with hands defiled'. Jesus' response is to accuse the Pharisees of putting 'the tradition of men' above the commandment of God (7.5–7). In what is doubtless a composite passage, the Pharisaic practice of 'korban' (the dedication of a sum to God and temple) is alleged to override the proper care of parents according to the commandment, so allowing the lesser obligation to take precedence over the greater. Thus, in matters of purity, it is inner defilement that is the key issue. There is a strong moral emphasis in such an interpretation, pertaining not only to the given list of vices (7.21–22) but also to motive, intention and purpose – 'the heart'. Jesus shared insights of this kind with his disciples, according to Mark (7.17). Mark has no doubt that, for the Christian community, all foods are therefore clean (7.19) – a stance which allows diversity of practice. Mark seems to be caught on two fronts here. On the one hand, such diversity of practice was by no means easy to achieve, as the 'unfortunate incident at Antioch' shows (cf. Borgen 1988: 126–41). On the other hand, his recommendation seems to go beyond Jesus' own practice. It should be noted that to insist on the priority of 'inner purity' does not mean that Jesus discounted external actions – it was the apparent emphasis on the external act alone that he opposed. He did not abrogate the purity laws but insisted on a radical reorientation of the interpretation given to them (cf. Bockmuehl 1996: 272). His charismatic practice seems to have presupposed that his own strength of holiness overwhelmed the impurity with which he came in contact. Contemporary Jewish practice was more concerned with contamination in the opposite direction. However, the conclusion is clear: dietary laws were not boundary markers of the Christian community. What marked out its members was recognition that the kingdom of God was impinging on their lives, bringing them to turn to God, believe the good news that God welcomed them into it and follow Jesus (Mark 1.15–20). Indeed, there is an openness about the table fellowship which extended to tax-gatherers and sinners and which stands in sharp contrast to the group at the last supper. From some angles, this may seem 'a very costly forfeiture of the exuberance that brought the movement into being in the beginning' (Mack 1988: 347). But, as Mark well knew, the founding of the Christian movement and its mission in the world could not be effected simply through open invitations to table fellowship and the optimistic bonhomie it implied – a fact amply illustrated by the narrative he had to present.

An ethic of tension

The moral dimension of Mark's Gospel frequently emerges in dialogue with resistant questioners. Is divorce lawful? (10.2). What did 'Moses' teach? (10.3) Is not divorce permitted in the Law of Moses (10.4)? Nothing Jesus says or does weakens the authority of the law, yet there is an apparent contradiction between the texts. The issue is one of interpretation, and the clash is resolved by the manner in which the texts are contextualised (cf. Daube 1956: 163). Mark's version of Jesus' interpretation of Deuteronomy 24.1–4 is that the law addresses human 'hardness of heart', stubbornness or wilfulness (10.5).

> Those whose hearts are, or may be, hardened; those who see with unseeing eyes or hear with unhearing ears (4.12; 8.18); those who lack knowledge (4.12; 8.17; 12.24); such persons are strangers to the insight which comes from involvement at the deepest level with Jesus. Those who are involved with, and secretly instructed by, Jesus do not bypass Moses.
>
> (Catchpole 1996: 75)

The insights at the deeper level relate to the purpose of the creator (10.6–9). While in the context of 'life as it is', Moses' command stands as a concession, the creator's intention constitutes 'the weightier things of the law'. To put it another way, the primary moral question is not, 'Is divorce permissible?', but rather, 'To what does God call us?' Mark uses the device of the private instruction of the disciples by Jesus to spell out the implications for practice in the churches: no divorce and remarriage, whether initiated by husband or wife (10.10–12). The secondary church origin of this reflection is shown by the fact that the wife could initiate proceedings under Roman law but not under Jewish law, yet the discussion was about Moses' teaching on divorce. This secondary passage also witnesses to the churches' desire or need to legislate, without apparent regard for 'hardness of heart'. This leads to bad legislation, for law (as 'Moses' knew) regulates the human situation. But Jesus' teaching does not regulate. Rather, it relates to the purpose of God in creation, which stands in tension with how creatures actually behave. This, it may be suggested, represents a primordial or proto-logical, rather than an eschatological, tension with human practice but, in fact, the beginning and the end are interrelated in this kind of theological overview. Either way, we find here the morality of tension and vocation (cf. Via 1985: 67–168).

The debate in Mark is not about the recognition of the Law of Moses but about the way it is understood and enacted. Mark affirms the validity of the love commandment as a summative concept (12.38–44). Other passages enlarge upon the context for effecting God's will, in spite of tensions of life 'between the times'. The peri-cope of the blessing of the children is not only about Jesus' acceptance of them as God's children (important as this is) but about 'receiving the kingdom' (10.15). It is a parabolic comment ('to such the kingdom belongs', 10.14) on turning to God and believing the good news (1.15). To be part of God's reign is to put one's trust in God with childlike confidence. For the childlike, tensions are resolved, for they walk humbly with their God. By contrast, the episode of the rich man in search of eternal life (10.17–22) is full of tensions. Unexpectedly, Jesus identifies a tension in the address 'good teacher'. Goodness may be predicated of God alone. It may be termed a divine attribute but, though tran-scendent, it is not an ideal Platonic form (although Philo would make it such). Rather, the implication is 'turn to God, the source of goodness'; it is a reinforcing of *teshuvah*, 'turning to God'. As the dialogue continues, the next tension is between observing the commandments or keeping the Torah in the context of a rich man's life-style. The man has followed the line taken by the Pharisees that one can accommodate the Torah to the demands of everyday life. Jesus warmed to the man, perhaps because he was aware of the tension and felt a spiritual dissatisfaction. He could resolve the tension by freeing himself from worldly attachments, becoming a disciple and turning completely to God. That, however, involved a fearful cost, a price he was unwilling to pay. He departed sadly, his problem unresolved. This pericope is thus concerned both with wealth and discipleship.[11]

Jesus and his disciples did not avoid all forms of accommodation to worldly situations. The problem of paying taxes to Caesar is a case in point. The pericope in question (12.13–17) involves a skilful debating technique (dialectics had been developed in Israel, at least partly from Greek roots). The critical formula outwitted Jesus' political opponents, who were left with nothing on which to base a charge against him, but appeared to draw a neat line between obligation to Caesar and to God (a fateful occurrence for Christian ethics). The 'inside' interpretation was probably that one was not to be indebted to the world nor allow the world to have an undischarged claim over one (cf. Rom. 13.7–8). In that way, the eschatological tension was seen as creative – one was fundamentally obligated to God alone.

The moral tensions of discipleship

The relation of the faith communities to the disciple group around Jesus received deeper treatment in Mark. The ethics of discipleship (cf. Best 1981) involved the eschatological tension which characterised Jesus' ministry. The beginning of the progressive relationship centred on Jesus as model. When they were sent out to be 'fishers of men', they were sent to do what Jesus had been doing. But that task was directly involved in the eschatological tensions of Jesus' mission, bridging the gap between the wretched situation they knew in Israel and the good news of the salvation being accomplished in their midst. However, not only were the disciples unable at times to demonstrate the power of the new age, but their very message, and Jesus' even stranger conduct, left them facing issues which were beyond them: issues which ranged from unresponsive subjects to disappointed hopes and, above all, the purpose of a self-sacrificing ministry. This was particularly true when the passion story began to unfold. Two moral strands should be noted. One is the morality of ministry which Jesus himself was following. The other is the corresponding pattern of discipleship which he enjoined upon the group.

According to Mark, Jesus clearly envisaged his rejection and death in Jerusalem (cf. 8.31–32; 9.31; 10.33–34). The suffering of the Son of Man was necessitated by his mission, which enacted the reign of God in the midst of a nation and world whose loyalty actually lay elsewhere. The eschatological tension now had the leaders of Israel, 'the elders, chief priests and scribes', as one of its poles, although he would also be 'delivered to the Gentiles'. The moral ethos of Jesus' ministry involved maintaining the integrity and truthfulness of his mission in the face of the pressures to desist from friend and foe alike. It meant persevering in the role of the vulnerable servant against the powers and authorities who held the land captive. Such faithfulness entails suffering and rejection, but it has a positive side expressed characteristically in terms of death and resurrection. Mark 10.45 speaks of 'giving himself as a ransom (*lutron*) for many'. The basic conception here is probably not the 'suffering servant' of Isaiah, with which the Marcan passage has not many similarities apart from the word 'many' (Isa. 53.11; cf. Hooker 1959). The word *lutron* denotes deliverance effected by the self-giving of others. It was particularly used of God's deliverance of his people (the redeemed) from Egypt and from Babylon (Isa. 51.10–11). Did Jesus claim that the climax of his ministry would effect something like a new exodus, or a new return from exile? Mark's narrative may well bear this out, and the connotation of 'many' is an indication of the answer. To understand this term as 'many individuals' is to Westernise it. But, as Morna Hooker has put it, 'the contrast is not between the many who are saved and others who are not, but between the many and the one who acts on their behalf' (Hooker 1991: 248–51). Interpretations contemporary with Jesus take 'many' to denote 'community', and in particular the covenanted community. Is the aim of Jesus' mission that a new covenanted community shall arise out of Israel in bondage, a new covenanted community responsive to the final work of God through his Christ? And are Mark's readers invited to identify with this redeemed community? We note the emphasis on resurrection in all the passion predictions. The new covenant community will only come into being through the faithfulness of Christ when confronted with the powers of darkness and death.

The disciples had to model their mission to Israel on Jesus' practice. Now they have to model themselves on his self-giving. They had to renounce self and 'take up the cross' (9.34). Their community must not be fashioned according to worldly power structures but have an ethos of service (10.42–44; cf. 10.35–41). The last supper Jesus celebrated with them confirmed them as a covenantal community (15.24), but the paradoxical calling of the disciple was to lose his life in order to save it (9.35). The painful scattering of the disciples was the working out of this process (14.27). Their community too had to die and rise to a new embodiment of the covenant community.

Conclusion

The tradition of Jesus, conveyed in its early forms through the sayings source on which the Gospels of Matthew and Luke relied and also through the Gospel of Mark, presented a powerful model to the early Christian communities of the Diaspora. Their separation from historic Israel was now an evident reality, even if their own moral aspirations were shaped to a considerable extent by the moral tradition of Israel. Mark supplied the narrative context which filled out the cosmic vision and the pattern of ministry presupposed by the sayings tradition. The 'word of the Lord' came not through Jesus' sayings only but through the story of his ministry and cross. The result was to distance the Christian communities further both from the current practices in Israel and from the pervasive culture of the times, however indebted they might be to both in certain respects. The 'tradition of the Lord' set up, in effect, a powerful counter-culture – a well-articulated cosmic vision grounded on the will of God, embodied in Jesus' ministry and passion and permeated with eschatological hope.

OTHER SAYINGS TRADITIONS

Since Matthew and Luke incorporate so much of Mark and 'Q', there is no call for an extensive further review here. Note will be made of the peculiar nature of Jesus' sayings in the Fourth Gospel, and slightly fuller comment made on the sayings tradition represented by the *Thomas* tradition.

Matthew and Luke

Matthew and Luke expanded Mark's narrative to present a more comprehensive picture of Jesus' ministry, including in particular teaching material from 'Q' and from other sources to which they had access. A feature of their presentation is their extended and contrasting use of parables, which figured only in limited ways in Mark and 'Q', even if the whole story of Jesus' ministry in Mark has a parabolic quality. Their concern lay not so much in producing a 'life of Jesus' as in offering an interpretation of his significance for salvation and in responding to needs felt in the churches.

Modern scholarship sees Matthew as addressing the predicament of faith communities in the aftermath of the débâcle of 70 CE. An urgent need was for a clear identity and purpose in face of the mounting hostility of Jewish groups. Matthew's Gospel therefore combines a narrative account of the messianic ministry of Jesus, which articulates the basic faith of the Christian communities for whom he was writing, with a statement of the messianic 'fulfilment' of the Torah – a consolidated collection of utterances (the 'Sermon on the Mount') which required a quality of righteous practice exceeding that of the scribes and Pharisees and which thus attempted a distillation of the wisdom of God. In studies of 'New Testament ethics', Matthew's moral interest tends to be characterised as 'training for the Kingdom of Heaven' (Hays 1997: 93–111), or in terms of the 'better righteousness' (Schrage 1988: 143–52), or 'a surpassing righteousness' (Verhey 1984: 82–92). It is important to realise that the context of his presentation is controversy with his Jewish opponents, which determines his perspective on moral understanding and becomes strident in some passages (cf. Matt. 23).

Studies of Luke/Acts, in which narrative predominates, have also focused on community concerns. One was the continuity between past and present in Luke (Conzelmann 1961: 14–16), but moral concerns were also prominent. New Testament ethicists speak of the portrayal of 'the Christian life in Luke' (Schrage 1988: 152–61), 'liberation through the power of the Spirit' (Hays 1997: 112–37) or 'an ethic of care and respect' (Verhey 1984: 92–102). Esler (1987), however, emphasised the need for a legitimation of the Christian communities over against the Jewish synagogue community and Gentile society. The programmatic sermon which Jesus delivered in the synagogue at Nazareth reflected initial acceptance and final rejection, stemming from his 'peshering' (interpretation) of scripture and the note of eschatological fulfilment which he struck. A fully contextual approach to these Gospels thus militates against reductionist claims that Matthew and Luke simply portrayed Jesus as a sage (contra Valantasis 1997: 17). The emergent picture is comprehensive, embracing cosmic significance, ministry in word and action, passion story and death and resurrection. Acts presents the continuity of the faith communities with the ministry of Jesus through the Spirit. The speeches in Acts supply the element of recital essential to an understanding of the churches' existence and faith.

The Gospel of John

John sheds light on important aspects of the tradition of the 'words of the Lord'. He does not reproduce a sayings collection, which by its nature is inert, but contextualises the sayings in the narrative of Jesus' ministry, particularly that of his passion, and presents them to his audience in the form of direct address. Thus Jesus speaks as the way, the truth and the life, as the light that shines in the darkness of the world, as the bread of life, as the resurrection and the life, and as the shepherd of his flock. The sayings thus interpret Jesus' person and function in relation to the faith community and, by contrast, the world which he would save in love. Meaning is apprehended within the community under the guidance of the Spirit of truth. An element of interpretative innovation is discernible here, its purpose being to recover the immediacy of engagement and encounter.

The danger is that such an approach might lead to the notion of Jesus as some kind of disembodied divine voice within the community, mediated by prophetic activity. Correctives are strongly enforced. The divine word became flesh, was incarnated, 'tabernacled' in the world (John 1.14, 18). Jesus' human characteristics are underlined. Meaning is generated in dialogue with the disciples, the crowds and his opponents. He sets the pattern of Christian discipleship by washing the disciples' feet. His entire ministry – including his passion – expresses cosmic purpose.

As we have already noted,[12] New Testament ethicists tend to be preoccupied with the love command in John. Jesus' requirement that they love one another is addressed to them in word and action. Much has been made of the fact that love is emphasised within the community, while love of enemy seems to drop out. Although there is enmity towards 'the Jews', there is no talk of hostile actions towards them. On the contrary, the loving community modelled on Jesus is itself a witness to outsiders (cf. Rensberger 1992: 297–313).

'Hidden sayings' of Jesus

A contrasting use of sayings traditions is found in the document described as the *Gospel of Thomas*. It is not in fact a Gospel but a collection of sayings which can be traced, in part and in Greek,[13] to the early second century CE. They are found in expanded form in a fourth-century Coptic document that came to light at Chenoboskion in the Thebaid and are included in the 'Nag Hammadi library'.[14]

As might be expected, this fascinating and tantalising document has provoked the liveliest discussion and speculation among scholars. In the modern ethos in which authority is suspect, the 'hermeneutics of suspicion' locks on to the notion of hiddenness and is tempted to sensational revelations of true but long-suppressed origins. The most startling version of this speculation is the view that elevates the *Gospel of Thomas* (or much of it) to equal status with 'Q' as belonging to the earliest stratum of Gospel tradition (cf. Crossan 1991), a move that has been described as 'highly tendentious' (Wright 1996: 48). Hiddenness had a rather different connotation for those who treasured *Thomas*. It denoted the precious 'word of the Lord' whose inner meaning was known only to the members of the community whose ethos it defined. It may well be that some parts of it are ancient, although it has been subjected to and preserved by exposition and interpretation.

The conclusion that the 'Nag Hammadi library' was some kind of Gnostic depository was understandable, given the range of Gnostic material in the documents and the underlying assumptions in *Thomas* itself. The collection, however, was varied, containing apocryphal and pagan works as well as Gnostic writings. The location of the find, together with internal evidence from the document itself, suggests a connection with the Pachomian monastic movement in the Nile Valley. Pachomius' Coptic communities can be dated to the early fourth century, and one of them was at Chenoboskion. They were coenobitic – that is, they lived in common rather than as hermits – and they pursued an ascetic lifestyle as monks. It may well be that their wide range of reading material fell foul of Athanasius' policy regarding apocryphal books, many of which were composed in Egypt. That there were purges of books in monasteries is well established – hence the burying of the books in a clay jar at Chenoboskion (cf. Morrice 1997). The library may well have been used by a variety of people, including coenobites and Gnostics. The one group should not be identified with the other (cf. Valantasis 1997: 23).

Were some of the sayings independent of the canonical Gospels? A succession of scholars, including Quispel (1975) and Patterson (1993), have argued for their independence. A contrary interpretation has been pressed by, for example, Tuckett (1988) and Stanton (1995). While the debate is in danger of generating more heat than light, one is impressed by Tuckett's conclusion that on the available evidence a precise solution to the problem is elusive.

> The fact that [Thomas] sometimes shows parallels with redactional material in the synoptics indicates that there is a measure of dependence between our version(s) of [Thomas] and our synoptic gospels. At the very least, that should prevent us from making any sweeping generalisations about [Thomas's] independence and from making further deductions based on such a theory.
>
> (Tuckett 1988: 157)

Our interest being primarily in the question of morality and moral teaching, we shall attempt to analyse and describe the dynamics of the discourse with this in mind. In order to focus on as early a version as possible, we shall largely confine our study to those sayings represented both in *Thomas* and the Greek papyri.[15] Later Coptic sayings have a more outright Gnostic perspective.

Cosmic vision

No attempt is made in these sayings (which we shall refer to as *Thomas*) to provide a formal account of the cosmic vision they presuppose, such as is apparent in 'Q' as we know it. *Thomas* is a sayings document, lacking narrative framework. It is not 'a systematic or even an organised theological tractate' (Valantasis 1997: 6). Its cosmic vision has to be read 'between the lines'.

The cosmic vision centres on 'the living Jesus' whose sayings were recorded by Judas Thomas. They comprise a secret or divine mystery which is shared by the interpretative community, who must seek until they find. Those who come to understanding 'will not taste death', for they have the secret of immortality. Self-knowledge is important to the process of understanding and also discovery about one's relationship with God. Thus the rank ordering of old and young, first and last, is inverted in a process of understanding which has as its goal an all-comprehending unity. The time will come when these sayings will no longer lead the readers to Jesus as authority, for they will themselves have reached enlightenment.

Moral and community ethos

The sayings presuppose an interpretative community, grounded in truthfulness, for whom Jesus' words are transformative. It has ostensibly an ethos of brotherly love: 'Love your brother like your own soul; protect him like the pupil of your eye' (Saying 25). This love command, however, is very different from that in John, let alone the other Gospels. The community has taken over from the devalued family and adopted a familial solidarity of the enlightened and of those (including beginners) on the way to it. Spiritual concern rather than social interdependence is the keynote of this kind of community. The enlightenment of the individual is the goal, which can be obtained only through self-knowledge. If one is to help one's fellow member, one must recognise one's own weaknesses and remove the plank from one's own eye. The potential of the human being is important. Humans rank above even the most noble animals because they have the capacity for light, and it is the community's duty to help towards the realisation of this capacity.[16]

Attitude to the world

The basic reason for human beings not realising their potential is because they are too close to the world. The world is alien to God and to the true nature of human beings. 'Jesus said, "Be passers by"' (Coptic Saying 42; Valantasis 1997: 118). Jesus stood in the midst of the world, indeed he appeared in the flesh, yet he was not overcome by its corruption. He 'aches for the children of humanity', to deliver them from their blindness and worldly intoxication. If fasting and sabbath observance are meaningful, it is only in so far as they promote detachment from the world. Worldly concern for food and clothing (cf. 'Q') is set aside, for God provides the garment (the reference is presumably to baptism). The enlightened are neither vulnerable to the world's pressures nor hidden from public gaze. Proclamation of the truth to the world is an important obligation. Those who have seen the light must shed light on the world. This is the basis of *Thomas*'s theology of mission.

Type of moral argument

The orthodox criticism of the morality of Gnostic groups or those with Gnostic tendencies was that they were either legalistic or anti-nomian: legalistic because of the requirements of ascetic rules, or antinomian because of their rejection of formal moral criteria. Hostile criticism tends to caricature, although there may be an element of truth in it. A more sympathetic verdict on *Thomas*'s moral procedure is that it

> does not revolve about a system of measuring up to an externally imposed ideal equally applied to all members of the community, but rather it revolves about individuals working on themselves among others who are also working on their problems in a process of mutual self-formation and corporate transformation.
>
> (Valantasis 1997: 100)

Is this a kind of personalism? It resembles it in some ways, but its view of the person, like its view of community, is extremely narrow and individualistic. If we take seriously its claim to stand in the tradition of James and Jewish Christianity, we must admit that it gives at best a one-sided interpretation of James' succinct definition of true religion: 'to visit orphans and widows in their affliction, and to keep oneself unstained from the world'. Nor does it take account of the centrality of the love command or royal law, whether in the Synoptic Gospels, John or James. In *Thomas*, social responsibility has been eliminated in favour of a dynamic of moral irresponsibility in relation to the world. *Thomas*'s negative view of the world leads to the avoidance of the incarnational language and the notion of God's love for the world of his creation which are salient features of John's Gospel. Jesus is a voice in the midst of the world, untouched by it. Hence there is no cross (other than metaphorically) and no resurrection from death (other than metaphorically).

It is extremely difficult to see these sayings, lacking context as they do, as representing the original form of the Christian message. They may well be 'old fashioned', not in the sense of recovering the ancient foundations but in the sense of being fragments and echoes of an unsatisfactory form (sayings without context) which the churches had left behind. 'Q' as we know it has a definite cosmic framework. The authority and cosmic significance of Jesus is under-lined. By contrast, these detached sayings virtually invite the hearer to fill in the cosmic blanks! They may therefore have been used by a variety of people, including monks and Gnostics, and they may well reflect a genuine spirituality. An assessment of them as 'sound words of the Lord' depends on the context in which they are heard. Their moral validity may be tested against the understanding of the person, the notion of community and the nature of moral excellence – subjects to be discussed in the succeeding chapters.

4

MORAL PERSONS

The dynamics of personal morality

How are we to understand 'the person' and, in particular, 'the moral person'? The question of moral being is canvassed as determinedly in today's scientific world as it was two thousand years ago, although frequently in more negative terms. Under the influence of the mythology of scientism, the person is reduced to a material system, a machine, a centre of appetites or a derivative of society (cf. Polanyi 1958: 163). It took courage for a scientist like Polanyi to affirm the personal character of all knowing – to insist on the significance of the fact that human beings can be truly creative, imaginative, responsible and moral.[1]

> In ordinary life we accept that only a person can know a person, and that emotions are involved as well as intellectual understanding. Only a person who suffers and rejoices, loves and fears and hates, can know another person. Polanyi speaks of the passions necessarily involved in the pursuit of truth.
>
> (Scott 1996)

Emphasising that 'we can know more than we can tell' (Polanyi 1967: 4; cf. 1959: 12), he argued that to eliminate all personal elements of knowledge would amount to the destruction of all knowledge (1967: 20). Human beings in fact operate at many levels of reality. They can attempt to integrate their insights to form a more inclusive picture of reality, and can even search for ultimate meaning in the universe, however contradictory the evidence may appear. 'So reality leads us on, and it is in such a universe that poetry, art and religion can give knowledge, and that persons can be real' (Scott 1996: 150).

In this chapter, we treat the moral as a relatively high level of apprehending reality and consider the light it throws on the personal as a fundamental level of human awareness. Not that the personal is an easy option for the student. Like all human life, it is complex and beset by tensions and problems. At least it is a concern which has occupied the best minds since ancient times, and which is no less evident in the New Testament.

TENSIONS IN THE MORAL LIFE

In the *Phaedrus* (246B) Plato presented his celebrated picture of the charioteer and his two contrasting horses as a metaphor of the moral struggle within human life. The charioteer of the soul is reason, which must direct the activities of the two-horse team. One of the spirited horses is responsive and obedient – 'guided only by the word of command and by reason' (253D) – representing the higher emotions, such as love of honour, temperance and modesty. The second horse is as indisciplined as a savage monster, 'the friend of insolence and pride' (253E). This horse, who represents the lower emotions or carnal lust, offers valuable strength to the team but is extremely unruly and resistant to the will of the driver, who struggles constantly to control it and thus operate a united team. The metaphor is intended to suggest not divisions within the soul – the *Phaedo*, for example, indicates clearly Plato's unitary view of the soul – but 'modes of the soul as it is affected by contacts with the body' (Fowler, Loeb edn, 409). Driver and horses are alike inspired by the vision of love (*eros*) and much of the *Phaedrus* is taken up with accounts of it. Reason strives to rule the soul and drive it on to attain the perfection of the transcendent world of ideal forms. Indeed, in the Socratic dialogues the role of the philosopher-god Eros is that of guide to 'the correct love of wisdom and of beauty' (cf. Osborne 1994: 92–3). In this quest reason has the co-operation of the spirited horse with its soldierly and honourable qualities, but the carnal horse 'springs wildly forward, causing all possible trouble to his mate and to the charioteer' (254A). The wild horse in fact wins out for a time until the charioteer recaptures his vision of true beauty combined with chastity and begins a long struggle to prevail, until finally 'the soul of the lover follows the beloved in reverence and awe' (254E).

This dramatic picture of the struggle of the soul highlights something of the dynamics of the moral life. The bedrock of morality involves taking responsibility for one's actions and implies a degree of freedom as well as moral choice. Moral awareness, however, also includes the recognition of constraining and even disabling factors, which may greatly reduce freedom of action and may leave one morally impaired or helpless. These forces inimical to the moral life may be located deep within the soul, or they may be external forces, restricting or undermining our ability to make moral choices and act on them. Ancient philosophers, like modern psychologists, have recognised the dilemma, made their own analyses, projected a corresponding model or cosmic view, and proposed therapeutical measures or a counter-strategy. Religions as diverse as Buddhism, Judaism and Christianity have involved themselves with the same human predicament.

Inherent in this discussion is the understanding of the self, the person within whom the emotions, reason, the will and temptations are such powerful forces. But this raises not only the question of the person as body and soul, or body, soul and spirit, but whether personal being can be understood adequately in individual terms. Is the best example of *homo sapiens* the autonomous, rational being of whom many post-Enlightenment philosophers speak, or is this a one-sided caricature of human personhood? Are not persons relational beings whose development is dependent on interaction with others? Must this relational aspect not form an important element in any definition of personhood? Indeed, one of the celebrated descriptions of the person in antiquity was Aristotle's dictum that 'man is by nature a political animal' (*Politics* 1.2) – that is, one who lives in a *polis* or city. The roles which human beings have to play in life are fulfilled not only in relationship with others but within the structures which human society has evolved for its own ends. Moral constraints are therefore important factors, whether they assert themselves in one's inner being, in interaction with others or in society at large. Thus many considerations impinge on human personhood and the moral life, all of which are relevant to our study of the roots of Christian morality. Implicit in the discussion are questions concerning the place of reason and its relation to the emotions, the relation between 'the individual' and the person, the importance of community, and the concept of 'the whole person'.

THE EMOTIONS AND OUR RESPONSE TO THEM

Two Greek words commonly used of the emotions are *pathos* and *epithymia*. The former basically denotes any experience that befalls one. It has a passive connotation, having as its root the verb 'to suffer', to be at the receiving end of action from outside. Hence it can denote misfortune or suffering. Indeed, most instances of the derivative word *pathema* in the New Testament denote 'suffering'. However, to be affected in this way can give rise to strong feelings. Hence *pathos* came to denote 'passion' in the sense of violent emotion, such as love or hate. Paul uses the word in Rom. 1.26 of 'dishonourable passions'; in Col. 3.5 it is used in the context of fornication, impurity, evil desire and covetousness; and in 1 Thess. 4.5 it denotes 'the passion of lust'. The word *epithymia* was originally a morally neutral term for 'desire' or 'longing', but it also came to denote sexual desire or lust. It is used in the New Testament in both senses. Paul can write of his eager desire to see the Thessalonians (1 Thess. 2.17), but more often it denotes lust, as in 1 Thess. 4.5, where both *pathos* and *epithymia* are used. 1 Peter warns against conforming 'to the passions of your former ignorance' (1.14) or living by human passions rather than the will of God (4.2; cf. Eph. 2.3; 1 John 2.16; Rom. 13.14). The gratification of the desires of the flesh is set over against walking by the Spirit (Gal. 5.16). To obey bodily passions is to let sin reign (Rom. 6.12).

In Jewish Greek – *epithymia* occurs eighty-four times in the LXX – the neutral sense predominates, but it has also a negative connotation as well as a religious application. It can denote physical craving (Num. 11.4, 34) and sexual desire (Prov. 6.25), but also religious striving (Isa. 58.2). In 4 Maccabees the four passions – desire, pleasure, fear and distress, arising from sensual and sexual excess – are given prominence and are to be combated by a combination of reason and law. In Philo, who also gives prominence to the passions, we find the Platonic modes of the soul – reason (*logos*, the head), dynamic spirit (*thymos*, the chest, in touch with reason), and desire (*epithymia*, the lower body, far from reason's royal seat and animal in nature). Before elaborating, however, on the dynamics of Hellenistic Judaism, some account of the Greek philosophical tradition on which it drew is called for.

The Graeco-Roman philosophical tradition

In Greek philosophy it was widely recognised that control over the sensual world was essential.[2] Desire or appetite was therefore listed by Zeno, the founder of Stoicism, along with pleasure, grief or distress and fear as leading passions which arise out of wrong attitudes to possessions, 'the waywardness of man in conflict with his rationality' (Büchsel 1965: 168). Zeno identified emotion with the sinking feeling of distress or the expansive feeling of pleasure, and reason had to be brought into play to exercise discrimination and control. Chrysippus, however, argued that emotion itself involved a double judgement – a judgement that the emotion itself was beneficial or harmful, and a judgement about the appropriateness of one's reaction to it. One was free to question the appearance of the emotion. Rationality is involved from the early stages of the experience, and a kind of cognitive therapy or discipline could therefore operate. By contrast, Posidonius was more concerned with psychodynamics. He recalled Plato's insistence on the irrational forces of the soul – the galloping horses, with reason as the hard-worked charioteer striving with difficulty for control. Posidonius questioned Chrysippus' claim that the emotions were judgements. For example, as emotion fades, judgements change (the horses are becoming exhausted); judgements may be inadequate through lack of imagination or foresight (we are not appreciating what the horses are doing); you can have contradictory emotions at the same time (the horses are galloping). Besides, animals have emotions but do not make judgements; and music can arouse emotions without judgements being involved.[3] Seneca took account of Posidonius' criticisms of Chrysippus but believed that a modified version of the latter's approach provided a defensible solution. Taking anger as his theme, Seneca distinguished between three stages:

> To let you know how the passions begin, grow and become uncontrollable: the first prompting is involuntary, a kind of preparing the way for passion but bearing its own threat. The next involves a voluntary judgement – a controlled judgement that I ought to get compensation since I have been injured, or that the other party should be punished since he has committed a crime. It is the third prompting that goes beyond control when it seeks vengeance not

simply if it is right to do so but at all costs, vanquishing the claim of reason.

(Seneca, *De Ira* II.iv.1; my translation)

The first stage was purely involuntary, a bodily reaction to a situation, like the warrior turning pale as he puts on his armour, the soldier trembling before battle, the commander with his heart in his throat before the battle-lines clash, and the most eloquent orator 'freezing' before a speech. This primary disturbance of body and mind is not anger, for 'anger is that which jumps over reason and sweeps it away'. Seneca has thus taken full account of the power of emotion, but he goes on to take up much of what Chrysippus said about rational judgement. 'No passion is more eager for revenge than anger and for that reason it is unfit to take vengeance' (*De Ira* I.xii.5). The second stage, involving the consent of the mind, is crucial. One judges that a particular response is appropriate. One assents to the action. It is best to resist anger at the outset, for if we once yield to the emotion reason is disabled. 'After that, it will do whatever it chooses, not what you permit it' (*De Ira* I.viii.1). In Plato's terms, the unruly horse will have won!

The philosophical debate was not purely theoretical. There was an intention to be 'relevant to life', and a practicable therapy could be derived from the analysis. The Stoic tradition generally pointed to the reinforcing of rational procedures as helpful in controlling irrational responses. The Stoics also encouraged qualitative judgements of externals and talked of the 'rightly dispreferred'. One should not direct the will to something that is 'indifferent'. Cicero and Seneca, among others, regarded precept and example as reinforcing right judgements. Detachment from the cause of disturbance – over-attachment to the world – was common to Stoics and Cynics alike. Other philosophers were attracted by other types of detachment, such as going to the gymnasium, or taking other forms of physical exercise. How one thinks about the past, present and future is also important for coming to terms with life and death, and while philosophers had conflicting views on the subject they provoked reflection on possible courses of action.

The Hebrew tradition

In the scriptures of Israel, the resort to law was much more than invoking an inert external code. Torah was God's teaching of Israel. In the Deuteronomic pattern, it was predicated on Yahweh's covenant love for his people, and on their love for their God (Deut. 6.4). That love is shown, above all, by obedience to his will and calls for response from the whole community. Hebrew psychology and psycho-dynamics differ from the Greek. The people's love for God was to be with all their 'heart' (Heb. *lebab*, a combination of mind and will, with related psychical emotions), with all their 'soul' (*nephesh*, the life force which vivifies the body), and with all their 'might' (*meod*, one's 'substance', including one's material resources). To achieve this total response to the divine will, the teaching of the law is to be memorised, internalised and conveyed to the next generation. Not only does it constitute the cosmic view, it becomes the absorbing interest of life, reinforced by constant discussion and reminders (Deut. 6.6–9). Above all, God's Torah must be remembered, never forgotten (Deut. 6.12), and translated into action. Hence, in the Hebrew tradition *par excellence*, moral practice was held to cohere with cosmic view.

Yet difficulties abounded. There was distortion through over-simplification, as in the kind of theonomy which effected a correlation between obedience to God and God's favour for Israel, between righteousness and prosperity, between cultic practice and God's approval. The world was a dangerous and tragic place, where atrocities were common and the unrighteous appeared to prosper. The practical life of Israel was hammered out on the anvil of political, economic and social contingency. Leadership was a vital ingredient, yet within the political and socio-religious life of Israel tensions were considerable among kings, priests, prophets, psalmists and wisdom teachers, with their interrelated concerns and antagonisms. The covenant was indeed a vocation and constraint, sometimes bypassed in favour of an alternative focus of the cosmic world, such as wisdom. Covenantal obligation often prompted rebellion and disobedience rather than a fulfilling relationship. Thus Israel's relation to Yahweh is frequently characterised by estrangement, and the anger of God is awesome. Hence the prophetic appeals for a turning back to God, for righteousness and holiness as the prerequisites of the covenant people; hence also the characterisation of God's people as a small group rather than the entire nation, as a remnant or faithful community rather than a racial or national people. This, however, was no easy transition, nor one made by common consent. Rather, there were those who took up arms against outrageous political fate, forging in the heat of the power struggles a concept of martyrdom as the ultimate test of loyalty and obedience. This was at once a recognition of the tragic derangement of Israel's life which called for costly devotion to set it right, and a distortion of the deeper prophetic insights into the outrageousness but inevitability of the suffering of the faithful in an unrighteous world and its vicarious possibilities. In the latter case, no armed rebellion was in view but simply devotion to God's justice. Hence the question of suffering – not least undeserved suffering – was part of the moral and theological quest, partnering dreams of a world remade and hopes of divine intervention to that end.

In the cumulative dislocation of Israel's hopes, Judaism tended to regroup round the notions of law and holiness. How were these to be given expression? The Pharisees opted for diligent study, exegesis and worldly observance and obedience; the Qumran community for monastic retreat and ascetic practice, with ritual cleansing, community study and eschatological hope of the renewal of land and temple. Both were heavily conditioned by the historical circumstances of post-Maccabean times, and both were urgently concerned, though in very different ways, that God's will should be realised on earth. Here is the crux of the problem. God's will was held to be revealed and discerned in the history and memory of Israel – hence the definitive statement of his moral requirements in the Torah and Prophets. However, this definitive statement was itself historically conditioned, in the exodus story as in the prophetic encounters with a resistant establishment in Israel. The interpretation of God's will was in this way progressively clarified (it could also be progressively obscured) in the sweep of continuing history. Thus, while moral requirements are seen to follow from God's nature, the latter is revealed not simply as the lawgiver whose codes of practice must be honoured if blessing is to follow, but as the suffering husband longing for reconciliation with Israel, his unreliable spouse. The combination of God's justice and mercy, typified in the covenant relationship at its best, issues not simply in a concern for the other but in a concern to overcome the alienation of the other. In the prophetic tradition (which includes Deuteronomy), this includes the poor and the dependent, as well as the outsider in the midst (that is, those alienated by economic and other circumstances). There is, however, a perceptible tension between this notion of God's openness, his reconciling justice, and the interpretation of purity as separation from the (ungodly) other. Hence at certain points Israel withdrew from such 'contamination', at the cost of inflicting suffering and division. Yet Israel's relation to the nations represented unfinished business. The prophetic tradition in particular had a concern – though it was by no means consistently expressed – to bring the nations within the compass of the faithful community, and for the ultimate reconciliation of the whole cosmos.

It is important not to 'get off the ground' here. There is indeed a dynamic of this kind in the ethics of Israel, but it was not acted out nor commended consistently. Nevertheless, it retains the element of vocation inherent in the covenant-making itself. In whatever circumstances the faithful find themselves – and they may be in dire straits, for the world in which Behemoth (the hippopotamus) and Leviathan (the crocodile) roam is brutal and dangerous – it is important to hear that call and respond to it, even if one is tempted to rebel like Job. This means that ethics must take account of suffering. Indeed, it is the experience of suffering that poses the deep questions of theodicy and moral orientation with which Job wrestled with such determination.

In some respects, the Greek and Hebrew traditions could not be more different. Suffering, in Greek understanding, is a wrong attachment of the emotions, a failure in judgement, to be overcome by therapy or philosophical technique. Suffering for the Hebrews was human reality, within which one was called to act morally. The Greek tradition was strong on analytic technique; the Hebrew tradition embodied unsurpassed insight into the nature of the human condition. Greek ethics formed a logical system, socially derived and humanly directed. Hebrew ethics were relational and drew upon the deepest level of understanding of alienation, reconciling justice and human vocation.

Hellenistic Judaism

4 Maccabees (probably second century CE) provides a useful illustration of at least one important strand of thinking. Professedly philosophical, the subject is whether reason is the absolute master of the passions (1.1, 13). The writer's cosmic vision combines Graeco-Roman and Hebrew views. For him, reason is fundamentally religious; it is the mind making a deliberate choice of wisdom, which he defines as 'knowledge of things divine and human, and of their causes' (1.16) – an exact reflection of the Stoic view adopted by Cicero (*Tusculanae Disputationes* 4.25.37), although he seems also to have some knowledge of Plato (Hadas 1953: 116–17). But he goes on to claim that this wisdom is 'the culture we acquire from the Law, through which we learn the things of God reverently and

the things of men to our worldly advantage' (1.17; Anderson 1985: 545). The writer's loyalty to Judaism is, in fact, his overriding concern. To be sure, his understanding of the moral person is one for whom reason is the guide of the virtues – he affirms the four cardinal virtues of prudence, justice, courage and temperance (see Chapter 6 below) – and the master of the passions. But he illustrates the compatibility of reason and Torah, as well as reason's ability to conquer the passions, from the stories of Joseph, David and, above all, Eleazar and the seven brothers and their mother in the Maccabean struggle. His eulogy focuses on the fact that they took no account of their fatal sufferings and thus 'they all proved that reason is lord of the passions' (1.9). Devout reason controls and guides, even if it does not eliminate, the passions (5.23). Eleazar, taken as the type of the Jewish philosopher, firmly endorses the basis of Torah and demonstrates what loyalty to it means (5.15, 17). To violate any commandment, including the prohibition on swine's flesh, is apostasy (5.35–38). Devout reason teaches one loyalty to the Torah, in all its aspects.

If devout reason provides the framework for understanding the suffering of the martyrs, two other features are to be noted. One is that, like the Wisdom of Solomon, the writer uses the Greek notion of the immortality of the soul rather than the Jewish belief in the resurrection of the body, as in 2 Maccabees. While this enables him to leave the martyrs in incorruptible glory, it testifies to a trend to devalue the corporeal. The second feature is his use of the notion of vicarious atonement. The martyrs' deaths had redemptive efficacy for Israel. 'Make my blood their purification and take my life as a ransom for theirs' (6.29); 'the tyrant was punished and our land purified, since they became, as it were, a ransom for the sin of our nation' (17.21). As H. Anderson says, there is no suggestion of a Christian interpolation here. The idea has its roots deeply set in the religion of Israel, as in the ordinances for the Day of Atonement (Lev. 16), the suffering and sacrifice of an elect group in Isaiah 53, apocalyptic literature and Qumran (Anderson 1985: 539). To this we would add the Aqedah, the intended sacrifice of Isaac. The notion had thus a certain currency in Judaism and contributed an important dimension to the problem of suffering.

THE MORAL DYNAMICS OF THE PERSON IN THE NEW TESTAMENT

In the New Testament, the understanding of the human being owes much to the Hebrew tradition and something to the Greek, but it is more than mere synthesis. Paul, for example, used a variety of terms without however developing a systematic psychology of the person. The range of terms he used not only suggests something of the complexity of his cultural inheritance but also indicates his highly nuanced understanding of human life. His linguistic struggle represents his effort to comprehend the moral and spiritual dimensions of human existence and to engage with the human predicament in its interiority, its interrelationships and solidarities, and its alienation, transformation and re-creation under God. Other New Testament documents reflected a similar understanding, albeit in a less articulate way.

Spirit, soul and body

In 1 Thess. 5.23, Paul prays that the Thessalonian Christians may be kept blameless in 'spirit (*pneuma*), soul (*psyche*) and body (*soma*)' for the coming of Christ. While the threefold formula might suggest a corresponding view of 'the whole person', it does not in fact represent an analytical statement nor does it adequately comprehend Paul's view of the human being. Nevertheless, it provides a useful starting-point.[4]

The term 'spirit' represents the transcendent horizon of human life. The word bridges the gap between the divine and the human. It may thus denote God, Holy Spirit, or Spirit of Christ in relation to believers, and the effects of the divine dynamic on human life, such as the 'fruits of the Spirit'. But it can also denote contrary spiritual forces, such as evil spirits exerting their bondage on human life. The human pole can likewise be designated by the word *pneuma*, whether as the new spirit generated within the believer from baptism and responsive to God's Spirit ('the Spirit himself bears witness with our spirit that we are children of God': Rom. 8.16), or the natural human spirit with its unrealised potential, unable to comprehend the things of God.

This last denotation is close to Paul's use of 'soul' (*psyche*). For him it carries the connotation of life or vitality, as in the Hebrew *nephesh* (cf. 1 Cor. 15.45). 'Whatever you do', says Paul, 'do it *ek psyches*' or, as we might say, 'with heart and soul'. This is as near as the word gets to expressing emotion or will (cf. also Phil. 1.27). But whereas in the scriptures the term was of central significance, in Paul that place is taken by *pneuma*. The word *psyche* was evidently too humanistic to encapsulate on its own the transcendent horizon which was Paul's primary concern. As Stacey observed, 'Paul's knowledge of the Holy Spirit set the basis of his anthropology', necessitating the emphasis on *pneuma* rather than *psyche* (Stacey 1956: 127).

The third term that calls for comment is *soma*, 'body'. Human existence is bodily existence, and the word can be used in precisely that sense. It can denote the physical body, the flesh, either in a straightforward sense without any moral significance or in the sense of moral and mortal weakness. But, as in Hebrew, the word is also used to denote the wider solidarity of human existence. Human life is not viewed in Paul in terms of the individual personality but in terms of corporate solidarity, corporate being. As human beings, we share in the solidarity – the body – of death. Separated from God, we inhabit 'the body of sin'. Through baptism, we are incorporated into 'the body of Christ'. This new solidarity involves identification with Christ in his death and resurrection. There is a solidarity with his cross – a 'dying' to the old body of the flesh, itself subject to death, and a 'rising' with Christ in 'the body of the resurrection', the whole process being that of a transformation with moral and eschatological import.

Important as the above terms were in Paul's thinking, they came short of giving a complete account either of the purposive self or of the emotions. Two terms, related to the Hebrew *leb* or *lebab*, require attention. One is *nous*, the Greek word for 'mind', and the other is *kardia*, 'heart'.

Mind and heart

In Greek philosophy, *nous* stood primarily for the rational faculty, intelligence, reason, mental perception, even 'academic' contemplation, removed from the exigencies of practice. It had, however, a second strand which connected it with feeling and purpose. If one 'has a mind' to do something, then one is intending action. In Homer, to do something 'with all one's mind' is to do it 'with heart and soul'. Hellenistic philosophy related the concept to the 'rational soul', the power of judgement related to the inner life. Greek-speaking Jews, with their penchant for connecting the moral and the rational, found it easy to take up this meaning. In Paul it denotes not the thinking faculty as a separate compartment of the human constitution but the knowing, understanding, purposive self, interrelating reflection and action. It can even be used of the 'mind' of God and the 'mind of Christ' (1 Cor. 2.16). In 1 Corinthians 14, Paul pleads with the Corinthian Christians not to separate spiritual feeling from understanding and intelligibility. The thinking self can, of course, be devoted to unworthy or corrupt ends. Paul condemns the 'base mind and improper conduct' of the Gentile world (Rom. 1.28) and the 'futility of their minds' (Eph. 4.17). It can also be directed to perceiving the will of God. This does not make it into some divine capacity. It is the thinking, willing self, renewed in the process of pondering divine truth.

What then of the emotions themselves? Influenced by his Hebrew upbringing, Paul on occasion used the term 'heart' (*kardia*) to denote the seat of the emotions, intentions and judgements. From it proceeds conduct, good or bad. However, unlike rabbinic usage where the 'evil tendency' (the *yetzer ha ra*) was located in the heart, Paul understood it in a morally neutral sense in relation to the purposive self. As in the LXX, Paul's use of the term 'heart' is close to *nous* (mind), *kardia* generally emphasising the self in relation to emotion and will, and *nous* the thinking, feeling self. But to appreciate fully how Paul regarded the emotions, one must turn to his use of 'the flesh'.

Flesh

The term 'flesh' (*sarx*) can denote the outward and physical self, marriage and sexual relationship, the tie of kinship, and other temporal and visible relations. Sometimes it can stand, Hebraically, for the whole being: 'our flesh [=I] had no rest' (2 Cor. 7.5), or for 'all mankind' (Gal. 2.16; Rom. 3.20; 1 Cor. 1.29). More particularly, it denotes humankind in its frailty and finitude, its worldliness and blindness to higher possibilities (Robinson 1952: 21). But Paul also gives to 'the flesh' a strongly moral connotation. To live in a fleshly way (*kata sarka*) is to be bound up in the sinful solidarity of the flesh and therefore to be hostile to God and resistant to his will (cf. Rom. 8.5–8). It is to render oneself helpless in the face of the power of sin (Rom. 7.25). In this line of thinking, Paul is clearly drawing on the Hebrew understanding of *basar*. The temptation to interpret Paul in dualistic terms should therefore be resisted. The world is God's creation and it is good. The life of faith

has to be lived 'in the flesh' (Gal. 2.20). Even in all our human solidarity the love of Christ controls us, so that we no longer live
simply for ourselves (2 Cor. 5.14). Nevertheless, the flesh also
provides a base for sin. A possible clue as to how this may come
about may be deduced from the last statements. Without the inspiration of faith and the love of Christ, the desires of the flesh
represent uncontrolled self-regard. This accords with the existential
interpretation developed notably by Bultmann, who took the
essence of sin to consist of devoting to the creature the honour that
properly belongs to God (Bultmann 1952: 235–9). The full dimensions of Paul's thinking, though, demand an extension of this view,
even if Bultmann would describe it as mythological. The power of
evil in the world transcends such an individualistic interpretation,
assuming cosmic dimensions. Paul therefore regarded sin as an inva-
sive power which sets up a destructive and disabling dynamic, a
'law' or regimen, within the human person, contending against
one's own better judgements (Rom. 7.23). In either case, one's
natural desires – and we are not talking here simply or mainly
about sexual drives – are no longer morally neutral. They are sinful
and rebellious, alienating one from God, disabling the will and
leading one into spiritual death (Stacey 1956: 163). The flesh
develops a mind of its own (Col. 3.16; Rom. 8.6). At his most
extreme, Paul adopts a form of dualistic language (Rom. 7.18; 8.7),
although this is not consistent with other statements he makes.

Freedom and conscience

The Christian community celebrated the freedom of the Christian
life. 'Where the Spirit of the Lord is, there is freedom' (2 Cor. 3.17).
This included freedom from the corrupt ways of paganism, with its
licentious passions, which were in fact a form of slavery, 'for whatever overcomes a man, to that he is enslaved' (2 Pet. 2.19). It
involved freedom from slavery to law, where an external imposition
took away the freedom of moral judgement (Gal. 2.4; 5.1). The
epistle of James spoke paradoxically of 'the law of freedom' (Jas.
1.25; 2.12) – freedom is real but has its limits. While one has the
right to make up one's own mind on a particular issue, one should
think of the effect of one's actions on others and exercise restraint (1
Cor. 10.29). One is called to freedom, not licence (Gal. 5.13; 1 Pet.
2.16). Paul longs for the day when the whole creation will enjoy
'the glorious liberty of the children of God' (Rom. 8.21).

An essential part of this freedom is the operation of conscience (*syneidesis*). The basic denotation of the term is 'consciousness', 'awareness'. It can therefore mean 'consciousness of sin' (Heb. 10.2); one can have a 'bad conscience' (Heb. 10.22; Tit. 1.15). To have a clear conscience, one must act honourably in all things (Heb. 13.18). It can mean having scruples – and knowing when to override them (1 Cor. 10.25, 27). Being unable to make an informed decision about an issue is to have weak *syneidesis* (1 Cor. 8.7). Thus the basic idea involves discernment or sensitivity to a moral issue. A good example of this occurs in Paul's advice on duty to the state. To have a right appreciation of all the issues involved means that one accepts the role of subject, not out of fear of God or the authorities but 'for the sake of conscience' (Rom. 13.5). One recognises the God-given role of the authorities, and one also recognises one's duty towards them. In the corresponding passage in 1 Peter, appeal is made to freedom. 'Live as free men, yet without using your freedom as a pretext for evil; but live as servants of God' (1 Pet. 2.13). Freedom and conscience are interrelated. One cannot have one without the other.

FURTHER APPLICATIONS

It must be emphasised that, depending on the human condition and motivation, emotions in Paul can be positive and healthy. After a period of absence, Paul speaks almost extravagantly of his great desire to see the Thessalonians once more (1 Thess. 2.7), and his letters show his warmth towards his churches, as well as the frustrations and disappointments he incurred in his dealings with them. Pastoral and community caring also involved emotional investment. 'Rejoice with those who rejoice, weep with those who weep.' (Rom. 12.15). Negatively, to gratify the desires of the flesh is the opposite of 'walking according to the Spirit' (Gal. 5.16). The Pastorals have much to say about the desires of the immature and foolish (1 Tim. 6.9; 2 Tim. 2.22), leading to enslavement to them (2 Tim. 3.6; Tit. 3.3). 1 Peter speaks of 'the desires that ruled over you formerly, when you were ignorant' (1 Pet. 1.14). Emotions are responses to external events: the word *pathos*, which denotes emotion, means anything that befalls one. The agent is, in the first instance at any rate, in a passive or receiving condition. Yet while Stoics spoke of first appearances which led on to judgements, the Christian standpoint was that reactions to events involve relationships – to other people, to the church, to God. There is an ethos, a way of life, to give general support and direction. More particularly, one's response as a person involves the exercise of judgement, will and feeling with a view to action. Each distinctive response is a test of faith, of character, of spiritual condition. One must ask whether the response is 'according to the Spirit' or 'according to the flesh'. In the making and controlling of such response, the help of the Christian community is important, for its members are called to bear one another's burdens. One has the help of the church's encouragement and memory – of the story of Christ who left us a pattern that we should follow in his steps – and of the church's worship, devotion and spiritual life. In the light of all this, possible responses are reviewed in relation to the solidarities they express. The spirits are to be tested to see whether they are of God (1 John 4.1). Thus discernment and will are strengthened, feelings clarified and appropriate action taken. In the end, everyone must bear his or her own burden (Gal. 6.5). The agent must take responsibility.

The process of controlled response can be illustrated in several ways.

Suffering

When one is the victim of misfortune, not only are emotions evoked but one may genuinely suffer. Concern to handle suffering is a prominent feature of New Testament moral teaching. It is bad enough, as the author of 1 Peter points out, when one suffers for one's own misdeeds but to be made to suffer when one is not at all at fault – a lot which often befell slaves (1 Pet. 2.20–21) – is particularly hard. This is the stage which the Stoics described as the 'appearance' or 'first impact' of the situation, requiring judgement with a view to response and action. As we saw in our discussion of freedom and conscience, a Christian response also involves assessing the situation, but to dwell on wrongs received and to foster bitterness or desire revenge is no way to control emotional pressures (cf. 1 Pet. 3.8). One must 'respond with blessing', for only in this way can one avoid inflicting or receiving harm and continue to have the blessing of God. This is not a flight from the reality of the situation, nor is it to retreat into an ideal inner world. One must understand the situation and appreciate why one must not respond in kind. The therapy or technique is to remember and concentrate on one's 'higher calling', that is, the implications of the vocation given in Christ. One can fix one's attention reverently on the example and story of the suffering Christ and his ministry of reconciliation and healing, and bring this powerful symbol into play in the difficulties with which one is confronted. Thus grace, blessedness, even credit replace fear of what unregenerate people can do (1 Pet. 3.14; cf. 2.19–20). When challenged, one should always be able to give a reasoned and courteous account of one's stance, one's conscience supporting one's reading of the situation (1 Pet. 3.15). Both Paul and the writer to the Hebrews are concerned with suffering in face of persecution, whether the latter took a social or political form. In Hebrews we find the notion of Christ, the companion in human suffering (Heb. 2.18), while Paul speaks of the consolation that one finds in Christ (2 Cor. 1.5–7). He can even speak of his joy in suffering in the service of the church and thereby completing the ministry of Christ (Col. 1.24). There is a sense here of the vicariousness of suffering. One's hardships can bring healing to others. The writer to the Hebrews, following the wisdom tradition in particular, held out the model of discipline (*paideia*) as a way of interpreting suffering (Heb. 12.3–13). This is a way of avoiding discouragement or faintheartedness – 'drooping arms and shaking knees' (Heb. 12.12). It turns on how one judges the circumstance. If one concentrates on the unfairness of it all or loses one's anchorage in the hope which Christ offers, one has adopted a self-defeating view. One should think of it as discipline, as a father disciplines his son. Discipline is never pleasant, sometimes painful, but produces in the end a life that is the better for the struggle.

Anger

The second illustration of controlled response is that of anger at wrong suffered. Again the question of relationships is primary; one should aim to be at peace with everyone (Heb. 12.14). Anger can produce a 'root of bitterness' which can disrupt the church (Heb. 12.15). The tradition of Jesus' teaching emphasises the need not simply to refrain from the act of murder but from the anger that prompts it and the uncontrolled abusing of one's brother (Matt. 5.21–23). In the worshipping community, here depicted in Jewish terms, one must seek reconciliation before bringing gifts to the altar. It is interesting that the Western and some other texts want to read 'angry without cause'; clearly, some felt that a complete proscription of anger was too sweeping. After all, there may be situations where one might judge it right to show anger. Were not the prophets angry at the unrighteousness of their nation? Was Jesus not angry at the hypocrisy of his opponents (Mark 3.5; cf. John

7.23)? And did Paul not suggest that one may well be angry but must not allow oneself to be led into sin – in particular, 'do not let the sun go down on your wrath' (Eph. 4.26)? Once again, the key is the enlightened judgement one makes of the situation. 'Do not be quick to anger', Ecclesiastes urges, for it is only 'the fool', or the feckless, who allow anger to fester in the soul (Eccl. 7.5). The responsible church leader must be slow to anger (Tit. 1.7); a sober judgement must first be made of the issue. The main criterion would seem to be whether the anger is conducive to the peace of the community (Rom. 12.18; Heb. 12.14–15). There is a particularly strong emphasis on not returning evil for evil. The tradition stemmed from the scriptures, where the law (the *lex talionis*) made the penalty fit the crime – that is, excessive punishment was outlawed. In personal disputes, however, the question of punishment or retaliation was ruled out in favour of acting rightly towards others, even if they were in the role of enemy (Prov. 25.21–22). Jesus as interpreter of the scriptures expounded the strategy of 'turning the other cheek', absorbing the violence rather than escalating it (a 'Q' tradition: Matt. 5.39/Luke 6.29), and of 'loving your enemy' as part of the call of God to the higher righteousness (Matt. 5.43–48/Luke 6.27–28, 32–36). Once again, we are into the language of vocation. Unless one shares the vision of the 'more excellent way' (1 Cor. 12.30), then the right judgement is unlikely to emerge through self-interested reasoning alone. Cicero, for instance, believed that an enemy should be treated as an enemy. A closed community view leads to a hatred of enemies, as in Qumranic teaching. In the relational ethic of Christian teaching, the scriptural prohibition on vengeance – the converse of loving one's neighbour (Lev. 19.18) – is reinforced. Vengeance is a divine prerogative (Deut. 32.35), forbidden to mortals (Rom. 12.19; Heb. 10.30). Resentful anger must be controlled before it usurps the authority of God.

Temptation

The third and final illustration of controlled response is that of temptation. In scripture, temptation has theological or eschatological significance. The exodus story, containing as it does celebrated episodes when the people succumbed to various temptations and rebelled against Yahweh, provides the archetype (cf. Num. 25.1–18; 21.5–6; Ps. 95.8–11; Heb. 3–4; 1 Cor. 10.8–9). 'Lead us not into temptation' presupposes the supreme test which will not be met without God's aid. Temptation is ascribed to Satan, not only in the story of Jesus' temptations but also by Paul – 'lest Satan tempt you through lack of self-control' (1 Cor. 7.5). The implication here is that we should so order our behaviour (in this case, marital relations) that we do not offer an opportunity for evil to overcome us. Temptation is therefore a time of test by which we can be damaged or from which we can emerge the stronger. 'Count it a joy when you meet various temptations', James says, 'for you know that the testing of your faith produces steadfastness' (Jas. 1. 2–3); 'blessed is he who has withstood trial' (1.12). Yet while the Gospels say that Jesus was led by the Spirit to be tested by Satan (cf. Matt. 4.1; Mark 1.12–13; Luke 4.1–2), James refutes any idea that God puts one to the test (Jas. 1.13). Each one is tempted by his or her own desires; 'then desire when it has conceived gives birth to sin; and sin when it is full-grown brings forth death' (Jas. 1.15). In the Pastorals, the desire to be rich baits the snare of temptation, and many senseless and hurtful desires lead to ruin and destruction (1 Tim. 6.9–10). Thus in human perspective the 'first movements' of temptation occur in a situation which suggests or prompts desires or evil thoughts. These may be ascribed to Satan, the adversary of God and all that God looks for in his creatures, but they arise within the human heart (cf. Mark 7.22). Sin lies in giving way to such promptings. A counter-strategy or therapy is needed; the struggle of mind and will in making a right judgement is intense. Yet 'God is faithful, and he will not let you be tempted above your strength, but with the temptation will also provide the way of escape, that you may be able to endure it' (1 Cor. 10.13). Indeed, left to one's own resources, failure is inevitable, as Paul powerfully puts it in Rom. 7.15: 'I do not understand my own actions. For I do not do what I want, but I do the very thing I hate'. The bondage of the will, as well as the power of worldly desires, is intensely felt in such passages. Hence one must turn one's attention outwards, away from self, to Jesus who was 'tempted as we are, yet without sin' (Heb. 4.15; cf. 2.18). The faithful, worshipping community, with its witness to and memory of Jesus, provides the necessary counter-culture.

NEW TESTAMENT PARAENESIS IN COSMIC SETTING

The bondage of the will illustrates a deeper perspective in New Testament understanding. Plato's analogy of the charioteer does not go far enough. The moral life is not simply about reason cajoling and controlling the emotions in order to steer a straight course. After all, chariot and charioteer can be hijacked. Reason is no longer in control. The will is helpless. Chaos reigns! There are forces which capture and compel the individual. Immorality, like morality, has a transcendent quality.

The modern Western mind finds it difficult to cope with this kind of notion, though people from other cultures may retain a deep appreciation of it. Yet, if we look back over the twentieth century or even concentrate on its final decades, it is difficult not to recognise the power and pervasive nature of evil or to minimise it as an aberration of reason. The Holocaust stands out as an ineradicable testimony to genocide, and ethnic cleansing testifies that its spirit lives on. War is regarded as a final resort, justifiable only within strict humanitarian limits, yet it almost inexorably develops an evil dynamic which leads to the justifying of the total destruction of cities or napalm bombing or chemical warfare. Then there are the great, seemingly inescapable economic systems. Communism, which encapsulated no small amount of human idealism, ended up as an 'evil empire'; yet capitalism too, which demonstrably has brought prosperity to some, is a pervasive, oppressive and divisive force. Both systems dominate where they hold sway. By contrast, there are the localised but tragic incidents – Hungerford, England; Dunblane, Scotland; Oklahoma, USA – the cases of the deranged gunman or bomber. We say 'deranged', yet the perpetrators were not without their rationality although they acted, apparently, under some terrible compulsion.

Thus we can at least recognise what Paul is talking about when he speaks of the bondage of the will and of being controlled by a force other than his own reason and volition. 'So then it is no longer I that do it, but sin which dwells within me' (Rom. 7.17, 20). He speaks of a perverse law that 'when I want to do the right, evil lies close at hand' (Rom. 7.21). Even the commandments that are holy, just and splendid in themselves arouse wrong desires within one (Rom. 7.7–12). Not that one can say that what is good produces sin, or that the law, which is spiritual and life-giving, is designed to undermine and kill off moral being. The fault is located within oneself. One's nature can be described as 'carnal', 'sold under sin' (Rom. 7.14). This sounds like bondage to the passions, which is nothing short of personal death (Rom. 7.5). There is a conflict within. 'I see in my members another law at war with the law of my mind and making me captive to the law of sin which dwells in my members' (Rom. 7.23). Here we seem close to the Platonic and Philonic model of the person, but this understanding of the person relates to a universal condition and to cosmic reality. If there is conflict within the person, there is also conflict in every area of the cosmos – the 'principalities and powers', the 'elemental spirits of the universe' that govern personal being, community life, empires, states and institutions, or higher spiritual realms of being. Each generates its own 'spirit' or dynamic, for good or ill, and human beings are at its mercy. These powers are the inner aspect of material reality (Wink 1984: 104–13), including human reality. Paul used this cosmic picture to interpret the reality of power – whether in individual or interpersonal experience, in corporate or political life, or in psychic terms – and to recognise the implications for freedom, determinism, responsibility, failure or despair in the moral life. Human life, for good or ill, is a bundle of connections, internal and external, as well as at the social, political, psychic or mystical levels, and all these levels impinge upon and lay claim to human existence.

This cosmic picture is, of course, mythological. It could not be otherwise. The 'modern mind' is inclined to be dismissive of such imagery, as of so much else – failing to recognise the operation of a reductionist mythology of its own. Bultmann bought into the mythology of 'the modern mind' as part of his 'demythologizing' programme. Whatever may be said in its favour (possibly a good deal), it was marred at least in his influential essay (cf. Bartsch 1954) by a caricature of the ancient world view as a 'three decker universe' without any real attempt to penetrate its inner workings, and by the assumption that 'existential interpretation' would reveal the only transferable truths that could be read out of such a strange world picture. Yet existential interpretation, with its tendencies towards individualism and rationalism, also represents a severe reduction of scope, neglecting as it does important areas of political and corporate life. Subsequently, the wheel has come full circle. The limitations of 'the modern mind' are becoming increasingly obvious as fundamental paradigms change from the old subject–object divide to much more participative models in which, as in the ancient world, the interconnectedness of all life is more fully recognised. This does not mean that the world view presupposed in Paul or other writers in the New Testament should not be translated into a different key in order to be more fully meaningful in the world of the interpreter, but it does mean that its inner significance must be teased out with greater diligence and humility.

As far as the moral conflict is concerned, with all its ramifications, Paul draws pessimistic conclusions. 'Wretched man that I am! Who will deliver me from this body of death?' (Rom. 7.24). At this point, he recognises that reason ('the law of my mind': Rom. 7.23), as well as the determination of the will (Rom. 7.18), is inadequate for the moral crisis. The humanist might consider him excessively pessimistic: 'I know that nothing good dwells within me, that is, in my flesh.' As we have noted above, the 'flesh' stands for human life in its frailty and finitude. What Paul is saying is that one cannot, by one's own efforts, change the reality of the human condition, bound up as it is with moral weakness, any more than one can escape from the pressure of the powers that be. Both human and cosmic realities require 'redemption', deliverance from their servitude. They need to receive a new spirit. They need not moral norms but a new dynamic – the power to keep these norms, and more. They need to be lifted out of the human and cosmic impasse. The answer Paul gives is a profoundly religious one. Not only in the cosmology of Colossians but throughout his letters, Paul focuses on the cross of Christ as the point where the 'powers that be' – the cumulative evil in the world, as evinced in the Roman authorities or the intransigent Jewish leaders, or the hostile mob, or Jesus' feeble friends, or the 'spirit' that they variously encapsulated – were unmasked, shown up in their true light, and defeated by one who evinced a different 'spirit' and gave a silent witness to the truth. 'Thanks be to God through Jesus Christ our Lord!'(Rom. 7.25). In his silent witness is the power of resurrection, and the destruction of 'sin's dominion' (Rom. 6.5–11). His death is thus a cosmic event, affirming the power of truth over against all the dissimulation of the powers. Here is the new creation, operative in everyone who is 'in Christ' (2 Cor. 5.17). Here is reconciliation with God, the author of our being and the giver of the ministry of reconciliation (2 Cor. 5.18–19). Christian morality presupposes 'conversion', transformation, change in the direction of the *imago Dei*, the face of God in Jesus Christ.

The 'worldliness' of the whole scenario should be emphasised. The powers that dominate the universe require to gain expression in bodily or corporeal form. They are not disembodied spirits, but the 'spirits' manifested on earth, in personal, social and institutional life. Hence those who hanker after gnosis miss the point when they denigrate matter and strive to detach themselves from it, thereby committing themselves to some kind of disembodied interiority. Under God's creation, for all its alienation from its roots, spirits are 'earthed'. They are expressed in the solidarity of creation. They are not, as some moderns might think, mere projections of the human scene. They constitute a reality which dominates the human scene. Evil is not simply a projection of the human but is a reality – cumulative and transcendent beyond doubt – which distorts and destroys the human. Hence, as Wink has put it, what is above is also below; heaven is the transcendent in the midst of material reality and within it (Wink 1984: 118–48). The Gnostic takes flight for the immaterial, and loses moral credibility.[5] The Christian way finds moral expression in the world of God's creation, and affirms it.

The mythology comes to fruition in the life of faith. Paul's faith may be described as a 'particularistic universalism', in that it touches on realities which are truly universal, although Paul comes to them through the particularity of Christ. But faith is, in itself, a universal structure, grounded in trust and expressed in faithfulness. Hence faith/trust is the ground of personal being (cf. Erikson 1980), while faith/faithfulness is the ground of personal morality (see above). Faith goes hand in hand with hope, the eschatological virtue, for hope grounded in faith gives one a future, a goal to strive for. And love (*agape*), undergirded by faith and hope, is the crowning quality of the Christian life (see Chapter 6), the 'more excellent way' for community ethos and personal life.

IMAGE OF GOD

One of the most striking features of the biblical description of the person is contained in the phrase 'image of God' (cf. Gen. 1.26). It was meant to be striking! The scriptures of Israel were all too aware that human beings were of the dust of the earth, to which they will return. Compared with the greatness of the creator God, 'what is man that thou art mindful of him?', asks the Psalmist (Ps. 84). God's care and respect for his creature is astonishing, and that astonishment is possibly mirrored in the daring phrase 'in our image, after our likeness'. It was virtually axiomatic in the scriptures that one did not deal in images and likenesses of God (cf.

Exod. 20.4). The phrase is thus deliberately provocative, even ironic (cf. Gibson 1981: 70–90; Cassuto 1961: 52–60). It expresses the paradox of the creature, who was of the dust, yet 'little less than God' (Ps. 8.5), doomed to toil and suffering (Gen. 3.16–19) yet crowned with glory and honour (Ps. 8.5).

Paradoxes of this kind are difficult to handle. A one-sided interpretation emphasises the power and glory of the human species. It can entertain the illusion of being 'like God, knowing good and evil' (Gen. 3.5) – 'glory to man in the highest!' If the elevated status given to human beings affords them 'dominion' over all other creatures, a one-sided interpretation takes this as the right to dominate and exploit. Yet goodness transcends human beings and is larger than they are; when they attempt to usurp it, it degenerates instantly. 'Dominion' in the scriptures of Israel is authority devolved by God for responsible rule, as in the case of the dominion given to kings. They were vassals of God, exercising stewardship over his people. Hence the dominion given to 'man', both male and female (Gen. 1.27), is a call to responsible stewardship over all God's creation, animate and inanimate. Yet even this notion – far exceeding actual human practice, with its gross exploitation of all creation, in the past and today – is not without ambivalence. 'Stewardship' is a call to responsibility, but it still sets 'man' above the rest of the created order, as if he/she had no affinity with it. Yet this is the other side of the paradox. Human beings are part of creation. If they are given affinity with God, they have also affinity with the animals, with the earth, with the dust.

'Image of God' shares in the ambivalence in so far as it suggests that human beings stand in a unique relationship to God which sets them over and above the rest of creation. It predicates an 'otherness' which can easily become alienation; and in an evil world, the alienation is extreme (symbolised in Gen. 3.14). Curiously, the personalist discourse adumbrated in this chapter can engender a similar product. If one emphasises personal interaction as the key to the human, one risks subordinating other relationships in which persons are involved. There is an element of this in the distinction Buber made between the 'I–Thou' and the 'I–It' relationships. To 'depersonalise' the human is indeed an offence to human dignity, but to fail to treat other levels of creation with respect is to 'depersonalise' ourselves, for these levels are also the good gift of the creator. 'Image of God' must therefore be used not simply to exalt the human but to reflect God's concern for all creation through the responsibility for it given to the human.

Colossians begins to address the problem in its treatment of the divine mission of the Son.

> He is the image of the invisible God, the first-born of all creation; for in him all things were created, in heaven and on earth, visible and invisible, whether thrones or dominions or principalities or authorities – all things were created through him and for him. He is before all things, and in him all things hold together. He is the head of the body, the church; he is the beginning, the first-born from the dead, that in everything he might be pre-eminent. For in him all the fullness of God was pleased to dwell, and through him to reconcile to himself all things, whether on earth or in heaven, making peace by the blood of his cross.
>
> (Col. 1.15–20, RSV)[6]

Here, the nature of the Son defines the image of God and the purpose of creation, since as the 'first-born of all creation' he was active in it. Just as creation is all comprehending, the nature and work of the Son is essential for the coherence of the whole, for otherwise it will fall apart and become fragmented into alienated elements. The church as the body that acknowledges him as head thus has the secret of 'the new nature, which is being renewed in knowledge after the image of its creator' (Col. 3.9–10). His ministry is one of reconciliation, to renew the harmony of creation, including the element of death within it, but this was effected only through his own self-giving on the cross – his renunciation of human power and the outpouring of his life to make peace in creation.

The 'image of God', so far from being the crowning glory that sets humankind apart from all others, is in fact to be understood as pertaining in some sense to all creation and as part of God's reclaiming of all creation. Hence it is not visible in human domination and exploitation of creation but in those activities which reflect the 'fullness of God'. The eucharist is an obvious focus, where elements of creation – bread and wine – symbolise the redemptive work of the Son and thus declare the witness of the church as 'the body of Christ'. The cup of salvation is not simply the pledge of salvation for human beings but of the restoration and reconciliation of all creation, visible wherever people act and live for others.

Various examples of theological rethinking could be cited here – from the 'panentheism' of the cosmic Christ and cosmic covenant to process theology and some forms of feminist and liberation theology today. Certainly, theology and biblical interpretation must continue to develop a creation spirituality, or sensitivity to the interdependence of all creation in the purpose of God, and to underline the role and limitations of human existence within the totality of existence. Ruth Page bids us speak, not of acts of God 'on the model of virile panache' but of acts of relationship. 'I have called this pansyntheism, God with everything and everyone, a state of being between God and nature or God and humans which makes concurrence with divine freedom and love possible among all other possibilities' (Page 1997: 85; cf. 1996: 40–52). Only by such an approach can the 'image of God' be fully expressed and realised.

CONCLUSION

As we have seen, there are many dimensions to the person – from the internal co-ordination of reason, feeling and will, to the interpersonal and the spiritual. Growth as an integrated person, internally mature and externally secure, is clearly an important dimension of the personal; hence the emphasis in the New Testament on the personal interaction of nurture in family and community. Here is laid the groundwork of spiritual and moral development, personal worth and character. Faith communities have a particular contribution to make to the fostering of a cosmic vision that extends moral horizons and supports and guides moral practice. They will therefore tend to embrace the family group and the infant from the earliest stages, so that moral and spiritual experience may evince a coherent pattern.

Moral persons are therefore relational beings, interacting with other people and with the whole world of creation and thus growing in moral awareness. Not that the dimension of 'the individual' should be ignored. Whatever help the community gives, we must each bear our own burdens and accept responsibility for our actions. Individual responsibility does not rule out group involvement. It is when the individual is regarded as a completely separate entity (if such a state can be imagined!) that distortion occurs.

There are various levels of moral apprehension. Socio-historical critics emphasise that elements of moral understanding and practice are culturally dependent. Some worldly perceptions may persist in spite of the moral teaching of the churches. These views we may take as the conventional level, although catechetics can also produce conventional responses (cf. Fowler 1981). At a higher level, a more critical stance may be taken, not only in relation to conventional morality but even in relation to the ethos of the churches. An example is found in the 'enlightened' party at Corinth, critical as it was of the 'weaker brother' with his scruples about meat offered to idols and of the church ethos that supported his views. Such 'enlightenment' may arise from contact with philosophical schools or religious movements which emphasised gnosis or knowledge, and could readily engender an alternative cosmic view. Paul endorsed the logic of some of their arguments but advanced other considerations which showed the dangers of an arrogant claim to knowledge and demonstrated the priority of love, concern for and empathy with others. The 'enlightened' party was not so enlightened after all!

It would be wrong to take the 'enlightened party' at Corinth as indicating the dangers of an over-emphasis on reason. There were probably other factors at work, from religious influences to social status. A better example is the notion of the 'autonomous rational man' of post-Enlightenment philosophy, with its inherent hauteur and its narrow individualism. For moral purposes, it is important to emphasise the 'whole person' – to affirm the interplay of reason, feeling, imagination, empathy, love – reinforced by experiences (such as worship) which express a cosmic vision which can integrate and transform the whole.

There are, of course, other visions of the cosmos, not least in modern scientific world views, which deny the reality of persons as well as trivialising morality. The quality of cosmic vision is thus important for morality as well as for religion. It is one of the strengths of 'New Testament ethics' that it highlights precisely this perception.

5

MORALITY, COMMUNITY AND SOCIETY

The public and political face of Christian behaviour

Alasdair MacIntyre's peroration to his *After Virtue* has become a classic comment on the theme of community and ethics. Referring to the reaction of the Christians to the decline and fall of the Roman empire, he observed:

> What they set themselves to achieve instead – often not recognising fully what they were doing – was the construction of new forms of community within which the moral life could be sustained so that both morality and civility might survive the coming ages of barbarism and darkness.
>
> (1995: 263)

MacIntyre seemed to have monastic communities in mind here, but his comment is no less applicable to the early faith communities. These groups, however, were not cut off from the world, in spite of some of the rhetoric they used. There were social and public dimensions to their lives which were integral to their discipleship. For this reason, and also because community has emerged in the foregoing chapters as fundamental to the shaping and nurturing of Christian morality from the earliest days of the churches, it is now time to take a closer look at the subject.[1]

COMMUNITY

Communities belong to empirical contexts and are accordingly shaped by powerful cultural forces. It is important, therefore, not simply to generalise about 'community' but to observe expressions of it in appropriate socio-historical contexts. Indeed, community is even more complex. The term can be used, for example, of religious and philosophical groups and movements, voluntary associations, households and enclaves, tiny sects and large cities, even (in some contexts) regions or peoples.

Definition is a matter of some difficulty. In modern times community has occupied the attention of a number of disparate disciplines, including sociology, social anthropology and, more recently, moral philosophy and New Testament studies. Long ago, Cooley made the fundamental distinction between primary groups, such as family and clan, and secondary groups such as city or state (cf. Sprott 1958), and household as well as duty to the state will occupy our attention in part of this chapter. The typology of church and sect has also been a related issue (cf. Weber 1965; Troeltsch 1960: 993–4). Social anthropologists like Mary Douglas have emphasised the notion of boundary, the delimitation of communities over against the wider world, and the rites of initiation that go with it. Some of these studies have been applied to New Testament communities (Barton 1986: 225–46). The boundary between church and household will be discussed below. Yet, for all these studies, a definition of community is noticeably missing. MacIntyre, in his final rhetorical flourish in *After Virtue*, lays great emphasis on the construction of local forms of community, but is consistently vague about the nature of community (1995: 263). In *Habits of the Heart* (1985), R. Bellah and others usefully define community, over against the more limited 'lifestyle enclave', as social interdependence, involving participation in the discussions, decision-making and definitive practices of the group. Members are shaped and nurtured by such community involvement as they internalise its ethos and story (1985: 333–5). R. Gill underlines the fact that values are fostered by community, rather than produced by rational argument in isolation, and sees a particular role for the worshipping community as the harbinger rather than exemplar of Christian values (Gill 1991: 16–21).

Christian communities were themselves the crucible of Christian morality and ultimately of Christian ethics. An understanding of the moral dimension therefore presupposes an awareness of the cultural inheritances which helped to shape Christian community. For this purpose, we turn to Graeco-Roman and Hellenistic Jewish traditions relevant to the subject.

Communities in the Hellenistic world

The Greek tradition, both in its aristocratic and its democratic forms, was noted for its sociability and even its conviviality. It thus produced an abundance of social practices – parties, associations, symposia – most often centring upon a meal or drinking session. As in most tribal societies, hospitality was a sacred duty in the Homeric tradition, serving to foster good will, give pleasure and contain excessive rivalry. Freedom of association was incorporated in the laws of Solon and was relatively seldom used for subversive purposes. As for the symposium, it has been observed that it would be difficult to overestimate its importance as a social form throughout the many centuries of Greek culture (Fisher 1988: 1175). In Hellenistic times, the gymnasium and the *ephebeion* or youth centre became focal for community life in the cities. Indeed, the Hellenistic age, when the centre of power had become more remote than ever from the ordinary person, saw a great explosion of social and religious clubs.

There was the family or kinship group (*genos*), meeting for fellowship and mutual support. On such occasions, there would be a brief dedication to the god or gods with which the family identified as a preface to the common meal and social celebration. The extended family group was also concerned with the great events of their members' lives, including their demise, and accepted responsibility for funerals and burials. The so-called *Haustafeln* in the New Testament witness to the strength and durability of the household as primary group within Christian circles.

There were also benevolent societies (*eranoi*), where each member brought his own contribution for the meal and afforded financial assistance to the members as well as caring for funerals. They were something like self-help groups: life-style enclaves rather than moral communities. The celebratory occasions could be somewhat boisterous. When Paul found that in the Corinthian Christian meetings 'each of you takes his own supper, one goes hungry and another has too much to drink' (1 Cor. 11.21), it would seem that the ethos of the *eranoi* was being reproduced within the Christian fellowship.

Trade associations had the additional function of receiving travelling members from other parts of the empire. Whatever trade Paul practised at Ephesus, he would have had contact with the trade association there. Curiously, we have a record of a first-century fishing cartel at Ephesus whose members had erected a new custom house near the harbour at about the time Paul was associated with the city. The social mix of the group, from Roman citizen to slave, is remarkably similar to that shown in the lists of church members in Paul's writings (Horsley 1989: 95–114; cf. Theissen 1982: 69–119).

Then there were cultic groups (*thiasoi*), centred on the service of a particular deity. These tended to be conventionally rather than deeply religious, attending to the upkeep and maintenance of the shrine and the offerings. They usually had a written constitution, a president, office-bearers and official records, and a programme of meetings (often monthly) at which the meal was the focal point, frequently attended by much conviviality (cf. Nock 1972: 414–43). The mystery religions had affinities with these *thiasoi* but were also significantly different. Their affinity is seen in the Dionysiac *thiasoi* at Athens, which took the form of private meetings open to members of both sexes and had their own initiation ceremonies and 'mystery' celebration. Their difference lies in their secrecy and in the intensity of their quest for and celebration of individual salvation. Apuleius described in detail his initiation into the mystery of Isis, exercising due care to protect the secrecy of the cult but speaking nonetheless of his near approach to hell, his vision of the gods celestial and infernal, his final sanctification and the feast of his nativity (*Metamorphoses* XI.23–24). He also uses the language of voluntary death, regeneration, new birth, grace and transformation. His devotion to the goddess is not exclusive, though, for he also goes on 'to embrace the great priest Mithras' and to be consecrated to Osiris, the father of all the gods (*Metamorphoses* XI.25–30). The strict moral requirement of chastity is related to the preparation for initiation rather than to a community ethic. In general, the mysteries did not form nor sponsor moral communities. However, parallels with Paul may be more than incidental, particularly since the terminology of *mysterion* occurs in Pauline literature. In correcting the selfish indulgence in the Corinthian fellowship, Paul not only evokes the memory of the last supper but interprets it as a Christian mystery. Christian celebration, however, is always linked with and permeated by Christian morality and the Christian story.

One inscription provides a fascinating account of a Hellenistic cult group at Philadelphia in Lydia towards the end of the second century or early first century BCE (Barton and Horsley 1981: 7–41). It contains the ordinances given to one Dionysius in his sleep. The cult met in his house (*oikos*), where altars to Zeus and a number of other gods were set up, and had concern for salvation (purifications, cleansings and the mysteries) and good moral and social standards. The moral emphasis is unmistakable (Barton and Horsley 1981: 25). Access was open, irrespective of gender or status – slaves were expressly included. There was an introductory oath, renouncing deceit and magic and anything harmful to young life; any infringe-ment of the oath by members should be reported and sanctions imposed. There was a strict sexual ethic, applying to males and females, infringement of which involved exclusion and the disfavour of the gods. There were monthly and yearly meetings of particular significance, when members renewed their vows by touching the inscription. The group is like a family – it may have been built on the household of Dionysius – and its dynamics support members in a shared moral life-style as well as in the esoteric rites of salvation. A voluntary group of this type offers a number of suggestive paral-lels with the early Christian communities.

The philosophical schools were not *thiasoi* although the Academy and the Lyceum both contained a shrine to the Muses and an altar. In the Greek tradition, the symposium provided the social context for philosophical, political and moral discussion, and the persistence of this model is attested by Athenaeus' *Deipnosophistai* or *Learned Banquet* from the third century CE. Nevertheless in Hellenistic times, the dominant Stoic tradition was not given to bibulous excess and, like the Cynics though in a less extreme form, their approach to life was individualistic rather than through community. It is often claimed for the Epicureans that they provided the outstanding Hellenistic example of the moral community. Epicurus is said to have tried to replace the lost home of the *polis* with the Garden as a substitute religious society (Koester 1995: 141). Inclusiveness and friendship were the keynotes of the movement. 'The Epicureans were indeed a Society of Friends' (Ferguson 1958: 72). In what he describes as the highly structured communities which the Epicureans formed, Wayne Meeks sees 'the closest social analogy, at least among the philosophical schools, to early Christianity' (1993: 26). Yet this may be a misjudgement. In the Epicurean perspective, influenced as it was by the teleology of Aristotle, one's pursuit of the goal of human well-being was a personal quest, to which interpersonal relations were instrumental. Thus the public and political dimension drops out of the picture, and instead of a genuinely communitarian Garden society one finds simply a supportive group to enable the achievement of private and personal goals (Nussbaum 1986: 69).[2] The paradox was not lost on ancient writers such as Cicero, Epictetus and Plutarch.

The affinity between Christian churches and Graeco-Roman associations can be readily illustrated from an unsympathetic second-century pagan writer such as Galen (cf. Walzer 1949) and from Tertullian, the Christian apologist. In Roman imperial times associations were scrutinised for subversive tendencies, and new associations, especially those of Eastern origin, were banned. The repercussions of this policy for the Christian churches provoked a more than spirited response from Tertullian. 'Ought not this community (*secta*) to have been classed with the legally accepted associations (*factiones*), since it is responsible for none of the actions which normally give rise to fear of illegal associations', he pleads (*Apologeticus* 38.1). Tertullian goes on not only to dissociate Christians from the games and other public events but also to define the nature of their community. 'We are a body (*corpus*) with religious convictions, united in discipline and with a common bond of hope' (*Apologeticus* 39.1). He describes their worship and demonstrates that it contains a positive, though limited, relation to the world. There are prayers for the emperor, for ministers and those in authority, for the stability of the world, for peace and the postponement of the end. The offerings (which are not entrance fees, as with some other associations) are not squandered on symposia or junketing but are used 'to feed the poor and to bury them, for boys and girls who are destitute and orphaned, and then for old domestics and shipwrecked sailors, and any who might be serving in mines, or islands or prisons because of their faith' (*Apologeticus* 39.6). The 'books of God' give divine guidance and rebuke. He describes how in extreme cases sinners are excluded. Thus the bounds are protected. The presidents are elders of known good character, who cannot buy their way into office. The ethos of the community is one of love and sharing. 'Everything is shared among us – except our wives!' (*Apologeticus* 39.11). With great spirit and not a little sarcasm, he defends their common meal, 'our little feasts', and also the *agape* (*Apologeticus* 39.14–19). Tertullian undoubtedly goes 'over the top', yet in his spirited if undiplomatic apology we find the profile of full community, combining moral ethos and liturgical practice.

Galen's interest in Jews and Christians is unusual for a pagan writer of the second century CE, even if his comments were little more than asides and his disapproval of their non-scientific arguments all too evident.[3] An unpopular figure in his day, his medical and philosophical work came into its own in later times, not least among the Arabs. His appreciation of Christian morality is preserved in Arabic quotations. He admired their contempt for death and their sexual ethics.

> For they include not only men but also women who, in their self-discipline and self-control in matters of food and drink, and in their keen pursuit of justice, have attained a pitch not inferior to that of genuine philosophers.
>
> (Walzer 1949: 15)

Clearly, the Christians – who relied on 'parables' rather than proper philosophical argument – had impressed as moral communities, and in this respect Christians and Jews were accorded a cautious recognition in terms of what might be termed practical philosophy. On cue, we turn now to Hellenistic Jewish communities.

Community and communities in the Hellenistic Jewish world

Much attention has been paid of late to the notion of community in post-exilic Judaism. Howard Kee has centred attention on models of community apparent in the life of the nation: the ideals of the scribal, legal, temple and mystical communities, and that of the ethnically and culturally inclusive people of God (Kee 1995). Yet definition of community is as elusive as its realisation in Hellenistic Judaism. In very general terms, Israel – or a remnant of it – can be called 'the community of God's people'. In times of stress in particular, the reality thus denoted was rather more than a secondary grouping. The Jewish home, of course, qualifies as a primary group on which the burden of nurture and instruction was firmly placed, while house groups were not unheard of (cf. Ezek. 20.1). The village was an extension of the homes it contained, but the city – which figures with the Temple in the symbolism of Israel – was socially fragmented and pluralistic, including alien forms of community such as the gymnasium and the *ephebeia*, not to speak of Greek schools. There may have been scribal coteries which qualify for the description of community, although the writer of Ecclesiastes is a scribe of a decidedly independent turn of mind – Ben Sira is a better example. The synagogue, whose origins are obscure, is certainly a community, although its heyday came after the collapse of the nation. As we noted above, there was an increasing tendency for 'Jew' to be defined by manner of life rather than simply by birth or nationality (Cohen 1990: 204–8). One chose to join, or was converted into, a particular form of Judaism.

Our concern here is with specific examples of moral community. Josephus singled out three distinctive movements (*haireseis*): the Pharisees, the Sadducees and the Essenes (*Antiquitates Judaicae* xiii.171), although Judaism before 70 CE was much more diverse than Josephus allowed (cf. Charlesworth 1990: 36–41). The three *haireseis* (the word means a 'choice' or 'thing chosen', hence a 'school': Josephus likened them to the Stoics, Cynics and Epicureans) embodied the three most distinctive responses to the Jewish crisis in Maccabean times. Their response centred on questions of ritual purity and faithfulness to Torah, although each pursued these ends in different ways. The Pharisees, aiming to be teachers of the people, remained committed to life in the political, economic and religious structures, and thus to expressing holiness and obedience to the will of God (as in the scriptures) in the midst of the world, with all its conflicting and compromising pressures. It was with an extreme form of this tendency within Judaism that Saul of Tarsus identified. The Sadducees were generally described as priestly, aristocratic, political and élitist. Whatever their precise view of the world (the evidence is even scantier than for the Pharisees), it is clear that they sought the resolution of the holiness issue through Temple and cult. Neither the Pharisees, who laid so much emphasis on instruction in the home and amid daily avocations, nor the Temple-based Sadducees can be said to form empirical communities.[4] The Essenes, a dissenting priestly tradition, followed a different line. For them, holiness or purity could be preserved only through withdrawing from the contaminated world and seeking sanctification through the monastic life. Indeed, it is in monastic communities – Qumran and the *Therapeutae* in Egypt (Philo, *De Vita Contempleva* 72–74; cf. Barclay 1996: 118–19) – that we find the strongest models of moral community.

At Qumran, which must be our example here, the community lived a life of strict discipline and piety, awaiting the coming of the Lord who most surely had a central place for them in the new age. 'They shall practice truth and humility in common, and justice and uprightness and charity and modesty in all their ways.' (*Community Rule* 5.4; Vermes 1995: 75). The ritual act of baptism marked the boundary, and careful preparation was made for it (cf. Allegro 1956: 105–8), but induction into the community seems to have been by progressive stages. Full membership, which involved community of goods and an assigned rank, enabled the member to participate in community decision-making. The ritual of the community emphasised purification and cleansing; purity was maintained by frequent washing, always in unpolluted water. There was also an annual renewal of the covenant, an internalising of the story of the people of the covenant.

In their communal life, members ate together, took counsel and searched the scriptures: 'They shall eat in common and bless in common and deliberate in common.' (cf. *Community Rule* 6.2–3). The group was hierarchical in organisation. The rules were strict, punishment severe; the extreme penalty was expulsion. There was continuous assessment, formal records being kept of progress.

The notion of morality inculcated within the community was entirely deontological. It was 'covenantal legalism' or rules ethics *par excellence*. Yet, for all its hierarchical and regulatory features, the movement enshrined the notion of moral community – an interdependent and interactive group, engendering the spirit of humility, obedience, mutual respect and loving kindness, bound together in the search for purity and righteousness. If the law of God was to be venerated and obeyed, certain qualities of character had to be generated and perpetuated within the covenant community: 'a spirit of humility, patience, abundant charity, unending goodness, understanding, and intelligence; [a spirit of] mighty wisdom which trusts in all the deeds of God and leans on his great loving kindness' (*Community Rule* 4; Vermes 1995: 73). A moral dualism, corresponding to their cosmic understanding, is clear in the 'ways of the spirit of falsehood' (*Community Rule* 4.9–10; Vermes 1995: 74). The dualism or polarity expresses awareness of the fact that moral character is shaped through conflict and struggle. The virtuous cannot rest on their laurels; the spirit of falsehood operates insidiously and effectively, to undermine and overthrow. Yet the spiritual resources of the faith community can sustain one against the wiles of the devil until the day of God's visitation brings healing, peace, blessing and joy for ever.

Community in the New Testament

New Testament communities were not monastic. It is true that the writer of Acts recalls a primitive apostolic community of the Spirit, practising community of goods and affording mutual support. 'There was not a needy person among them, for as many as were possessors of lands or houses sold them, and brought the proceeds of what was sold and laid it at the apostles' feet; and distribution was made to each as any had need' (Acts 4.34–35). Difficulties were apparently experienced from an early point (Acts 5.1–11), and this pattern of community life did not become typical of the churches as a whole. In the Diaspora, most of the churches were set in busy cities, and most of the members had worldly duties to perform. In this respect, Paul's notion of righteousness accorded with Pharisaic rather than monastic notions. But for him the creation of genuine community was essential; it was nothing short of the calling of the church.

Broadly, his notion of the covenant people, the people of God, was that of a solidarity of faith: a *soma* or whole body encompassing God and his people, even his creation, in a relational unity (cf. Robinson 1952: 26–33). Since this organic relationship had been renewed and redefined through the work of Christ, he can speak of the church as the 'body of Christ' and its inner dynamic as the Spirit of God (and of Christ); and since the calling of God's people is the work of God's righteousness, he can understand the focal web of relationships as characterised by moral excellence. All this had final (ultimate) or eschatological significance. His moral groundwork is therefore complex, comprising covenantal, theological, christolog- ical, pneumatological, eschatological and community aspects. The making of Paul's ethics, however, is not a simple deduction from nor systematising of these premises. His thinking was related to the situation that confronted his ministry, namely that the communities he was addressing were far from being 'the body of Christ' in their moral practice. His teaching – like that of other New Testament epistles – was therefore shaped in the dialectic between the tradi- tion he had received and the empirical reality that confronted him.

In other words, the life of the faith community shared in the indicative and imperative that governed all moral action. Baptism was the boundary marker. Baptism in the name of Christ marked them out as the people of God, God's holy people, a united and interdependent community of the Spirit, and the object of his love. They were therefore called to live a godly and holy life, to be the body of Christ in their solidarity with him and in the sharing of their gifts in mutual service, to express their oneness through the avoidance of factions and prejudice and through bearing one another's burdens, and to bring forth in their common life the 'fruits of the Spirit'. Baptism also marked them off from those of the circumcision (the marker of Jewish identity) and from the centrality of law. The life of the Christian community was modelled on

Christ's self-giving – his life, suffering and death for others – and his real presence in their common life.

The catalyst of all this is the worshipping community. The very act of worship expresses Christian humility – the recognition of human inadequacy and need in the presence of the sovereign God of love. Worship is therefore intrinsically moral; the arrogant cannot offer spiritual worship. Its ethos is that of thanksgiving, which Paul reflects in almost all of his letters, and thanksgiving generates a spirit of gratitude and appreciation of all gifts. It is the place where the story of the church – the story of Christ, of salvation – is narrated and internalised, so that it is productive in the common life and in face of all circumstances. It offers the place and time for remembering Christ's self-giving, thus marking off the community from either worldly celebrations, with their tendencies to excess, or household customs, with their clannishness and exclusiveness. Yet, as we have been at pains to underline, the communities had many faults, which the various writers addressed. The indicative always requires underlining. Calling is always a summons to go forward towards the realisation of true destiny. As Gill put it, worshipping communities are harbingers rather than exemplars of Christian virtue.

Yet, while these elevated comments have point, we must not forget that Hellenistic civilisation, in its Graeco-Roman as well as its Jewish forms, prepared the way in many respects for the Christian mission. There was a searching for salvation, a move towards inclusive community, an admiration for moral integrity, which the Christian mission could address. The cult at Philadelphia had similarities of location – the *oikos*, or household – with that of Christian groups, to which we could add family ethos. Both sets of community were inclusive, although the Philadelphia group was probably much more localised than the Christian groups. Both sets of groups emphasised moral purity, although (as far as we know) the Philadelphia group seemed to focus more narrowly on the morality of the family, which included respect for all forms of human life from conception onwards. The Christians certainly had a different cosmic vision, which gave a particular motivation and dynamic to its moral practice. The Christians had probably a much more intense community life, with more frequent meetings for worship. Yet, when all is said and done, we must beware of reading a too rarefied theological understanding into the ethos of the early Christian communities. As Barton and Horsley justly observe:

The moral requirements of the Philadelphian cult-group provide a valuable insight into that sphere of popular moral thought and practice in hellenised Asia Minor which, in addition to the undoubtedly more important influence of their ethical heritage in Judaism, may have moulded the behavioural norms of the early Christian groups.

(Barton and Horsley 1981: 40)

As we have seen, the Christian communities had also a very close relation to households. They were in fact house groups, and their membership was reckoned in terms of the households it comprised. To this subject we now turn.

THE HOUSEHOLD

There can be little doubt that the household was the matrix of the early faith communities and therefore of early Christian moral practice. The household pattern in question was very much part of the social and political fabric of the times. In Roman society the household was an aristocratic tradition, but as the power of the old senatorial families waned, the order which replaced it was intent on maintaining the social base of the *familia* – a more inclusive group than the *domus*, which tended to denote the more closely related family members in a house. Augustus secured the social cohesion of Roman society by fostering the system of interdependent households, the emperor himself being paterfamilias. He was then able to exploit the traditional paternalism of the household as a means of securing ties of loyalty and friendship to himself as emperor. Households were extended families which could include in their fellowship and support system outsiders who regarded the head of the household as their patron. The head of the household had a legal responsibility for his dependants but the unit as a whole was sustained by economic, psychological, social and religious considerations (cf. Malherbe 1983: 69).

It is important, however, not to transfer this stereotype to Christian families without reviewing the evidence (cf. Theissen 1982: 83–7). There was a certain fluidity in terminology; Roman and Greek usages were not identical; Jewish influence continued to operate among Christians. Was the Christian household (*oikia*) more like the Roman *domus* or the extended *familia*? It seems to have features of both. The so-called *Haustafeln* clearly comprise husbands

161

and wives, children and household servants or slaves. The head determined the ethos of the household and thus baptism could be administered to the whole household, establishing it as a household of faith. However, personal assent, at least of the adult members, was assumed, and not all households acted with similar solidarity. Paul had to advise on the problem of divided households and mixed marriages, as had Tertullian. Heads could not therefore simply dictate the policy and had to exert moral influence in the management of their households. Thus in the Pastorals, deacons are required to be 'the husband of one wife' and to 'manage their children and their households well' (1 Tim. 3.12). A woman could act as head of household, like Lydia from Thyatira, whom Paul met at Philippi (Acts 16.14–15). Ignatius indicates that a widow with her children constituted a household (*Ad Polycarp* 8.2). To be a head of household conferred a certain status in society, although this does not mean that Christian householders belonged to the upper echelons of society. Most of them did not, but they nevertheless headed a recognisable group and were able to offer hospitality to itinerant members of the church. The fact that they were able to host church meetings suggests a transformation of the Roman idea of patron. They were, in effect, the patrons of the church that met in their house and clearly had some responsibility for it, if only in promoting what Theissen has called 'love patriarchalism', evincing acceptance irrespective of status and promoting reciprocal concern and respect (Theissen 1982: 107–8).

Ethical interest centres on the so-called *Haustafeln* or 'house tables' denoting the series of household rules which are found in Col. 3.18–4.1, Eph. 5.21–6.9 and 1 Pet. 2.13–3.7. Two basic features are to be noted. The first is the acceptance of a socially determined stereotype which appears to reflect the upwardly mobile urban society of the Hellenistic world. As a stereotype, it consists of the typical range of constituents: husband/father, wife/mother, children, and household slaves. The atypical are not included: widows, orphans, members of the wider family not otherwise attached, and single people. The model is patriarchal. The head of the household enjoys a certain status and authority. Each member has his or her expected role to play. The second feature is the conflict or tension between the inherent structure of the model and the Christian adaptation of it. Thus in Ephesians – probably the most highly developed example – the ethos in which the model must operate is that of mutual respect ('be subject to one another': Eph. 5.21) born of reverence for Christ. Thus reverence for Christ conditions the entire set of relationships, but christology is interpreted in such a way that it does not negate the hierarchical authority inherent in the structure. Wives must be subject to their husbands – a christological reason is given for the male leadership role (Eph. 5.23–24) – but in spite of the note of mutuality struck at the beginning, husbands are not instructed to be subject to their wives. The very suggestion is contrary to the tendency of the model. Instead, husbands must love their wives, in a manner also suggested christologically. This love implies total dedication; indeed, it involves loving one's wife as oneself – the basis of Christian marriage (5. 25–33). In spite of the clear implication that this applies to both parties, though, the writer continues to use the formula of the love of the husband for the wife, and the reverence (the word is 'awe' or 'fear', *phobetai*) which the wife should have for her husband. A certain degree of reciprocity is assumed, but mutuality is sold short! Children should obey their parents and thus fulfil the commandment and the promise it carries (6.1–2); fathers, as the leading figures of authority, are warned against over-punitive discipline which might break the children's spirit. Nurture is an important function within the household. The key terms are *paideia*, which can mean discipline, instruction or education, and *nouthesia*, which has overtones of warning, perhaps against the dangers of the world. Personal formation is thus clearly an interactive concern. It is interesting that in the Haustafeln there is no mention of the tutor, as there is, for example, in John Chrysostom's sermon *On vainglory and the right way for parents to bring up their children*.[5] It was usual for a well-educated slave to fulfil this role, and the Haustafeln do not preclude this, but the absence of formal mention suggests that the stereotype does not relate to upper-class life. In any case, the final responsibility lies with the parents. What the Haustafeln do encompass is the master–slave relationship. Thoroughgoing obedience is required of slaves. The christological model reinforces the requirement: they should look on their servitude as service to Christ, to whom all owe obedience, whether slave or free. Masters are considerably chastened by the thought of Christ as master (Eph. 6.9). Nevertheless, the effect is to ameliorate the condition of slavery rather than challenge the institution.

Two positive estimates of the ethic of the Haustafeln are of note. Focusing on its elements of reciprocity, John Yoder has described its ethic of subordination as a 'revolutionary innovation' (Yoder 1994: 163). All must submit to God; all authority and all subordinate roles are carried out in the context of this ultimate and universal submission. The acceptance of a given order of society is but the necessary framework for a radical change in the quality of relationships expressed within it, based on the Christian affirmation of the worth and dignity of all under God, and the worth and dignity of their service (cf. Gal. 3.28). In 1 Peter, there is more than a hint that the household served as a 'home for the homeless', offering shelter to those who had become outcast for their faith (Elliott 1982).[6] Thus the church was probably able to exploit for good its accommodation to the conventional structures. There was also a failure here, however, which was to reverberate in later ages of church life. The acceptance of conventional authority structures was also a capitulation to them. Authority can be shared in a partnership. It need not be patriarchal. The radical possibilities of Gal. 3.28 could be more truly realised if they were expressed not simply within the structures but by the structures. Then christological thinking would not be distorted to accommodate and subserve cultural assumptions as it is in this passage (cf. Eph. 5.23–24). The shaping of Christian character within such an ethos would be beneficial in many ways but it would include accepting the rationale of worldly society as unchangeable, notwithstanding fine sentiments about equality under God. The 'revolutionary innovation' has gained a measure of expression, but it is half-baked. Must it ever be so?

Gerd Theissen contrasted the Haustafeln with the earlier, rural Palestinian ethos, which was much poorer in a literal sense, as Paul's collection for the poor of Jerusalem shows (Rom. 15.27; 2 Cor. 9.12). 'The history of primitive Christianity was thus shaped even in the first generation by a radical social shift which altered important socio-cultural, socio-ecological, and socio-economic factors through the processes of Hellenization, urbanization, and penetration of society's higher strata' (Theissen 1982: 107). The radical disciple-ethic of Jesus, with its surrender of family and property, simply did not fit the new scenario. In its place there emerged the new Christian love-patriarchalism – seen elsewhere in Paul's teaching apart from the Haustafeln (cf. 1 Cor. 7.21–24; 11.3–16) – which accepted the prevailing social differences but required the superior to show respect and care for the inferior while the latter were obedient, faithful and respectful in return. As Theissen argues, this ethic was successful in many ways. 'It produced the church's fundamental norms and fashioned lasting institutions' (1982: 108). It had great social consequences. 'Constantine was able to succeed with his religious policy only because Christian love-patriarchalism, as the creative answer to radical social changes, was able to have an effect even beyond the small Christian minority' (1982: 109). There is much to ponder here, much that is true, and much that remains problematic. In ethical perspective, one must try to preserve the 'revolutionary innovation' which Yoder highlighted. What happens when the assumptions of patriarchy are themselves rejected? Is the Gospel to be rejected also? Has Christian ethics nothing to say? Yet love-patriarchalism is only one of the possibilities for Christian ethics. What seems essential in such a situation is that the love-patriarchalism is deconstructed and the revolutionary innovation given creative freedom to engage with a new age.

Such cautionary notes indicate inherent tensions in the model broadly adopted by the churches. Stephen Barton has underlined the complexity of the relation between household and church patterns, which gave rise to differing expectations. Two cases in point, as we reflect below, were women and slaves. In response to their claims, overt or tacit, the churches – and Paul in particular – opted to reinforce patriarchal authority. One consequence was that such a stance 'made possible the intrusion into the church of house-hold patterns of allegiance and competition of the kind which found expression at the church meal and proved to be very divisive' (Barton 1986: 243). Paul might have avoided some difficulties, as Barton has suggested, if he had more often insisted on a sharper and more effective distinction between church and household, as he did when requiring that normal eating and drinking be done not in church but at home.

WOMEN: STATUS AND ROLE

There was, on the face of it, little argument about the status of women in the churches. They were full members of the community and as such enjoyed the same status as all other baptised members. In this respect, Paul's celebrated statement in Gal. 3.28 went at least as far as the most liberal practice of the Greek philosophical schools (such as the Cynics, for example), and much further than synagogue practice, where the community was constituted by the adult males. As far as one can see, there was more controversy over the relative status of circumcised and uncircumcised (Rom. 10.12; cf. 3.29), and of Jews and Greeks and other racial and social divisions (Col. 3.11) than over gender difference. The Roman empire was a cultural amalgam in which traditional patriarchal patterns persisted but to varying degrees, women in Egypt (for example) enjoying legal and economic rights not common elsewhere. In Roman imperial society patrician women at least were more liberated than in earlier ages, having access to education and frequently managing the business of the household in the absence of their husbands on public or military service (Witherington 1988: 19). Ambitious or 'upwardly mobile' groups were influenced by such patrician models, including the Christians among whom Priscilla, Lydia and others emerge as people of initiative and enterprise. Nevertheless, when the husband was present he took precedence.

The role of women, particularly in a religious organisation, was a different matter. Women had little role in traditional Roman cults and there is some evidence that they deserted them in droves in the first century CE (cf. Petronius, *Satyricon* 44.84–7), but they responded eagerly to the new religions which swept in from the East – above all, that of Isis. Here, in a cult that was apparently devoid of barriers of gender, class or race, women found religious sentiments and sanctuary to meet their needs and were not debarred from holding the highest offices.

The radical openness of the early Christian communities was thus by no means unparalleled in Roman imperial times, even if the theological and moral emphases were distinctive and far reaching. To some extent, these emphases differentiated between the public and private domain, and thus between the church and the household. The church was a public place in the sense that outsiders could enter it (1 Cor. 14.23) – 'public gatherings which assembled in private space' (Barton 1986: 232). Some aspects of its ethos were therefore problematic. Might women carry over the freedom and authority they exercised at home into the house church, meeting as it did in the same kind of location, and thus extend the social range of their activities (Barton 1986: 233), or were they to be governed by public accountability and convention, even if social roles in society were themselves changing? Paul clearly regarded social propriety as an important aspect of the church's interface with the world. Thus it was 'unnatural' for a man to wear long hair (1 Cor. 11.14), and it was 'disgraceful' for a woman to be cropped and shaved (11.6). Christian traditions (1 Cor. 11.2), probably reinforced by Jewish proclivities, affirmed social convention. Let women cover their hair with a mantle (*peribolaion*), and let men refrain from covering their heads! The result is to emphasise the patriarchal assumptions precisely at the point where public life was being distinguished from private. The household is thought of as coming to Christ through the action of the husband/father as its head; the woman comes to Christ through her husband (11.3). The convoluted theological and exegetical justification of this stance (11.7–12) was apparently not guaranteed universal acceptance in the church (11.16). Church authority had the last word on the matter.

What then of the notorious *crux* represented by 1 Cor. 14.34–35, which bids women keep silence in the churches? If this is a general rule (as it would be if 14.33b – 'as in all the churches of the saints' – is taken with this passage) and if 'speak' refers to prophecy (as the general context suggests), the passage would seem to contradict 1 Cor. 11.5, where the possibility of a woman praying or prophesying in church is clearly accepted. It is in fact possible to challenge both 'if' clauses. 'As in all the churches' could well be read with the preceding statement (14.33a), and 'speak' may denote gossip or chatter. This latter suggestion is not convincing, since the verb *lalein* (to speak) is the regular word for speaking prophetically or under inspiration. One common response to this passage is to argue that it is an interpolation (cf. Hays 1997: 54–5). Without these verses, the passage makes good sense. Besides, it is argued there is evidence of manuscript dislocation at this point. A common suggestion is that a scribal recollection of 1 Tim. 2.11–12 has been incorporated here. The case, however, suffers from two defects. The first is that the manuscript evidence, when carefully assessed, is much less strong than first appears. The dislocation, in fact, appears to be very late (Niccum 1997: 242–55). The second is that it is an incredibly convenient solution for interpreters who wish to explain the passage away. It cannot simply be excised by a flourish of the textual critic's scalpel. Nor is the suggestion that it is non-Pauline paraenesis subsequently appended by Paul as a footnote (Ellis 1981: 213–20; Barton 1986: 229–30) capable of substantiation.

The context of 1 Tim. 2.8–15 suggests a later stage of paraenesis. Now it is the men who are leading prayers, and who must do so in the proper spirit. Women should be modest in dress and manners. A picture is conjured up of the fashionable lady with hair piled high and bedecked with jewels, as in the best Graeco-Roman fashion. Women should be silent and should not be teachers, with authority over men. Once again, appeal is made to the Genesis story (Gen. 2.7, 21–22), in a less than convincing exegesis. A woman's vocation will be fulfilled by raising a family. Pauline reservations have become institutionalised in the next generation. Patriarchy has strengthened. It is tempting to take the glamorous woman as a wealthy or powerful female who has become too dominant in the church, but the comparison with 1 Peter suggests she is more of a stock example (cf. 1 Pet. 3.3–6). The refusal to permit a woman to teach may arise partly through anxiety about false teaching and partly from a desire not to overburden women. Paul is the archetypal teacher (1 Tim. 2.7), and teaching is such a morally weighty occupation that James recommends that few should become teachers at all (Jas. 3.1).

While 1 Tim. 2.8–15 is thus general paraenesis, 1 Cor. 14.34–35 deals specifically with the difference between church gathering and household, and therefore reflects an early stage in the evolution of the church community (cf. Barton 1986: 229–34). 'If there is anything they desire to know, let them ask their husbands at home' (1 Cor. 14: 35). The passage refers to married women, who can pursue further interpretation in the household context but cannot obtrude domestic discussion into the church context. There is probably more to it than this. The bid for public space which some women were making may well reflect the enhanced status of some women in imperial society, while the fact that the command for silence relates to prophesying or related interpretation suggests the emergence at Corinth of a powerful charismatic or 'spiritual' group of women who claimed enlightenment (*gnosis*) and who threatened to dominate, or at least to disrupt, church proceedings by their activities. They claimed divine inspiration without regard to the revelation grounded in the community itself (1 Cor. 14.36). Hence Paul's rebuke, his plea for order and his insistence on his claim to express dominical authority, resistance to which would lead to exclusion from the group (1 Cor. 14.36–40).

The entire chapter, of course, is about the right ordering of worship. The prophets themselves are subject to the discipline of ordered worship. It is in this context that the women too must accept the discipline of the community; that is, they should be 'subordinate, as even the law says' (1 Cor. 14.34). Here is a clear indication that Paul thought in terms of the Jewish tradition, though he cites no relevant passage. Yet subordination did not apply to women alone. All have to be subordinate in appropriate ways. Paul urges them all to be subject to Stephanas and his household and to every fellow worker and labourer (1 Cor. 16.15–16). Thus everyone in church must be subject to the leaders, and ultimately to Christ (cf. 1 Cor. 11.3).

It is evident that Paul felt he had to take a strong line in the interests of eliminating scandal and abuse (1 Cor. 14.40). Since elsewhere he countenanced women prophesying, he would seem to be addressing particular abuses in 1 Cor. 14:34–36, rather than denying prophecy to all women. Besides, what about unmarried women, or widows? What about Philip's four daughters who prophesied? Paul was intent upon the circumstances at Corinth, rather than on other situations and possibilities, although later tradition could readily extrapolate from what he wrote. An assessment of context is always an important safeguard against the dangers of generalisation.

The whole issue of women in the early church is fascinating not because one wants to interpret Paul or anyone else as male chauvinist, revolutionary 'feminist' or even middle-of-the-way liberal (the case provides, in fact, a chastening lesson on the presuppositions of interpreters), but because it reveals something of the social dynamics of the house churches. The Gospel message is one of freedom and impels the church to overcome all barriers, including that of gender. Moral considerations arise in relation to the expression of this freedom in given contexts and within the structures which society provides.[7] There is, however, another issue, one not resolved in the New Testament: at what point must the structures themselves change in order to express more fully the justice and equality of subordinate groups?

SLAVES

Slavery was endemic in the ancient world. In the Roman empire, it was part of the basic social and economic structure. It was also a status symbol. Senators and prestigious public figures would have a very large contingent of slaves. These numbers reduced in relation to the social status of the owner, but even relatively humble citizens would regularly have a few slaves. Households of any standing could not operate without them. Epictetus mocks the unenlightened man who is overcome with the fear that he may lose the good things of life:

> You are afraid that you will not have a professional cook, you will not have another servant to buy the delicacies, another to put on your shoes for you, another to dress you, others to give you your massage, others to follow at your heels, in order that when you have undressed in a bath, and stretched yourself out like men who have been crucified,

you may be massaged on this side and on that; and then
that the masseur may stand over you and say, 'Move over,
give me his side, you take his head, hand me his shoulder';
and then, when you have left the bath and gone home, that
you may shout out, 'Is no one bringing me something to
eat?' and after that 'Clear away the tables; wipe them off
with a sponge.'

(*Arrian on Epictetus* III.xxvi.21–22, Loeb edn, II.223–5)

You were nobody if you did not have your slave in attendance! And
the master–slave relationship inevitably turns up in the household
pattern.

Several factors may be noted here. One is that slaves were of
many degrees, from the personal secretary and educated tutor to the
lowliest menial in kitchen or washhouse, and there were differences
among them in status within the household as in personal bearing,
language and interests. Another is that, slavery being in effect
forced labour, slaves often behaved as the victims they were and
accorded minimum effort to their labours, and running away –
dangerous as it was – was not uncommon. Epictetus takes the
runaway slave as the type of the cowardly and ignoble, who in their
battle for survival 'steal just a little bit to last them for the first few
days, and then afterwards drift along over land or sea, contriving
one scheme after another to keep themselves fed' (*Arrian on Epictetus*
III.xxvi.1, Loeb edn, II.227). The result was the souring of
master–slave relations, the whip and other modes of punishment
being *de rigeur*. The more ambitious slaves could save towards the
purchase of their release, when they would become 'freedmen' – still
not entirely free of obligation to their erstwhile master, but
certainly of higher social status. To save towards freedom, however,
was a long haul and impossibly difficult for the majority. Yet some
masters at any rate were aware of the claims of humanity. To be
sure, slaves were often treated as household chattels, which was
indeed their legal status. Cicero cites the moral philosopher
Hecaton's discussion of the master's moral duties and dilemmas.
Should he let his slaves starve if there is a famine and food prices go
through the roof? In a storm at sea when cargo has to be jettisoned,
should he prefer to sacrifice a valuable horse or a worthless slave
(Cicero *De Officiis* III.89)? Cicero was well aware of the aridity of the
moral philosopher's discussion and distances himself from its elevation of expediency over humanity. He himself emphasised that even
the humblest deserved to be treated with justice, and it was not a

bad maxim to treat our slaves as we should treat our employees (*De Officiis* I.41). But Cicero, we guess, was not an average employer! Be that as it may, some slaves did not want to leave the womb of slavery, especially where they were well fed (slaves were costly), relatively secure and well treated. Freedom and independence were terrifying prospects. Some long-term prisoners in our own culture feel the same way (cf. Kyrtatas 1987: 25–54).

There is some evidence that Paul was studiedly ambiguous about the institution of slavery. With his Hebrew background and probably also an awareness of the more cultured Graeco-Roman attitudes, he showed a humane concern for slaves yet probably did not regard seeking freedom in the formal sense of becoming a freedman a priority for Christian slaves. The crux is the (intentionally?) difficult phrase *mallon chresai* in 1 Cor. 7.21: 'if you can gain your freedom, use it the more'. Did Paul in fact mean that becoming free would give greater opportunity to serve Christ? Did he mean that if the slave was obtaining freedom, the more important thing was that he should serve Christ? Might he even have meant that the opportunity of freedom was irrelevant and that he should concentrate the more single-mindedly on Christian service? Holding as he did that the present order would soon be swept away, he was certainly concerned that slaves, like everyone else, should use their position as an opportunity of serving God (1 Cor. 7.20–21, 24). All of us are the slaves of Christ – a sentiment which may have come more easily from the lips of non-slaves! Yet he was against Christians becoming the slaves of men (7.23).

Certainly, the household pattern dutifully reinforced the necessity for slaves to obey their masters. The system depended on such obedience, and Christian slaves should be most diligent, performing their duties as part of their service to Christ (Col. 3.22–25; Eph. 6.5–8). There is a partial parallel with the inner freedom of the Stoics and Cynics. Epictetus cited the example of Diogenes, who did not let slavery at Corinth trouble him but lived according to the freedom which philosophy afforded him. 'From the time that Antisthenes set me free, I have ceased to be a slave' (*Arrian on Epictetus* III.xxiv.66–67, Loeb edn, II.207). Paul has something of this attitude when he describes the converted slave as 'a freedman of the Lord' (1 Cor. 7.22). However, the inspiration for such an attitude is found in participation in the worship of the church, with its lofty emphasis on moral virtue and a community ethos sustained by agape and imbued with the peace of Christ (Col. 3.12–17). Christian teaching reflects awareness of the temptations and difficulties of the slave's position. 1 Timothy warns Christian slaves against taking undue advantage of their status within the Christian community. They must respect their masters and not take liberties, giving all the better service since those for whom they work share their faith and love (1 Tim. 6.1–2). Some slaves, however, may serve hard masters and be the recipients of savage injustice. This, according to 1 Peter, is an occasion not for rebellion but for living out a Christian vocation, for Christ too suffered unjustly yet did not retaliate (1 Pet. 2.18–25). The weight of Christian teaching is applied to masters in order to ensure justice and fairness to slaves (Col. 4.1), not using threats but remembering that masters and slaves alike are subject to God who shows no respect for human status (Eph. 4.9).

Finally, we come to Philemon – not as the Christian *Magna Carta* for the emancipation of slaves but as the supreme demonstration of Paul's ambivalence on the issue. One of the difficulties is that we do not know precisely what the situation is that he was addressing. Was Onesimus a runaway slave, or had Philemon lent his services to Paul (for whatever reason)? Had Onesimus converted to Christianity under Paul's influence, or had he been a representative of Philemon's church in the first place? At any rate, Onesimus had not distinguished himself in Philemon's service but had won Paul's respect and affection (Philem. 10–11). Paul now feels bound to send him back, although he would have liked to keep him, but he claims to respect Philemon's prerogative and will not presume on his kindness (Philem. 13). Whatever the precise issue is, Paul goes out of his way to win Philemon's sympathy and even, in spite of protestations to the contrary, to pre-empt his response (cf. Philem. 17, 20). We must remember that if Onesimus was a runaway, Paul was asking a great favour in persuading Philemon not to enforce a legal penalty. At any rate, Onesimus seems to have wronged his master in some way, or run up a bill, for Paul offers to stand good for any debt (Philem. 18–19). But what exactly was Paul asking? What does it mean to take him back 'no longer as a slave, but more than a slave, as a beloved brother' (Philem. 16)? Was Paul asking Philemon to emancipate Onesimus, in recognition of the latter's services to Paul? Or was he simply asking him to accept him or reinstate him (as the case may be) as a member of the church? Certainly, Paul makes it clear that he expects positive action. What does he mean by hinting that Philemon should do more than Paul is asking (Philem. 21)? And why does he take the step of reserving a guest room (Philem.

22)? Was it to bring additional pressure, thereby ensuring that Philemon could not quietly ignore Paul's request?

We must not overlook the fact that the letter is addressed to 'the church in your house' (Philem. 1–2). It is thus not a personal letter, although it calls upon Philemon to act. The involvement of the church suggests that Onesimus' membership is at least part of the request. It suggests that the church will support Paul's request that Philemon looks favourably on Onesimus. It also implies that the church is involved with the question of how to deal with slaves. It need not mean that the church will understand Paul to direct that Onesimus should gain his freedom. The consequences for the other household slaves would be considerable. As John Barclay suggests, the church was probably dependent on their services in a number of ways, including preparing the room and the food and generally ensuring that the household coped (Barclay 1991: 176–7). After all, the household was the setting of the church meeting. Besides, the church would hardly want to encourage baptism as a short cut to emancipation![8] The extra step at which Paul hinted may have been that Onesimus should be given a special role in the church – for example, as secretary or amanuensis to the apostle, or as his emissary.

Barclay is probably right in suggesting that, even if we had a clearer picture of its context, Paul's letter would remain ambiguous and that the ambiguity was deliberate. It was designed to compel Philemon and his church to think through the issue and to make their own response to the case of Onesimus as the apostle requested. At this point we can recognise that an element of ambiguity is almost always involved in Christian ethics in relation to worldly issues. The worldly structures and agendas are often intractable, and neither pietistic nor dogmatic solutions will serve. Philemon and his church would have to reckon both with the questions of justice and forgiveness and also with the range of consequences that might attend the various options open to them. Christian ethics does not have, nor can it engender, a fail-safe answer to every dilemma. What is notable, as we have seen, is that the case is referred to the faith community. Moral debate within it, using the accepted criteria of moral discourse, is part of the requirement, but to avoid the aridity of moral philosophy, something more is needed. The moral community can supply that need, and – for all their deficiencies and struggles – the church communities fulfilled that role. As they put on 'compassion, kindness, lowliness, meekness, and patience, forbearing one another and . . . forgiving one another' (Col.

3.12–13), they were creating a context in which moral decision-making was possible.

It is difficult to evaluate the stance of the early Christians on slavery without engaging in non-contextual exegesis. We may feel justified, with Margaret Davies, in castigating their failure to abolish slavery within their own households rather than simply at the church meeting, and contrast their attitude unfavourably with the provisions for slaves in the Hebrew scriptures, as well as at Qumran and in the writings of Josephus and Philo (M. Davies 1995: 315–47). On the other hand, the significance of the fact that they were treated as full members of the church – and, in some cases at least, very responsible members – should not be overlooked. Nor should Paul's ambivalence on delicate matters be made a ground for censure. He could not have shown more acceptance to Onesimus than he did, nor is it at all likely that he was unaware of the Jewish tradition on the matter. He had to address his own context, to which the Jewish laws were not immediately applicable. It is true that, with the foreshortening of eschatological perspectives, the early Christians did not develop a policy for the emancipation of slaves, whatever may have happened in individual instances. For similar reasons, they did not have a highly developed view of work, beyond affirming the necessity to earn a living and avoid idleness (cf. 2 Thess. 3.6–13). Davies attempts to contrast the New Testament 'charity of consumption' – for example, the missionary's right to be supported by the community, although limitations were placed on it – with the 'charity of production' necessary to sustain loving concern for one's neighbour. A clearer vision of the latter, she maintains, might have drawn attention to the anomalous situation of the slaves. Yet Paul, in 2 Thess. 3, certainly insists on productive work, citing both tradition and personal example, 'that we might not burden any of you' (2 Thess. 3.8). Modern notions aside, it is not clear that Paul was unaware of the distinction. Finally, to castigate the New Testament impoverishment of traditions 'which allowed gross injustice to flourish in Christian countries through the centuries' (M. Davies 1995: 347) is to betray a non-contextual view of how tradition works. Paul was speaking to his own times, not to all generations, and each generation interprets tradition afresh for its own context. The recurring problem is that of expressing the Gospel within and to the structured society in which we live. Paul and his fellow teachers cannot be held responsible for the use others made of their writings. Nor is the logic of the argument persuasive. After all, the determined non-militancy of the early Christian centuries did not prevent later ages adopting a highly militant stance.

THE STATE

Two similar passages require our attention here. The first is Romans 13.1–7, with further commentary in 13.7–10 and an echo in Titus 3.1. The second is 1 Peter 2.13–17. That they share a common basis is obvious, although they are equally clearly directed to different situations. It is tempting to see Rome as the common factor. Paul was writing to the Roman Christians at the heart of the empire, perilously close to the seat of imperial power. 1 Peter may have been written from Rome to Christians in a turbulent area of the empire, namely Asia Minor. It was important that the recognised Christian teaching on submitting to human institutions should be well understood.

No issue illustrates the dilemma of the interpreter more clearly than this one. Church–state relations have been such a live and sometimes explosive issue down the ages that it is difficult for interpreters not to bring a load of baggage with them. Sometimes the passages have been cited to cement church–state relations. Karl Barth used the Romans passage to undermine the claims of revolutionaries in the early twentieth century while qualifying the pretentious claims of governments to absolute power. A more recent commentator is equally sure that its bequest has often been negative.

> These seven verses have caused more unhappiness and misery in the Christian East and West than any other seven verses in the New Testament by the licence they have given to tyrants, and the support for tyrants the Church has felt called on to offer as a result of the presence of Romans 13 in the canon.
>
> (O'Neill 1975: 209)

Strictly, however, it is not the verses but their interpretation which causes the problem. Without resorting to untenable claims for neutrality or objectivity, as if we could be exempt from the ambiguities of the interpreter's role, we shall attempt to achieve a balanced view by considering contextual, comparative and ethical perspectives on the interpretation of the passages.

Both Paul and the writer of 1 Peter proceed from community considerations to public commitments. 1 Peter has just described believers as 'aliens in a foreign land' (2.11). Their policy, in the face of prejudice, must be morally unexceptional and capable of winning the respect of outsiders. An important way to 'silence ignorance and stupidity' is to defer to every human authority, whether thought of in personal (Michaels 1988: 124) or institutional (Selwyn 1964: 172) terms. The emperor and his governors or provincial magistrates are specifically indicated in terms of the offices they hold, though they are not in fact personally identified. Christians must 'give honour due to everyone' (2.17). In Romans Paul proceeds from his emphasis on living at peace with all (12.18) and 'using good to conquer evil' (12.21), to the universal requirement of respect for the governing powers (13.1), from which Christians are not exempted. Paul adopts a decidedly optimistic view of imperial administrators. They hold no terrors for the law-abiding citizen (13.3). Persecution, as opposed perhaps to a degree of inconvenience or prejudice, has not yet been incurred at the hands of the imperial authorities. 1 Peter is more reserved. It is certainly the authorities' role to punish those who do wrong and commend those who do right, and Christians must take their cue from that fact (2.14–15). With skilful diplomacy, he sets his discussion of unjust treatment in the context of his advice to slaves, but he has just described Christians as 'slaves in God's service' (2.16). It is reasonable to conclude that the addressees have experienced unjust treatment, and the pattern of Christ's suffering is not cited simply for the benefit of those who have the formal status of slaves. In his summing up addressed to the whole community, he asks, 'Who is going to harm you if you zealously pursue the good?' (3.13). And even if they should suffer in the process, they can count themselves blessed (3.14) – a very different emphasis from Romans 13, yet they no less than the Roman Christians should 'honour the emperor' (2.17).

The requirement to submit to rulers was, of course, a fundamental obligation in Graeco-Roman society, inheriting as it did the hierarchical structures of Greek imperialism as well as the philosophical ramifications of the Stoic view of the natural order. This does not mean that Paul or the editors of Romans have simply borrowed a convenient portion of Stoic doctrine in order to provide the churches with an apostolic ideology of empire. In fact, Paul in particular gives a carefully nuanced statement of human authority. All authority comes from God; the powers that be derive their authority from him (13.1). They are 'God's agents working for your good' (13.4), and God's agents, backed by force, for the punishment of offenders (13.4). This is evocative of the Jewish tradition, where the king is the vassal of God and it is by divine wisdom that rulers decree what is just (Prov. 8.15). Dominion was given from the Lord and sovereignty from the Most High (Wisd. Sol. 6.3). But there is a critical strain in the Jewish tradition that is not explicit in Romans or 1 Peter. 'Though you are servants appointed by the King, you have not been upright judges; you have not maintained the law or guided your steps by the will of God' (Wisd. Sol. 6.4, REB). But neither Paul nor the writer of 1 Peter are attempting either to instruct imperial rulers in the execution of their task or to develop an explicit philosophy of kingship. They are interpreting the role of Christians in relation to the governing authorities. They do not raise the real or hypothetical issue of the unjust ruler or magistrate, even if there is more than a suspicion in 1 Peter that some of those addressed have experienced something of his works. There is no encouragement for the rebel – quite the reverse (cf. Rom. 13.2). The writers have a pastoral concern for the communities they address.

There may be an indication in Romans that the purpose was even more specific (cf. Friedrich *et al*. 1976: 149ff.). One of the ways in which Romans and 1 Peter are most clearly different is in Paul's reiterated insistence on the payment of taxes (13.6, 7). Paul thus suggests that submission to the authorities has to take this tangible form. He even specifies two types of taxation: tribute and revenue (cf. McDonald 1989: 546). Agitation over taxation reached a high point during the early part of Nero's reign, and it may be that Christians in business were tempted to join it. Perhaps, in the aftermath of Claudius' edict which had the effect of expelling them from Rome (Suetonius, *Life of Nero* 44), they were smarting under the two forms of taxation: the tribute, not levied in Italy but levied on subject nationals, and customs duties, which were a deeply resented imposition on traders. Paul would therefore be doubly anxious to insist on submission to the authorities. The Christians had already been expelled from Rome and had quietly returned, but if they proved troublesome it would be simple for the authorities to act against them. Paul urges a prudent course – one which, when they gave it proper attention, would be confirmed by their own conscience (*syneidesis*: 13.5).

If both passages relate directly to a specific situation, have they any wider relevance? This kind of issue has been widely discussed, and a sharp distinction is sometimes drawn between Paul's 'concrete ethics' and the principle of agape of the great commandment.

Although the latter, it is suggested, has permanent value, while most of Paul's teaching is so context-dependent as to have no continuing significance, 'the claim of the relevant instructions is not necessarily applicable only once, but is repeatable' (cf. Schrage 1960; English translation in Rosner 1995: 335). One would not, on principle, engage in non-contextual exegesis, nor attempt to strain out some kind of 'permanent truth'. Rather, one is engaged in the dynamics of the modern situation as Paul was engaged in his. However, it should be noted that, in his continuing discourse, Paul links the specific or 'concrete' moral issue with agape. In this last age, Christians must discharge all their debts, including their debts to the authorities. The principal and inclusive debt to one's fellows is to love one's neighbour. Therefore, to discharge one's civic obligations is one form of neighbour love which, in the crisis of the times, cannot be omitted. To behave responsibly is part of Christian formation as the night passes and the Day draws near (13.12).

As a postscript, let it be noted that the contribution of these passages to the subsequent Christian attitude to the emperor was by no means negligible. While they harness Jewish understanding, they also relate to a debate about imperial kingship which would be familiar to intelligent Romans. One view with roots in Stoicism gained Latin expression in the notion of *clementia* (clemency or benevolent rule). 'The king is first and foremost custodian of the laws he makes and his *potestas* (power, authority) finds its own limits in the *potestas* of God, to whom he too is *subditus* (subject) and to whom he owes his empire' (Sordi 1994: 172). This view, which as it happens is in line with Jewish understanding as well as Romans 13 and 1 Peter 2, was embraced by Augustus and Claudius and given remarkable expression in a speech by Tiberius (cf. Tacitus, *Annales* 4.37–8). The alternative view, of oriental origin, is that of the theocratic *imperium* of Antony, Caligula, Nero and Domitian. It is this view which is the target of the furious denunciation in Revelation 13. In effect the Christians, while remaining true to the Jewish/apostolic tradition, fostered the moderate view of the emperor's role. One can see it in 1 Clement 60–1, where Christians must obey their rulers and governors who in turn derive their imperial power from God, in the Apologists, such as Melito, and above all in Tertullian, who claimed that Caesar was 'more truly ours' because he was put in power by our God (*Apologeticus* 33.1). To quote Sordi once more:

Paradoxically, we could say that the Christian empire, made into reality by Constantine and his successors, was already potentially present in this claim of Tertullian's, a claim which comes at the end of such a deeply committed declaration of loyalty to Rome and its empire that it should surely suffice to disprove the theory that a so-called 'political theology' was the fruit of Constantine's peace.

(Sordi 1994: 173)

6

MORAL EXCELLENCE

Virtue in Hellenistic ethics and the New Testament

Every culture has some notion of virtue or moral excellence. To raise the question in relation to early Christianity is therefore to ask about the varying cultural contexts and moral traditions of the Hellenistic, Roman and Jewish worlds, and to observe the development of the notion of moral excellence from tiny beginnings within the Christian communities themselves, until like a mighty rolling stream it reached Augustine and Aquinas and beyond (cf. MacIntyre 1985).

To take such an inclusive view of moral tradition may reopen a debate that is almost as old as the Christian church itself. Classic stances include that of Justin: 'Those who live according to reason (*logos*) are Christians, even though they are accounted atheists. Such were Socrates and Heraclitus among the Greeks, and those like them' (*Apologia* 1.46); and, in opposition, Tertullian: 'What has Athens to do with Jerusalem, or the Academy with the Church? Away with all projects for a "Stoic", "Platonic" or "dialectic" Christianity!' (*De Praescriptione Haereticorum* VII). Tertullian was unable to maintain this view with consistency, yet the power of his argument gives pause for thought. Is there not a sense in which virtue or the basis of morality is context-invariant? Is this not doubly so if the Bible or the notion of revelation is admitted to the equation? There is a philosophical or theological issue here which lingers in the mind. Yet when we consider the concept of virtue held by various communities and peoples, the matter has a different aspect. As we shall see in what follows, notions of virtue, or goodness, are demonstrably bound up with cultural identity, with ethnicity and life-style and, therefore, with history, tradition and story. This is true even of communities that figure in the Bible itself. Moreover, as W. Burkert has emphasised, societies and communities interact with one another, learn from each other, and grow in strength and vitality through a degree of cultural indebtedness that often greatly exceeds their awareness of the process. Even 'the miracle of Greece', the source of Hellenistic morality, did not emerge out of the blue but 'owes its existence to the simple phenomenon that the Greeks are the most easterly of the Westerners' (Burkert 1992: 129).

Whatever merit may lie in Tertullian's perceptions, the culture of the early Christians, like that of the contemporary Jewish communities, was deeply affected by the pervasive Graeco-Roman world, within which virtue was articulated as the leading moral concept. The Hellenistic context in which the early Christian communities lived and moved and had their being had a long pedigree which can be traced at least to Homer, 'the first and the greatest creator and shaper of Greek life and the Greek character' (Jaeger 1939: 35), and to the 'noble' concept of virtue which exerted its influence on many subsequent centuries. This forms the first section of our study.

VIRTUE AND THE NOBLE VISION

The epics of Homer reflect a heroic, if physical, society, where skill was admired and the power to prevail over one's opponent was all-important. *Arete* (generally translated, not too felicitously, as 'virtue') was essentially excellence, the power to achieve, to be effective in action. In a society in which one's role and status, like the privileges and duties that accompanied them, were predetermined and well defined, *arete* denoted honour, eminence and success in one's field, the full flourishing of one's personal talents and even endowment with special power. It was the mark of the leader or warrior, who carried out his duties in war with the same skill and flair as he governed his household, tenants and property back home and thus more than held his own in the *agon*, the contest of life. As such, he was worthy of the praise and esteem of his people. Since such a premium was placed upon action, life itself had a narrative quality, and narrative portrayals of it provided the historical and value-laden memory of the culture.

Arete therefore did not in itself denote a moral quality, although moral qualities are found in its connotation. The moral world of the Homeric hero united the intrinsic values of the warrior society – honour, glory, courage, nobility of purpose, excellence – with a prudential ethic which enjoined respect for parents and others who merited it, and respect for the gods. A person who possessed *arete* would act fittingly – in accordance with *dike*, which denoted social custom and came to include the recognition of the rights of others and the wider moral order. In effect, *dike* constituted a rudimentary moral law (*themis*). To act otherwise was to be antinomian and anarchistic (*athemistos*), without respect for the rulers, laws and customs which were given with the social structure and cosmic vision, and which were reinforced by intimations of doom for the disobedient. Order and rank in society were not negotiable. A certain equality obtained among the aristocracy, but it had no wider application. Equality in Homer was as unwelcome as death, old age and misfortune, which levelled out the proper social distinctions (Ferguson 1958: 21) and gave life its tragic quality. 'It is defeat and not victory that lies at the end' (MacIntyre 1985: 124). It took courage to recognise this, just as it took courage to sustain the demands of true friendship and meet one's obligations to household and community: hence the claim of courage to be a prime virtue.[1]

Two further moral controls may be noted briefly: *nemesis*, retribution or righteous anger, which in Homer is often expressed in social terms as disgrace, and *aidos*, 'sense of shame', often close to 'sense of honour'. The charge against Achilles, when he desecrated Hector's body, was that he did not show *aidos* (*Iliad* 24.44), which seems here to combine respect for the person, the gods and oneself. The Argives are rebuked by the god for their poor performance in the battle at the ships, as the mighty Hector makes war by the ships themselves: 'Let each reflect on the shame and disgrace (*aido kai nemesin*) his conduct may bring him' (*Iliad* 13.121).

The ethic of 'nobility', however, was not confined to the warrior class, as in Homer, or competing athletes, as in Pindar. Hesiod, the peasants' poet, presented more than simple tales of country folk. His *Works and Days* offered a view of life seen from below, where might and money talked and ordinary people suffered (Hesiod had suffered much at the hands of his brother who, having apparently squandered his own patrimony, then threatened him with a lawsuit). The whole of life – not just the battlefield – was an *agon*, a struggle. Competitiveness or strife (*eris*) was an all-too-present, if ambiguous, reality. It might be evil, as in the jealous unscrupulous striving which oppressed others, or it might be good, prompting achievement and economic success. The peasant farmer had his own excellence: *arete* was now the ability to achieve results through work. But Hesiod saw clearly that the peasant world view required to be anchored in justice. Zeus who presided over all had 'justice' (*dike*) as his daughter, ever anxious to uphold the cause of the righteous and seek punishment for the wicked. With her were associated 'order' (*eunomia*) and 'peace' (*eirene*), who together provided the conditions that supported the life of the country. *Arete* thus required to be yoked to respect for *dike* and the abandoning of wickedness.

It was Sparta that gave the most uncompromising twist to the aristocratic ideal. The Spartans were a deeply conservative people, married to the ancient ways and traditional values as they saw them. In their system, the aristocratic *arete* was commuted to the service of their city-state and a dominant ruling class which observed the principle of equality within itself but which kept in subjection a Helot or serf population ten times its number while exploiting its industry and manpower. In its landlocked fastness, Sparta banished every suggestion of softness, shut its gates against the stranger and international trade, and devoted itself to cultivating military prowess and the martial arts. Here was the complete military ethic, subserving the ends of the state. Physical fitness and discipline were essential – the weak were eliminated and potential enemies, especially among the Helots, ruthlessly exterminated. Children, male and female, were handed over to the state at the age of seven for the education and discipline which would equip them for life in such a society. As its greatest poet, Tyrtaeus (seventh century BCE), put it, what matters is not simply fleetness of foot or skill in wrestling, or one's great strength or fine stature (a playing down of the traditional athletic *aretai*):

> Were he more beautiful in face and body than Tithonus, and richer than Midas and Cinyras, and more kingly than Tantalus' son Pelops, and sweeter of tongue than Adrastus, I would not honour him for these things, even if he had every glory except warlike valour. For no one is a good man in war, unless he can bear to see bloody slaughter and can press hard on the enemy, standing face to face. That is *arete*.
>
> (Tyrtaeus, frag. 9, cited in Jaeger 1939: 88)

On the basis of such a review of the virtues in heroic societies it is reasonable to conclude, with MacIntyre, 'that all morality is always to some degree tied to the socially local and particular'. Our study below offers more evidence. He is possibly correct to suggest too that 'the aspirations of the morality of modernity to a universality freed from all particularity is an illusion'. His further conclusion is also important: 'there is no way to possess the virtues except as part of a tradition in which we inherit them and our understanding of them from a series of predecessors in which series heroic societies hold first place.' (MacIntyre 1985: 126–7). First place – but by no means final place. Greek society underwent many changes, and the quest for moral excellence was compelled to take new forms.

VIRTUE IN THE CITY CONTEXT

With the decline of the aristocracy, the political solidarity that assumed greatest significance was the city-state, the *polis*. The values reflected in the epics were increasingly challenged. The Ionian poets, like those of Greece proper from Hesiod to Solon, had long mirrored the struggle for 'self-sufficiency' (*autarkeia*), the right of citizens to frame their own policies and settle their own disputes. At Athens (and it is important to be specific, for the ethos of the various city-states differed greatly), Sophocles' *Philoctetes* openly challenged the notions of cunning and honour in the story of Odysseus. *Arete* now related more directly to the moral quality of the citizen. As early as Pindar, it had acquired a certain tetradic form: 'mortal life brings forth four virtues, and bids us face the present with prudence' (cf. *Nemean Odes* III.70ff.). Aeschylus presents us with a man who is self-controlled, just, good and pious (*Seven against Thebes* 610). Plato spoke of four principal virtues: courage, godliness (later he substituted philosophical wisdom), justice and prudence. Referring to this canon of four virtues, Jaeger comments (1939: 104), 'Plato took it over *en bloc* from the ethical system of the Greek city-state.' Yet in emergent city-states such as Athens the citizen's charter of four cardinal virtues was variously interpreted and applied. There was no agreement about the nature of virtue as such, or whether *dike* (or *dikaiosyne*) was the fundamental virtue, or what it stood for even if so accepted. The nature of *arete* in fifth-century Athens, so far from being consensual, was something of a storm centre.

The conflict gave *arete* a tragic quality in the dramatists. Among other things (for it was a complex drama) Sophocles' *Antigone* questioned whether the will of the civic head should prevail over eternal, unwritten *themis* or law. Antigone, with feminine devotion to family ties and traditional values, invoked the latter as expressed in age-old clan custom, even if it meant defying her uncle, Creon, ruler of Thebes, in the matter of the burial of her brother. Such disobedience, said Creon, signalled the ruination of civilised society, since as tyrant he embodied positive law and justice. Yet for Antigone there was a higher claim. Even rulers and elders had to respect fundamental moral obligation. Who was right? Do state and tyrant define justice, or is there something more? How does one balance virtue, power and tradition? It is possible that both parties found themselves tragically in an irresolvable dilemma. Again, how does one come to terms with the fact that by following one virtue one may deny another? What then is virtue?

A second view of *arete* was proposed by the sophists. In the public life of the city it was essential to speak and argue effectively. The sophists offered their skills for the education of young aristocrats for political achievement. What mattered was not necessarily the merits of the case viewed objectively or theoretically – the sophists remained sceptical or agnostic about questions of truth – but its effective presentation, in order to persuade the assembly or the jury. And, since juries differed from city to city, a highly situational or relativistic factor was apparent. In one context one might praise as just certain actions which would be thought unjust in another. A latter-day interpretation of Homeric *arete* might highlight effectiveness, the power to accomplish one's goal, individual success. Does this mean that the entrepreneur has free rein to use intelligence and initiative to satisfy his desire for power, without reference to any other moral control? This places a premium on the question of what virtue is.

The window which Plato opens on Socrates permits us to discern a third approach. In various dialogues, Socrates questions his fellows on the virtues: courage (in the *Laches*), godliness (in the *Euthyphro*) and justice (in the *Gorgias* and the *Republic*). The result is to highlight the confusion and imprecision which characterised such moral discourse. In the *Meno*, Socrates protests when he is confronted with a mere list of virtues. But what *is* virtue? That is the question! For Socrates, the elucidation of the concept of virtue could be achieved only through the exercise of reason, through understanding (*phronesis*) and wisdom (*sophia*), involving clarity of definition and argument. Refuting the sophists, he argued that wrongdoers were surely mistaken when at a given moment they perceived a bad action as being good, for everyone does what he or she believes will produce happiness. Like his immediate successors, Socrates linked virtue and the desire for happiness. The good is also the useful; ignorance is the root of evil. Socrates embodied that streak of individualism and independence (*autarkeia*) which was inherent in the Athenian spirit but carried it to a point where, in critical times, it was no longer tolerable for the *polis*. He was sentenced to death in 399 BCE. Now, what price virtue in the city-state of Athens?[2]

Plato lived through the eclipse of Athens as a city-state, and came to distrust the workings of the democracy that had put Socrates to death and had caused Plato himself much pain in public service. While he found a new kind of heroism – of nobility – in Socrates' death, as well as a woeful breach between truth and appearance, he developed a pessimism about politics and society and began to distance himself from the politics of the city-state as he knew it. If the city-state could fall into turmoil, so also could the inner state of the person at the mercy of uncontrolled passions. Plato's writings, with their overtones of Orphism and distrust of the epics, witness to his pursuit of dialectical truth, and the search for permanent forms. He gave much attention to the concept of justice (*dikaiosyne*): was it no more than the interests of the prevailing political powers? His response was to demonstrate that *dikaiosyne* was the ideal of moral excellence which should permeate and unify the whole and also reflect a deeper cosmic pattern. The need for it was inherent in the life of persons and community. Its opposite was the opposite of every virtue: like *pleonexia*, acquisitiveness (the vice of the consumer society!), and the desire to dominate (the vice of every bully). Ideally, the cardinal virtues should be exemplified in the interplay of the parts: rulers should evince wisdom (*phronesis*: in Plato's ideal scheme in the *Republic*, the philosopher-kings possess understanding of good and evil and thus make right moral judgements); soldiers display courage (*andreia*); and the whole community should exercise moderation or self-control (*sophrosyne*), which includes the avoidance of extremes and the promotion of *homonoia*, harmony or consensus. In such a context, justice required that each constituent of the community played his proper part and did not usurp the role that belonged to another. Justice also applied to the inner world of personal being, where it fostered harmony within the soul and so resolved the conflicts of passion. Conflict in society, as in the inner world of the self, was not creative; it had to be overcome. It was through the vision of justice that one was in touch with final reality – the form of the good itself. Hence in the *Laws* Plato recommended a rewriting of Tyrtaeus' poem, substituting justice for courage as the leading virtue.

Aristotle's experience of Athens was also disconcerting. Rising literacy, trade and diversification in society, which brought greater opportunities for personal advancement, promoted the rise of a new and powerful middle class, a bourgeoisie, with its self-serving values. For Aristotle, the city-state defined the cosmos – man was a being fitted by nature to live in a *polis*, a carefully delimited city community – and the paradox of his life was that when, as a resident alien from Thrace, he had to leave Athens in face of a rising tide of anti-Macedonian feeling, he became tutor to the young Alexander who did more than anyone else to overthrow the city-state. Another paradox was that, while he absorbed some of the most limiting features of the *polis* and of Greek culture generally – he can be said at times to reflect 'a prosperous Greek citizen's philosophy of living at its most narrow-minded and complacent, dominated and limited by the prejudices of his class, civilisation and period' (Armstrong 1949: 98) – he also offered the most penetrating analysis of ethics as the quest for universal principles and values.

Aristotle made little of the cardinal virtues, preferring 'high mindedness' or 'great heartedness' (*megalopsychia*) in a sublimation of the noble vision. Besides, he found Plato's mysticism and idealism little to his taste. Hauerwas comments that 'he was forced to rely on the clumsy device of the mean in order to compile what is almost a grocery list of virtues' (1981: 122). More to the point, he contextualised virtue within the view that, in common with all other species, human beings by nature move towards a specific *telos* or goal. Discounting the lower types of goods entertained both by aristocratic and bourgeois society, he related human good to the goal of *eudaemonia* – 'well-being', 'human flourishing'; the word is almost untranslatable and is not materially defined by Aristotle. While the cultivation of the virtues was essential to attain this end, they were never merely means but were always intrinsically right. They represented the exercise of moral choice that produces right action. They thus presupposed the development of good judgement or discernment. To this end, moral training was important, so that one was not at the mercy of one's desires and emotions but acquired and exercised the virtue of self-control and self-direction, for as MacIntyre emphasises, 'virtues are dispositions not only to act in particular ways, but also to feel in particular ways' (1985: 149). Character is built up through good habits and practice.

There is no place here for a detailed critique of the Greek philosophical notion of virtue. A modern philosopher such as MacIntyre can take Aristotle as '*the* protagonist against whom I have matched the voices of liberal modernity' (1985: 146). It may be observed, however, that the dramatists touch on areas of moral reality which escape the philosophers' attention. This is true particularly of the tragic dimension of life, as in Sophocles' *Oedipus Rex*. Rational thought alone does not allow us to escape from the awful dilemmas which life can impose and which do not simply arise from some defect in ourselves. There was a too general assumption in moral discourse that virtue and happiness were bound up with each other, and when the going got rough retreat was made into an ideal world which stood in dialectical relation to the real world. In the elevation of harmony as a basic concept, there was no recognition of the role of conflict as providing a source of learning about virtue or a context for the practice of virtue. Not surprisingly, therefore, there was a lack of historical awareness, of tradition and therefore of life as narrative – although Aristotle's discussion of virtue, with its emphasis on training and habit, cried out for it. Great as their contribution was, these Greek philosophers did not have the last word on *arete*.

VIRTUE IN A GLOBAL CONTEXT

The Hellenistic age, inaugurated by Alexander's conquests, marked a new phase of East–West relations and brought great change to Greece itself. Increasingly Greek society, already deeply affected by Macedonian dominance, became pluralistic and syncretistic, while on the world scene the diversity is illustrated by Briant's comment that 'the Graeco-Macedonians simply added their own traditions to a multi-ethnic and multi-lingual state, but did not know how, or did not wish, or were not able to achieve a unity (least of all a fusion) centred on their socio-cultural values' (Briant 1990: 61). A new cosmic scale now operated, in which the city-states were no more than small secondary units. The city of the future (the *politeia*) – Alexandria, Antioch, Rome – was comparatively large, complex and anonymous; Aristotle would have been appalled! Where now was virtue to be located? No consensus view emerges from this kind of society. Moral transformation, which as Wayne Meeks has observed, was the business of philosophy rather than religion, involved personal choice and conversion into a particular school or discipline (Meeks 1993: 23). Virtue was now at the mercy of a pervasive individualism which, however, often claimed an objective rationale.

The Cynic life-style

Difficult to define, controversial even among Cynics, the way of life of the Cynics involved living according to 'nature', although then, as now, 'nature' was capable of wide interpretation. Nature defined *arete*; its antithesis is found in the false values of so-called civilisation, which the Cynics parodied in dramatic ways. Self-styled as citizens of the cosmos (rather than a localised *polis*) and completely individualistic, they were no mere drop-outs but insisted on self-discipline and training (*askesis*) as the way to *arete*; as Diogenes Laertius put it, 'by physical training we arrive at *arete*' (D.L. 33.1). At their best, they proposed an alternative *praxis* for society. *Arete* itself did not require academic elaboration (the tetrad was not endorsed) but was a matter of deeds and, as F. G. Downing has emphasised, was the same for females as for males. From time to time it encompassed various terms, none of which were definitive: freedom, self-sufficiency, boldness or free speech (Downing 1992: 47). The main point, the hub of their world view, was that one had real choice in life.

The Stoic response

The Cynics were followed in their cosmopolitanism by the Stoics, whose view of virtue was essentially individualistic yet also objective: to pursue the rational goal of human well-being (*eudaimonia*) understood as harmony with the cosmic *logos*, found deep within each being. By this adaptation to the way things are (*oikeiosis*), they were able to affirm virtue as comprising justice and magnanimity (*megalopsychia*) and as directly related to attaining the goal or *telos* of existence (Engberg-Pedersen 1990: 50–1, 120–1). As part of this view, the Stoics had no difficulty in accepting the tetrad of prudence, courage, temperance and justice as 'according to nature', as they did the fundamental unity of humankind. They finally cut the Gordian knot that had tied virtue to the satisfaction of desire and placed value on *apatheia*, the imperturbability that sprang from freedom from emotional entanglement. To achieve it – as only the sage could – entailed indifference to all externals and attachments, such as wealth and success, and to those emotions and affections which constituted pathological states, but Stoics nevertheless accepted, with Aristotle, that the emotional attitude which accompanied actions was an indication of moral character (Long 1974: 207). Wise teaching was therapeutic, a healing of the soul. Many

Stoics devoted themselves to public life and, in the tradition of Chrysippus, pursued appropriate and seemly policies without being unduly affected by the outcome. True to their notion of virtue, all such involvement was qualified by an 'as if not'. It did not pertain to one's true being.

The Epicurean movement

The typical expression of this was found in life-style rather than in logical analysis, in the friendship of a community in a garden rather than in academia, in an inclusiveness which gladly accepted women and slaves, rather than in social élitism. Since virtue had ostensibly a communitarian aspect, the Epicureans went some way towards recovering the lost intimacy of the city-state. Virtue lay in creating conditions of well-being (such as a calm disposition) which is called *hedone*, pleasure as opposed to pain or disturbance. To attain this 'natural' *telos*, one may have to remove some disturbing factors (e.g., the pain of hunger) and avoid other forms of pain which may arise from an unwise course of action (e.g., over-indulgence). Pleasure was to be interpreted as *ataraxia*, freedom from trouble. The pleasure of the mind was to calculate the limit of desire and assess possibilities of disturbance or repose. There was no place here, however, for the traditional tetrad of virtues. For Epicurus, justice simply rested on a compact, an expedient agreement, not to harm or be harmed. To act justly was to avoid trouble. To act unjustly was to store up trouble for oneself. He gave a low rating to involvement in political life. It was a prison to be avoided! Not so, friendship. The Epicurean virtues were wisdom and friendship. Friendship 'goes dancing round the world exhorting us all to awake to the enjoyment of happiness' (Ferguson 1958: 70). In some ways, among the philosophic schools the Epicureans approach most closely to the early Christian notion of community, but in view of the nature of their cosmic vision such judgements, as we noted earlier, are subject to serious qualification.[3]

There are, of course, dangers in trying to trace the global fortunes of virtue through the schools and by a generalising method. Thousands of people in Hellenistic times continued to live in local communities and to follow traditional ways. Yet with the development of the great imperial common markets (to put it no higher), syncretism was in the air, not least in social and religious terms. Through the efforts of the schools, the issue of virtue was kept alive, and the Stoic solution in particular proved influential.

VIRTUE AND THE ROMAN POWER STRUGGLE

The Roman tradition came to the question of virtue with the baggage of the Latin word *virtus*, although Stoic influence greatly assisted its further development. *Virtus* was a homespun quality, denoting the 'manliness' of the paterfamilias as head of the extended family in a society of citizen farmers. Its three main qualities were courage, as of a soldier; power and authority; and finally, as society changed and Greek influence spread, *arete*, moral courage or, as Cicero put it, 'a state of mind in conformity with reason along the lines of nature' (*De Inventione Rhetorica* II.53.159). However, the strength of popular views should not be underestimated, holding fast as they did to the first two meanings. John Ferguson commented that 'the generic word *virtus* never shook off its narrower associations, and one cannot help feeling that there remained a certain narrowness in the character which the Republican Roman honoured' (Ferguson 1958: 164).

For brevity's sake, Cicero must be our guide through the higher development of *Romana virtus*. Professing to follow the Academy but eclectic in philosophy while inclining to Stoicism in ethics, Cicero deferred to the republican virtues of *pietas* (sense of duty) and *gravitas* (dignity). Within this world view, we find once again the tetradic view of virtue, which he cited almost as a commonplace. It involved firstly the universal search for truth (*veritas*), which is wisdom or prudence. Its second feature was justice (*iustitia*), 'the crowning glory of the virtues', which was held to provide the common bond in society and to be expressed in the personal sphere as charity (*caritas*), kindness and generosity. The third aspect was courage (*fortitudo*), which can be linked to moral goodness through the Stoic understanding of it as 'virtue which champions the cause of right'. Courage of this kind required indifference to outward circumstances so that the soul, thus disciplined, could prompt one to noble action. The fourth and last division of moral goodness was self-control (*temperantia et modestia*), which led to propriety (*decorum*) in one's actions. The interdependence of the virtues was underlined. Justice came from wisdom; courage was an expression of wisdom and justice; self-control related to all three. Cicero sometimes added piety as a fifth element. With such a moral armament, he directed his career in troubled times and sustained himself as the dream of the Roman republic crumbled around him. He loathed tyranny and totalitarian rule, maintained by fear and force rather than by the good will of the people (*De Officiis* II.23–9). Nothing can be expedient, he insists, that is not morally right (*De Officiis* III.35.85), though killing the tyrant is not ruled out on that score, for in such a case, right and justice go hand in hand with expediency (*De Officiis* III.19).

Just how little the subsequent *imperium Romanum* could be said to be the guardian of virtue emerges from even the briefest consideration of imperial values. Much of the rhetoric is propaganda. Augustus wanted to be known as the champion of virtue and clemency, justice and piety. Within the ethos of Rome, his claim to manliness and piety may be justified; in the same context, however, justice tended to be reduced to law as imperially defined and clemency to the advancement of imperial policy. These and other attributes – such as *providentia* or foresight and *liberalitas* or generosity – were invincibly paternalistic.

> There is something pathetic in the spectacle of men of vast riches in a world of mal-distribution throwing a sop to the Cerberus of their conscience by redistributing some part of their excess, or the men in power in a world where power is inequitably divided claiming it as a virtue that they have refrained from an arbitrary use of that power.
>
> (Ferguson 1958: 206–7)

For Cicero, virtue or moral excellence was not simply a personal quality; it also pertained in a fundamental way to the actions of politicians. His work served to transmit Plato's tetrad of the virtues, with minor variations, to the Roman world. One feature that should be underlined here is his very real piety. Modern readers too quickly deduce from Plato's attack on the gods in the *Republic* that ancient Greek religion and its Roman successor were bankrupt concerns. This is very far from the truth. Plato himself could include piety among the virtues. The Hellenistic age was intensely religious,[4] and Cicero had a deep piety which provided the context for his morality, even if his moral philosophy had intellectual, rather than theological, roots. Plutarch, who had been a priest at Delphi, evinced a deep spirituality, illustrated well in his dialogue on 'Divine Vengeance' (*Moralia* VII) in which God is the primary model in that he does not rush to punish and allows the offender time to make amends. There is thus a transcendent dimension to Plutarch's moral world. Plutarch, like Cicero and Seneca, exercised considerable influence over later ages. Plotinus, for instance, incorporated the four-fold scheme of virtues, comprising intelligence, justice, self-control and courage. But before we hail Cicero, Plutarch and company as the great transmitters through whose influence the four virtues passed into Christendom (cf. Ferguson 1958: 48), it is necessary to look more closely into the crucible of Christian morality, which contained not only Graeco-Roman but also Jewish Hellenistic elements.

VIRTUE: A TRANSCENDENT NOTION

Hellenistic Judaism denotes a complex moral context, fed by Israel's experience (its 'story') and Hellenistic cultural and political imperialism. The Jews had already acquired much experience of living under foreign domination, and under Alexander's successors it was normally possible for local cultures to prosper. Even when relations reached their nadir with Antiochus Epiphanes and the Maccabean Revolt, the essential issue was not the rejection of Hellenism. There were specific causes, including the plundering of the Temple treasure and political offences against Jewish religious susceptibilities. The outcome certainly did not bring an end to Hellenism. The victorious party proceeded to form an alliance with the Romans, Greece's cultural debtor and eventual successor; the written accounts of the Maccabean Revolt reflected Greek historiography, and the praise of the martyrs was a form and adaptation of the heroic vision.

If Greek culture had its value-laden epics and classics, Israel also had its multi-stranded epic story and scripture, setting forth as Torah the vision and implications of divine election and covenant. The question arises: what happens when Greek concepts dominate moral thinking and when the Hebrew scriptures themselves are translated into Greek language? Interestingly, the Greek translation of Isaiah (LXX) provides *arete* with a transcendental reference. Excellence belongs to God. *Arete* denotes the 'glory' or 'honour' (*kabhodh*) which, like worshipful praise (*tehillah*), properly belongs to God and can be given to no other, least of all to idols: 'my glory I give to no other, nor my praise to graven images' (Isa. 42.8; cf. 42.12). In Isaiah 63.7, it is used in the plural to denote 'praiseworthy deeds' which were recounted in worship at festivals and celebrations. Such usages reflect the heroic model of *arete*, but its connotation of excellence, effectiveness and glorious exploits has been transposed into the covenantal context. Yahweh possesses *arete*, praiseworthiness, because his *arete* or glorious might is expressed in his mighty acts of creation, salvation and covenantal election by which his people – and in principle all creation (cf. Isa. 43.20–21) – recognise his *arete* and offer the *aretai* due to him (cf. Hab. 3.3). Here *arete* has practically been overwhelmed by the theological, liturgical and relational connotations of the text.

The language of virtue was used by Jewish apologists, such as the writer of 4 Maccabees, Josephus and Philo, most of whom were also at home in Greek philosophy, especially Stoicism. Their general position is that what in Greek is termed *arete* is contained within and reinforced by Torah. We look briefly at each in turn.

4 Maccabees

This book is variously dated to the period *c.* 18–55 CE (Bickermann 1945; Anderson 1985) and the early second century CE (Breitenstein 1978) and ascribed to Diaspora locations as varied as Alexandria and Asia Minor. It has been described 'as a synagogue sermon, a lecture, a genuine commemorative address, or as a fictive discourse' (Anderson 1985: 535). Its moral presuppositions recall both Plato's *Gorgias*, with its emphasis on living and dying faithful to justice and the other virtues (Hadas 1953: 116–17), and Stoicism in particular, with its advocacy of devout rationality as the key to control over the passions that destroy. But the writer's expertise in Greek philosophy is put at the service of Judaism, both for apologetic purposes and, in Anderson's words, 'to show that the cardinal virtues, self-control, courage, justice, and temperance, indeed the very essence of Greek wisdom, are subsumed under the Law or obedience to it' (Anderson 1985: 538). Indeed, the author makes relatively extensive use of *arete*, which occurs sixteen times. Rational judgement is described as the highest virtue (1.2) and therefore guides all the others. *Arete* also denotes courage and is exemplified by the story of the Maccabean heroes, Eleazar and the seven brothers and their mother, which occupies much of the book (1.8, 10) and which invites the readers to identify with it as their own story and the paradigm of their faithfulness.

> You deride our philosophy, as though our living by it were contrary to reason. But you are wrong, for it teaches us temperance (*sophrosyne*), so that we control our pleasures and desires; and it trains us in courage (*andreia*) so that we willingly endure every hardship; and it instructs us in justice

(*dikaiosyne*) so that throughout all life's intercourse we can act proportionately; and it teaches us piety (*eusebeia*) so that we magnificently venerate the only living God.

(4 Maccabees 5.22–24; my translation)

The intention in both cases is to use the language of philosophy in the service of the Jewish faith and way of life. Indeed, in the confrontation between Eleazar and Antiochus, it is the latter who appears to articulate the Stoic view alone and totally fails to understand the Jewish loyalty to the Torah which, as Eleazar makes clear, is unqualified and excludes eating unclean food or food sacrificed to idols (cf. Anderson 1985: 538). The view that the author clearly commends is that reason reinforces the law, as when it forbids covetousness and controls desires, and even overrules affection for parents, wife, children and friends, so that one takes appropriate action when necessary. Reason and law together can prevail even over enmity. 'The fruit trees of the enemy are not cut down, but one preserves the property of enemies from the destroyers and helps raise up what has fallen' (2.14).

As indicated above, the virtue of courage is interpreted primarily in relation to suffering and is exemplified from Jewish tradition. As one recognises that it is blessed to endure any suffering for virtue's sake, as the Maccabees did – the atoning power of suffering and death is endorsed in 4 Maccabees – so one can overcome the power of the emotions (such as fear, despair, cowardliness) through godliness (*eusebeia*). Virtue has as its reward life with God (9.8, 31; cf. 17.12) – the writer seems at home with the Greek view of the immortality of the soul – while the tyrant will be punished eternally. Where virtue is concerned, the faithful are invincible (9.18) through their godly training (*paideia*, 10.10); there is a hint of *askesis* here. By their endurance of torture and death for the sake of *arete* (11.2; 12.14), the brothers provide irrefutable proof that devout reason possesses the power to master the emotions (13.1–4). Thus they attained self-control, having benefited from the quality of their common upbringing and 'from both general education and upbringing in the law of God' (13.22). Improbably, even the tyrant Antiochus, impressed by 'the courage of their virtue' and their endurance under torture, cited their example to his soldiers, with apparently telling effect (17.24)!

Josephus (c. 37–100 CE)

In the *Contra Apionem*, Josephus bases his apologetic on the Jews' love of good order, law, moderate behaviour and virtue in accordance with nature. Moses is the fountain-head of virtue, which has a metaphysical context as in all the best Greek philosophers (2.17). Moses emphasised justice, fortitude, temperance and universal law, virtues which are sympathetic to piety. Moreover, he linked instruction with the practice of virtue. Truly, the laws of Moses 'teach the truest piety in the world' (2.42). This discussion lays the foundation for a cosmic view which Josephus commends to his readers. While Roman philosophy was not incompatible with the teaching of Moses, the heritage of the Jews placed them in a particularly strong position to appreciate the full cosmic picture.

Philo of Alexandria (c. 20 BCE–50 CE)

Philo's cultural identity effectively fused together Hellenistic culture and Jewish tradition. He had imbibed the former through his Greek-style education, patterned on the *encyclia* (literature, rhetoric, mathematics, music and logic), and he valued mental training as the basis of higher intellectual and spiritual achievements. His Jewishness, however, was never in doubt, whether in terms of community membership or religious conviction. Indeed, in 39–40 CE he was part of a delegation of Alexandrian Jews who made representations to the emperor Caligula concerning persecutions which fellow Jews had incurred. He remained loyal to Jewish practice, such as sabbath observance and circumcision, while his spirituality was nourished by the allegorical interpretation of scripture, a method which corresponded to Hellenistic norms for the interpretation of Homeric poems. While eclectic in philosophy, the diverse philosophical elements he derived from the Stoics, Plato, Aristotle and even the astrologers, were comprehended within a theological vision of the cosmos, in which the transcendent God was infinite and the divine immanence was expressed through the *logos*, the cosmic rational principle, and in the operation of other cosmic powers, including the power of goodness.

Philo's access to God was through the scriptures of Israel (for him, the LXX), which undergirded the notion of moral law. Moral laws cohere with the cosmic pattern, as in the creation story. Philo devoted much attention to the Decalogue. These particular or special laws given by Moses exemplify 'the virtues of universal value': 'wisdom, justice, godliness, and the rest of the company of virtues' (*De Specialibus Legibus* IV.134). He went on to refer to piety and holiness as 'queen of the virtues' and further cited wisdom and self-control (IV.135). Piety in Philo has been described as 'a kind of super-virtue which stands above the other virtues and is presupposed by them' (Runia 1995: 97). Philo devoted special attention to justice (*dikaiosyne*) in relation to kingship. Judicial policy must respect particularly the weak and helpless, the stranger, the widow and the orphan. More generally, justice demands honesty in commerce, prompt payment of wages, proper treatment of the disabled, and respect for animals and the land.

Philo expanded on the virtues in *De Virtutibus*, the first critical edition of which was published by L. Cohn in 1906. There is uncertainty about the title and original contents of the treatise, although this is less serious for our purposes than might be expected (cf. Runia 1995: 77–101, esp. 96–101). Apart from justice, Philo discussed four virtues, although the title may originally have specified three (Mangey 1742; cf. Runia 1995: 97). The first was courage. Carefully distinguishing it from war fever, reckless daring and savagery, which betokened invincible ignorance, Philo took knowledge or understanding to be its hallmark. 'Those who train themselves in wisdom cultivate true courage' (I.4). Many circumstances in life called for such courage – protracted illness or frailty, poverty, obscurity, disability or disease. True courage, based on wisdom, enabled one to rise above such adversity. So far, so good. Courage is a kind of critical consciousness, the mark of a vigorous and gallant soul that discounts all that vanity tends to glorify to the destruction of true life. Courage is required in time of peace and war. In a confused argument, Philo betrays a tendency to think of courage as essentially a masculine quality (literally *andreia*), which should never be compromised, but the passage he glosses (Lev. 22.5) is as concerned with women as with men. Returning to the military theme, he held that courage in war, while the reverse of savagery, was expressed rather in the dedication of sound and active bodies to gallantry, which elevated a glorious death far above a life of dishonour. Such was the courage which defeated the Midianites of old. Unlike the author of 4 Maccabees, he did not illustrate from latter-day martyrdoms.

The second virtue is humanity or benevolence (*philanthropia*) 'the virtue most closely related to piety, its sister and its twin' (IX.51): a theme which recalls Cicero's *caritas* and also *clementia*. The word had a chequered career in Graeco-Roman culture. Coming into prominence in Hellenistic times, it was related by Diogenes Laertius (III.98) to greeting people, charity, and the kind of hospitality which would suit the *bon viveur*. Ferguson comments that his account 'reads almost like the aims and objects of a Rotary Club' (1958: 102). It had, however, much more serious work to do, although in Graeco-Roman society it was usually used in a limited rather than a universal sense of 'humanity' or 'humaneness'. Philo did much to enhance it. Illustrated from the life of Moses and the Law, *philanthropia* within Israel included loans without interest, wages promptly paid, the debarring of the creditor from infringing the privacy of a debtor's house, the gleanings of the harvest for the poor, and so on, together with the provision of the sabbatical year and the Jubilee. Humanity was to be shown also to strangers, who were assumed to be proselytes, and to 'those who have immigrated under stress of circumstance'. Even enemies at the gates had to be offered a peaceful settlement before recourse was made to war. Women captives had to be treated with respect. Animals had to be returned to an enemy in order to attempt the ending of a feud. The Mosaic Law taught peace and brotherhood. Special provision was also made for slaves, for kindness to animals and even plants, and respect for new-born children (cf. *De Virtutibus* 25). The obverse was pride, arrogance, or the presumptuousness which usurped divine prerogatives. All in all, this was, in Colson's words, 'Philo at his best' (Colson 1939: xv).

Repentance, the third of Philo's values, in so far as it is a virtue at all, is the virtue of rectification, like recovery from disease or deliverance from danger at sea – a second prize, but valuable for humankind, for only God is completely without sin. Those who repented of idolatry, proselytes, are to be given a particular welcome and serve as examples to all Israel. Colson argued that Cohn (the translator of the book in the Loeb series) over-emphasised the proselyte as the target of Philo's sermon and pointed out that the second part seemed to be addressed to the people at large (Colson 1939: xv-xvi). Certainly, in *De Praemiis et Poenis*, after discoursing on the punishments for disobedience, Philo declared that confession and acknowledgement of sin, with clear conscience and open declaration, would find favour with God and bring blessing to personal as to national life. Strictly speaking, Colson is correct in observing that repentance is not a virtue but a stepping-stone to the virtues (Colson 1939: xvi). It is a *sine qua non* which is brought into prominence by the fact that 'turning to God' (*teshuvah*), 'choosing God' (*De Virtutibus* 184), is central to covenantal faith and thus a virtue of faithful living.

Finally, Philo considered nobility. This section probably does not represent a further virtue but is 'a somewhat polemical development' of the previous section on repentance (Runia 1995: 98). True nobility is not the prerogative of the well born but of the wise, as the fool is the exemplar of all that is ignoble. As in *Quod Omnis Probus Liber sit*, it is the virtuous person who is free. Here we find not simply the final rejection of aristocratic values but a warning to fellow Jews not to stake their salvation on their noble lineage alone. Cohn took this to be a warning against regarding proselytes as second-class citizens. Colson took it as a reinforcing of the general call to repentance, not unlike the message of John the Baptist. Runia is in broad agreement with Colson's view.

Philo is a complex figure, difficult to sum up briefly. Like all expatriates, he is exercised about the question of identity. He is a Jew and an Alexandrian, a scholar educated in Greek culture and reared in the faith of Israel. He is an urbane citizen, yet is true to Hebrew morality. As a Jew, he is conscious of his heritage. He reads and prizes the scriptures, while interpreting them in Greek fashion. He acknowledges the sublime morality of Israel's tradition and uses Greek moral concepts to interpret it. Yet he never compromises its distinctive contribution to moral understanding. It may be helpful to single out four aspects.

1   To acknowledge the sovereignty of God is to affirm human accountability before him and to counteract human arrogance. In spite of Philo's emphasis on reason and wisdom the stark picture of the autonomous rational man, sovereign over his destiny, was not for him. He had a strain of scepticism which informed his awareness of human ignorance, weakness and folly, and underscored his view of human finitude and sinfulness.

2   Repentance as (re)turning to God was a central moral and religious concern. Hebrew tradition affirmed this notion, while Greek philosophical practice had increasingly incorporated the need for conversion. In Philo, conversion involves repentance, and this seems to combine the notions of turning from idols to the true God and release from sin through confession.

3   Philo's deep respect for the scriptural narratives, encompassing Israel's memory of her calling, reinforced his sense of history and tradition, which in the style of the day provided moral examples and could fire the imagination. His historical sense also translated into concern for contemporary moral issues, from the welfare of the Jewish community to concern for social

malpractices and the environment. In spite of the 'mystical' elements in his thought, Philo retained a sense of history.

4   Philo has the notion of virtue as a response to sovereign Goodness. Since the moral life was thus associated with *eusebeia* (piety) or *theosebeia* (godliness), morality and the virtues were never acts of human self-assertion but were in tune with the Creator's purpose and the divine *logos* within.[5]

VIRTUE IN THE NEW TESTAMENT

Before taking up the theme of virtue, it should be recalled that virtue belongs to the long tradition of Greek values, beginning with the noble vision. The early Christians, including Paul, were influenced in language and concept by the social world thus created. To be sure, with the importance of transcendent perspectives, major adjustments take place. Honour, praise, excellence and power are located in the divine. Good conduct has always a responsive quality. To resist God is arrogant (cf. *hybris*). The language of 'shame' persists. 'I am not ashamed of the gospel', Paul declares (Rom. 1.6), for it is the power of God for salvation. But he would be shamed if his churches were not obedient to his message, for he would then be an inadequate channel of God's power. It is shameful that the Corinthians are unable to settle disputes within their own fellowship, for that is to deny God's purpose (1 Cor. 6.5), although Paul normally writes not to shame them but to give counsel and correction. To obey the emperor and the established authorities is an honourable course, for they express some aspects of the divine economy. To be rebellious is to incur wrath and to meet a deserved fate (cf. *nemesis*). To fly in the face of convention in the matter of hair style or silence on the part of wives in church is counted shameful (1 Cor. 11.6, 14; 14.35). There are literally catalogues of vices and immoral acts which are shameful and characterise the lives of the unconverted – 'such were some of you'. The Christians devote themselves to holy living. Holiness is virtually the converse of shame in the New Testament, for the transcendent God who alone is good is the holy God, and holiness 'helped create a separate universe for the Christians which distinguished them from others' (Moxnes 1988: 215). Moxnes suggests that the Christians accepted the system of honour operating in the public areas of Hellenistic society but rejected it in relation to the private world of sexuality and sex roles.

It is misleading, however, to make such a sharp differentiation of the public and private realms. Sexuality and sex roles – marriage, for example – are lived out in public, and they have implications for structures. It is better to focus on the ethos of the community into which they are baptised – a holy community, into which they are incorporated. They must express that holiness in their behaviour.

What then of *arete*? The word *arete* is not common in the New Testament. In 1 Peter 2.9 it is used of the 'excellences' – the wonderful deeds – of the God who called the faithful out of darkness into his marvellous light. 2 Peter 1.3 speaks of the divine power which admits us to and sustains us in godly life 'through the knowledge of him who called us to [or 'by'] his own glory and *arete*.' Both these instances are consistent with LXX usage. However, the realm of discourse to which 2 Peter 1.5 belongs is clearly that of the virtues. The recipients should add *arete* to faith, knowledge to *arete*, self-control (*engkrateia*) to knowledge, courage (*hypomene*) to self-control, piety (*eusebeia*) to courage, brotherly affection (*philadelphia*) to piety, and love (*agape*) to brotherly affection – and all without further explanation except for the observation that these qualities are of the essence of Christian nurture. Their general signification seems to be widely accepted and uncontroversial, and they provide a classic description of the developing ethos of the Christian communities, or at least the ethos to which they aspired.

When we enquire more closely of the specifically moral denotation of *arete* in the New Testament, we need to distinguish between the use of the term *arete* and its field of reference. Thus in Titus 2.12, where the word *arete* is not used, the bishop's training course in character formation (*paideia*) exhorts his hearers to be true to their renunciation of impiety or irreligion and worldly passions (*epithymiai*) and to live with self-control, justice and piety. We find here both a negative and a positive reinforcement. The negative side is renouncing the impiety and irreligion of the pagan world together with desires that are stimulated by the negative side of that world; the Christian struggle with *epithymiai* – sometimes 'the desires of the flesh': cf. Rom. 1.24; 13.14; Gal. 5.16, 24 – parallels the philosophical concern for the control of the passions. In this context the reference may be to honouring the vows taken at baptism ('having renounced' is in the aorist tense and may recall the decisive event). The positive reinforcement cites three of the virtues which commonly occur within the four-fold formula. Only courage is missing, but its Christian equivalent (*hypomene*) has already occurred in Titus 2.1.

As for *arete* itself, the *locus classicus* is Philippians 4.8:

> All that is true (*alethe*), all that is lofty and noble (*semna*), all that is just (*dikaia*) and pure (*hagna*), all that evokes love (*prosphile*) and is attractive (*euphema*), if there is anything that may be described as virtue or excellence (*arete*) and worthy of praise (*epainos*) – concentrate your thinking on these things.
>
> (Phil. 4.8; my translation)

The majority view of scholars is that this statement would be at home in Hellenistic morality and rhetoric (Hawthorne 1983: 185–6), or that it reflects popular Hellenistic philosophical usage (so Beare 1959, and others). To be sure, the terms used do not all occur in the familiar catalogues of vices (Wibbing 1959) nor do they reflect the usual tetrad of virtues. The fact that they are also unusual in Paul probably reveals a degree of LXX influence (Lohmeyer 1956; Michaelis 1935; Martin 1976). Truth or truthfulness and justice are basic. Lodged between them is a curious reprise of aristocratic society. *Semnos* is used in Homer of gods and things divine: 'revered', 'holy' and, subsequently, 'grand', 'splendid'. Plato used it of 'noble' qualities. Like *semnos*, *hagnos* has religious overtones, meaning literally 'filled with religious awe' and thus 'pure', 'unsullied'. *Prosphiles* has the root meaning of 'beloved', 'pleasant', but also 'that which calls forth love' (Hawthorne 1983: 188), while *euphemos* is another religious word meaning 'of good omen', 'auspicious' or, perhaps better, 'winning, attractive' (Lightfoot 1894; Plummer 1919).

Paul's purpose in commending virtue in these terms is not entirely clear (Michael 1928: 202). We may conclude that the 'if' clause – 'if there is anything that may be described as virtue' – is not intended to be a grudging comment. Often he had to be critical of pagan morality (cf. Rom. 1.20; 2.14–15) and to present a sharp contrast between it and the Christian life-style (cf. 1 Cor. 6.9–11). This passage, however, shows an appreciation of the positive side of Gentile morality. No doubt Christians were aware that some of their Gentile neighbours followed a recognisably moral life-style, however they differed in cosmic understanding (cf. Keck 1996: 9; Marxsen 1993: 215), and even that some of their writers took morality very seriously. Morality is not simply a deduction from a fixed cosmic view but is a response to life. However, while Paul shared the moral quest of humankind, he believed that there was much more to be said. The Christian story which informs the

Christian vision is important for the understanding and development of personal and community morality, even if it also affirms the best of pagan insights. Paul himself draws heavily on his own Jewish tradition, virtually equating virtue with the fulfilment of the Law (cf. Raisanen 1986: 49, 118). For him, *arete* was essentially a relation term, assuming a response to God's *arete*. In this realm of understanding, human action is empowered by God's Spirit. Hence, while Paul could enter into dialogue with Gentiles about virtue, his aim was to lead Gentile Christians at any rate beyond the level of consensus to deeper Christian understanding. He therefore enjoins them to 'put into practice the lessons I taught you, the tradition I passed on, all that you heard me say or saw me do' (Phil. 4.9). Paul embodied the Christian message and story and communicated them through his words and actions. Indeed, the *imitatio Christi* is transmitted as it is lived out among the people of God. Christian virtue has a specific focus in Christ.

Such theological interpretation resulted in considerable enlargement of some Hellenistic virtues. Justice (*dikaiosyne*) is an obvious case where the Christian story, with its roots in Hebrew covenantal discourse, substantially transforms the connotation of the moral term. *Andreia* is replaced in New Testament discourse by *hypomene* or *makrothymia* or some similar term because the moral concept is qualified in the Christian community by a wholly different story and context, centred on Christian experience and, above all, on the Cross. The intersecting of moral understanding and Christian story is dramatically illustrated by a sentence such as, 'Those who belong to Christ Jesus have crucified the flesh with its passions and desires' (Gal. 5.24). The virtues themselves were reinterpreted by the notion of gift and quality of character. Paul's most dramatic *tour de force* is found in his use and interpretation of *agape*, itself stemming from covenantal discourse. In the hymn of love in 1 Corinthians 13, the 'downside' of the poem relates to charismatic or prophetic extremism, intellectualism or early Gnostic manifestations, wrong conceptions of charitable works, and the glorification of martyrdom. In all this, there is no attack on *arete* as such. What emerges, however, is a triad of Christian or theological virtues – faith, hope and love – which translate the Christian story and tradition into the leading features of Christian *praxis*. In time, the theological virtues would take their place at the head of the cardinal or general virtues which have commanded attention in this chapter.

VIRTUE IN THE FATHERS

It was in the post-apostolic age that many of the strands discussed above came together in creative association. Justin Martyr set the tone with his openness to the Greek tradition. Alexandria was, not surprisingly, a key centre, apparently as early as the second century. The Nag Hammadi discoveries[6] include *The Teachings of Silvanus*, which according to Zandee, reflects Stoic, Platonic and above all Philonic influence, and emphasise the importance of virtue as well as the struggle against the passions (Zandee 1977, 1991; Runia 1993: 127–8). Runia cites Pearson (1986: 216): 'It was the Philo-like Christianity of *Silvanus*, rather than the primitive apocalypticism of Barnabas, or the acosmic radicalism of the Gnostics, that ultimately carried the day in the development of Christian theology in the patristic age.' Clement held that truth is a unity, the key to which is to be instructed by the Son of God, but that the search for truth is a co-operative enterprise in which philosophy shares. Similarly, virtue is one, yet it is seen as prudence, temperance, courage or justice: the tetrad surfaces again! (*Stromateis* 1.20). Later his extended treatment of the virtues (2.78–100) draws heavily on Philo, underlining his use of the Torah which points to Christ, the final Teacher, and refutes the Gnostics (Runia 1993: 139–40). Origen, against the Gnostics and their fellow travellers who denied that the Old Testament God was a God of love, insisted on the unity of the virtues (*De Principiis* 2.5), and therefore treated goodness as generic and virtues as species (Runia 1993: 177). Later, Ambrose presented a Christian reinterpretation of the tetrad of virtues which he drew primarily from Cicero and the Stoics (*De Officiis* 1.27). Wisdom and piety are now theologically based. Courage is related to the withstanding of temptation, although more traditional senses are not excluded. Self-control seems to be taken over without qualification, while justice was extended (as in Cicero) to comprehend benevolence (Ferguson 1958: 50). Ambrose also drew extensively on Philo's debate between pleasure and virtue (*De Cain et Abel* 1.4.13–6.23) and related it to christocentric biblical interpretation and Christian worship (Runia 1993: 301–4). Augustine, advocate of classical education and exponent of biblical interpretation (*De Doctrina Christiana, passim*), represents the full flowering of this tradition, in which the virtues are comprehended by Christian love. Following Ferguson (1958: 50), we illustrate his redefinitions of Christian virtue from *De Moribus Ecclesiae Catholicae* 25:

courage: love cheerfully enduring all things for the sake of God;

self-control: love keeping itself entire and inviolate for God;

justice: love serving God only and therefore controlling all else
that is subject to humanity;

wisdom: love discriminating between those things which assist
and those things which retard its approach to God.

The love which informed all other virtues was not just another human idealisation of moral virtue. It was rather the moral reality which encountered and laid hold of them, conveyed in the covenantal language of Israel and portrayed *par excellence* in the story of Jesus. 'See how they love one another', the pagans sneered (Tertullian, *Apologeticus* 39.7). But in expressing in practice the moral dynamic which they encountered as transcendent reality – in allowing the Spirit of love to inform and transform their community – they were in fact laying the foundations of an edifice much greater than they realised, for it was with such groups that lay 'the continuation of civility and moral community' after Roman *imperium* was no more.

CONCLUSION

The theme of virtue is a fascinating and important topic, illustrating the complexity of the elements in the crucible of Christian ethics. In what must be a brief conclusion, three points may be underlined.

1   There are limits to the usefulness of the attempted systematisation in terms of 'cardinal virtues'. Ferguson (1958: 50–2) advanced three criticisms. Such formulae represent inadequate analyses, particularly in relation to questions of unity and diversity, leading virtue, precise components, outcome and so on; the Greek approach tends to be over-intellectualised; finally, an introspective standard of virtue is presupposed. Ferguson in effect underlines the Pauline objection to the adoption of such abstract principles as the basis of moral behaviour. It leads either to despair at moral failure or to self-righteous complacency at having apparently attained. It must be emphasised that New Testament writers, like Augustine after them, did not use the formulae in this way but related the whole moral life to the story of the grace of God in Christ and to the dynamics of forgiveness.

2   Virtue, however, is important as a category which interprets the
    moral experience of humankind. To take it seriously is to affirm
    not only that Christians can enter into moral discourse with
    non-Christians in a pluralistic world, but that the Christian
    moral tradition itself has drawn on the wisdom of others in
    interpreting and clarifying the moral dimension of life. To that
    extent, Justin has been proved right. Virtue relates to the moral
    agent, to character and life in community, and to generating a
    vision of the world as it should be: all of which fall within the
    central compass of Christian moral concern. That is why Paul is
    constrained to affirm virtue, even if the concept comes to him,
    as it were, in a foreign tongue.

3   The presence of 'virtue' within the crucible of Christian ethics
    says something about the task of 'New Testament ethics'. One
    endorses, of course, proper distinctions between moral practice
    and ethical reflection (cf. Keck 1996: 3–16). 'New Testament
    ethics', by definition, is reflection on practice: primarily, the
    moral practice of the early Christian communities and the
    moral teaching in their received tradition and story. Today, that
    is available to us through texts; hence 'New Testament ethics'
    has always an exegetical and hermeneutical aspect. But through
    the texts – Christian and otherwise – we encounter the *mores* of
    communities, Christian and otherwise, and observe the interac-
    tion between them, all of which witnesses to the moral quest of
    humankind. Thus 'New Testament ethics' is not simply
    concerned with in-house issues of the early Christian communi-
    ties, but with questions of truth and right. 'Virtue' thus leads
    us to contemplate a renewal of dialogue – or is it the establish-
    ment of dialogue? – between 'New Testament ethics', Christian
    ethics and even moral philosophy (not to speak of practising
    teachers of morality) for the better understanding of the moral
    dimensions of human reality.

> For all the authors were able to see the truth darkly,
> through the implanted seed of the Logos dwelling in
> them. For the seed and representation of reality, given
> according to human capacity, is one thing; far different
> is the reality itself, the sharing of which (and its repre-
> sentation) is given according to his grace.
>
> (Justin, *Apologia* 2.13)[7]

POSTSCRIPT
The significance of the crucible

As T. S. Eliot observed, there is a notable coherence in our endings and our beginnings. We began with the notion of the crucible of Christian morality, suggestive perhaps of a seething cauldron, a dynamic admixture, something new brewing up! More specifically, the use of 'crucible' in connection with moral communities conjures up not only the inescapable factor of socio-historical context and situation but also moral reflection and moral search as a lively, interactive process, testing disparate cultural factors and bringing selected elements into a powerful compound which takes its decisive pattern from a new focus – from the tradition, story, memory and interpretative activity of the Christian communities themselves. The resultant product had to withstand strains and tensions in the life of these same communities. It had also to absorb the assaults and opposition of inimical competitors, and it had to be able to resist the corroding acids of pagan culture and politics.

That it was able to respond vigorously to these challenges can be ascribed to a number of factors. The community life of the Christian groups was itself a helpful setting, cultivating the conditions in which moral dialogue could take place (as 1 Corinthians, for example, demonstrates). As dialogue continued, their understanding of community life deepened, as did their grasp of personal being and moral excellence, for their moral stance was underwritten by *agape*, the creative and transforming love that sprang from their awareness of the transcendent God in history and experience. There was also the possibility of dialogue with the world – partly through mission but also through responsible citizenship and able articulation of a critical obedience to the state. At the same time, it is important not to idealise their procedures. Even Paul, who could work through a moral issue with much precision and openness to truth (cf. 1 Cor. 8), also laid down the law! As the churches became more ordered and hierarchical, they tended to follow catechetical style and resort to rule or command, as in the *Didache* or *Barnabas*, where the crucible is much less in evidence. Catechetics typically makes use of mass-produced samples rather than material freshly crafted in the crucible. Moreover, popular moral teaching seldom avoids 'negative ethics', which paradoxically had its positive side, for it includes not only conventional moral denunciation (as in 1 and 2 Romans) but also the awareness that all human action takes place under the judgement of God. Gradually there emerged in the Fathers something more than casuistical skill; rather, the realisation of a moral dynamic grounded in the love of God and expressed in moral excellence. All this was part of the interaction within community that is the genius of the Christian moral enterprise at its best.

In this book we have attempted to characterise the activity within the crucible as the interaction of fundamental cosmic vision, personal and community identity and *mores*, and social and political stances and action. Inherent in this dynamic is the location of authority and its nature. Also relevant is consideration of the types of moral criteria to which appeal is made and the nature of the emergent moral discourse. By and large the material has responded well to this attempt to represent the nature of the moral dynamics of the early faith communities. It is a reasonable conclusion that this kind of process is endemic to Christian ethics when we look to the baseline of moral community rather than propositional statements.

And so, from our contemplation of the beginning, we come now to the end – at least of this book! More importantly, we come to the question of the crucible of Christian morality today. As in earlier times, Christian moral decision-making takes place in a pluralistic and multi-cultural world. The thrust of our argument is that all Christian morality worthy of the name is forged in the crucible of moral test and search. Situation and context raise the clamant questions. Indeed, many elements in the debate derive from the prevailing culture, to be tried and tested and perhaps found wanting. Yet some of these elements will endure – like toleration and understanding of others, or virtue – for Christians have no monopoly in ethics. Inter-religious dialogue may also contribute to the rich mixture. But distinctive and essential elements are also contributed from the Christian story and tradition. While these may come through biblical or church interpretation, they encourage particular perspectives on given issues; they do not foreclose them!

There are no simple Christian solutions to moral problems. There is, however, a Christian ethos, expressed in relationships, community, worship and service, which is the location of the crucible if not the actual crucible itself. Its working out is at the behest of the Holy Spirit. If this moral community is to be worthy of the name, however, for its essence is vocation or calling, it will not simply resort to defiant, simplistic answers. Some actions may be judged intrinsically evil, but they are not well expressed in prefabricated lists (even Paul's lists of virtues and vices have to be subjected to contextual assessment). Thus issues in bio-ethics and sexual ethics (including, for example, abortion and euthanasia, as well as homosexual orientation and practice) are much too complex for simple categorisation. The adoption of language such as 'intrinsic evil', leaving no scope for situation or circumstance, contributes to the polarisation of public debate and takes the issues into the area of campaigning and power politics, thus impeding reasonable solutions. Christian ethics should be able to do much better than this. If moral community is at its heart, then at the very least we must attempt to understand other viewpoints, for assuredly no single viewpoint, however authoritatively reinforced, has the monopoly of truth. Hence the crucible is unavoidable. This is not to reduce faith communities to debating societies but to insist that Christian morality is engendered through community and identity, through Christian story and memory, through openness to life's problems, through worship and the guidance of the Spirit. Truth is transcendent. Our knowledge and our prophecy are imperfect (1 Cor. 13.9). The insight granted to us by the Spirit must be expressed and shared in love.

NOTES

INTRODUCTION

1 In Egypt a century ago, Grenville and Hunt discovered some Greek fragments of the sayings of Jesus at Oxyrhynchus (Grenville and Hunt 1904). Half a century later, the Nag Hammadi codices in Coptic came to light (Robinson 1979). They included a number of so-called Gospels, including the *Gospel of Thomas* (see Chapter 3), which is clearly linked to the Greek fragments. Both discoveries were of great value for the study of Christian origins. The discovery of the Dead Sea Scrolls in 1947 and succeeding years is well documented. For an authoritative account of how they came to light and a review of fifty years of Dead Sea Scrolls research, see Vermes 1997: 1–25.

2 I am indebted to Professor A. Lindemann of Bethel, Germany, for drawing my attention to this reference. For further discussion, cf. Merklein (1989).

3 In relation to basic models in Paul, cf. Hasenstab (1977).

4 See further, Chapter 3.

1 MORAL CONTEXT

1 Cf. Barton 1986: 225–46. There is a helpful discussion here of boundaries, with reference to Mary Douglas' work in anthropology. For an overview of the process of the parting of the ways between Christianity and Judaism, cf. Dunn 1991.

2 Cf. Rom. 2.11; Col. 3.25; Eph. 6.9; 1 Pet. 1.7; Acts 10.34.

3 Cf. J. G. Gager 1975, which studies millenarian movements, giving attention to factors such as conversion, cognitive dissonance, social conflict, early Christian missions and tensions with the Jewish communities.

4 Hays 1997: 21–7 may usefully be referred to here.

5 Cf. *The War Rule* at Qumran, between 'the sons of light' and 'the sons of darkness'.

6 For a notable discussion cf. Theissen 1982: 69–119.

7 Cf. Schmithals 1965: 22–37 emphasises this point.

8 Cf. Haenchen 1982: 360, 469, 471.

9 Jewish Christianity in the strictest sense seems to have been perpetuated in the Ebionites, the Nazoreans and the Elkesaites. According to patristic evidence, their main features were adherence to the Jewish Law and an adoptionist christology. Earlier examples of Jewish Christianity are found in *The Epistle of Barnabas* and the *Didache*, both of which are discussed in Chapter 2.

10 Cf. Cohen 1990: 204–23 for a careful exposition.

11 For a succinct account of Jewish Christianity, cf. Murray in Coggins and Houlden 1990: 341–6; also Simon 1986.

12 Cf. Theissen 1982: 27–67 for a distinctive discussion.

13 Cf. Wilson in Hooker and Wilson 1982: 102–14.

14 Cf. Dunn 1990. The term has been variously interpreted and the question of the group's identity is still debated. Only in Galatians does 'Judaisers' seem to indicate a Jewish Christian group which attracted some Gentiles by its rigour. At Corinth and Philippi, the reference is probably to a kind of Jewish gnostic tendency.

15 Derrett 1988: 206, 218 n.13. The whole article is intriguing and is reflected in our discussion of the issue.

16 As Derrett 1988: 205, 218 n.8 notes, patristic evidence indicates that Gentile Christians did observe dietary restrictions, although their origin had been forgotten and their practice had nothing to do with salvation.

17 A much discussed incident! Cf. Schmithals 1965: 63–78; Dunn 1983: 3–74.

18 Derrett 1988: 213 argues the point.

19 For a more detailed discussion of these issues, cf. Sanders 1983 and Watson 1986.

20 The distinction is between a movement for change within Judaism and a distinct group marginal to Judaism or even beyond its accepted parameters. Sociological studies, however, have as yet thrown little light on this distinction. Weber's classic church–sect typology is of little assistance.

21 The language of 'conversion' can be misleading in that it invites various kinds of stereotypical interpretation. Paul's experience does not offer a precise parallel with conversions which transform an ungodly into a godly life, or lead from unbelief to faith, or involve a move from one religion to another. Although he could be described as 'chief of sinners' (cf. 1 Tim. 1.15, probably a secondary text), this statement does not relate to a personal moral crisis but to his mistaken role as persecutor of the church of God (cf. 1 Cor. 15.9, Phil. 3.6). His 'sin' lay in not recognising the true nature of the will and purpose of God and thus, at the crisis of the ages when the church of Christ was being born, he was on the wrong side! The enormity of this misplaced devotion, of which Paul was always aware, was overwhelmed by the mercy and patience of God (cf. Gal. 1.15; 1 Tim. 1.16), which was directed not only to Paul but to all the nations. Hence Paul's 'conversion' cannot be understood apart from the revelation to him of the transcendent Christ as Lord of all creation and of the place of the Gentiles in the purpose of God (cf. Gal. 1.15–16). This does not mean that Paul

understood all this in one blinding flash of inspiration, but it is the source of his interpretation.

22 It is important to note that Paul was neither a systematic theologian nor a systematic ethicist. His teaching is not only generated within but also addressed to the needs of the churches. This in part explains the 'difficulties and inconsistencies' (cf. Räisänen 1986: 264) which a more systematic presentation might have modified.

23 This criticism has frequently been made of socio-historical approaches to the New Testament: cf. Scroggs 1979: 164.

24 Cf. Sanders 1977 for a fuller discussion.

25 The term is a recognised part of discourse on ethics. It is derived from the Greek *dei*, *deontos*, meaning 'it is necessary' or 'required'. It denotes action that is intrinsically right or required by authoritative rule, command or maxim. See further Fairweather and McDonald 1984: chapter 1.

26 The term is derived from the Greek *telos*, an end or goal. Cf. Fairweather and McDonald 1984: chapter 2.

27 See Chapters 4 and 5.

28 Martin 1988: lxi–lxix is relevant here.

29 For a discussion of the implications of audience and genre, and reflections on the Jewishness of 1 Peter, cf. Michaels 1988: xlix–lv.

30 Its alleged deutero-Pauline nature is as ancient as the tradition of New Testament ethics: cf. Jacoby 1899. Common moral traditions include christological statements and paraenetic passages with their use of the indicative and imperative, eschatology and ethics, baptism and the Spirit. That there are so many common features in a letter to a Diaspora Christian group reflects no more than the common life of the churches, but we cannot ignore the distinctive features of the letter.

31 Cf. Schrage 1988: 281–6 on this point.

32 Cf. Baker 1995 *passim*.

33 On perfectionism in James, cf. Martin 1988: lxxix–lxxxii.

34 Schrage 1988: 281 should be consulted here.

35 See further Schrage 1988: 286–90.

36 Ignatius is seen to have elaborated Pauline ideas, with his emphasis on christology, church, ministry and sacraments, and hierarchical order modelled on Christ and his first followers. Church offices – including that of bishop – were thought of not in terms of power but of service and care for others: cf. Koester 1982: 281–7, esp. 285.

37 On this whole subject, cf. Hays 1997: 138–57.

2 MORAL INTERPRETATION

1 The phrase is used and developed by Steiner 1989.

2 Cf. Lindbeck 1987. Wink 1973 also provides a good discussion of this point.

3 The reference is to McLuhan 1962.

4 Cf. de Lubac 1968; Fowl 1997: 3–25; Louth 1983.

5 Cf. Neusner 1973, 1979; Rivkin 1978; E. P. Sanders 1985, 1990; Lieu 1990.

6 On Qumran, cf. Vermes 1995 (4th edn), especially the Introduction and 'The Community Rule'.

7 The subject is discussed further in Chapter 3. Eschatology is literally discourse about the last things (or end-time) and was embedded in the prophetic tradition. Apocalyptic was an 'unveiling' of the divine plan and purpose for the universe, revealing the cosmic secrets vouchsafed to some legendary figure from the past – Enoch, Moses, Baruch, Daniel – who ascended into the secret place of the Most High to receive the revelation. Its characteristic medium was dreams or visions, and it frequently contained a welter of astrological data, angelologies and popular lore. For an examination of the ancient roots of apocalyptic faith, cf. Cohn 1993.

8 Attention is given to this problem in Jewish-Christian dialogue today; cf. Charlesworth 1992; my own contribution is found in McDonald 1995.

9 Cf. Vermes 1995 on the War Rule (1QM).

10 Cf. Vermes 1995 *passim*.

11 Cf. Chilton 1979 *passim*; Chilton and Evans 1994. For a critical response, cf. Kvalbein 1997, who emphasises that the kingdom of God is a concrete expression for the gift of salvation, the place of salvation and the time of salvation. 'It is not an abstract phrase for God's position or rule as king' (p. 65). It is not a necessary part of the performative view outlined above to suggest that it is.

12 On *Didache* and the *Epistle of Barnabas*, which provide important evidence on the Jewish foundations of moral education in the churches, see Koester 1982: 157–60, 276–9.

13 This follows accepted haggadic practice in the rabbinic tradition; cf. M. Bockmuel in Barclay and Sweet 1996: 267–70.

14 Community ethics figure prominently in the first letter of Clement. The writer has to deal with dissension over church appointments! As the story of Daniel shows, the wicked always cause problems for the righteous. The initial appeal is to emulate the conduct of the saints (46.1–4), as scripture bids (cf. Ps. 18.26–27). There is a call for unity – indeed, organic unity – that is reminiscent of Paul. The recipients are warned to 'recall the words of our Lord Jesus' (46.7; cf. Matt. 18.6–9; Mark 9.42; Luke 17.1–2, etc.), and to contemplate the harmfulness of schism. 'Pick up the letter of the blessed apostle Paul', he tells them, inviting them to apply Paul's strictures on schism in Corinth in his day to the present troubles in the Corinthian church (cf. 48.1). Taking his cue again from scripture (Ps. 118.19–20), Clement argues that 'the gate of righteousness is the Christian gate', and if they act 'in holiness and righteousness' (Luke 1.75) they will be blessed and will remove disorder from their midst.

15 1 Peter 2. 24–25; cf. Isa. 53.5–6, 12 (LXX); the image in fact evokes many other scriptural passages.

16 Parallels have been noted between 1 Peter and the first letter of Clement, which cites 'the words of the Lord Jesus' (13.2), teaching consideration and patience. His dominical source seems to be Luke 6.31, 36–38 (cf. Matt. 5.7; 6.14–15; 7.1–2, 12), although variations

from the Gospel forms of it suggest an earlier collection of Jesus' sayings ('Q'?) and also interaction between the tradition and the LXX (cf. Best 1969: 112). The writer seems to distinguish between 'the commandment' in scripture and 'these injunctions' of the Lord which clarify its meaning. The outcome of this process of interpretation is moral action, with humility and faithfulness as the keynotes. In difficult times, it is a comfort that the devout 'oppressed and afflicted' enjoy the favour of God (cf. Isa. 66.2).

17 There has been a long debate over the nature and content of catechisms in the early churches, including notable contributions by Seeberg (1903), Carrington (1940) and Selwyn (1946). No attempt is made here to substantiate complex catechetical patterns, although there was a recognisable catechetical tradition (McDonald 1980), including the 'two ways' motif so evident in the *Didache* and teaching traditions relating to the household (the *Haustafeln*). We concentrate here on the moral foundations of the lists of virtues and vices.

18 For example, the *Shechinah* or cloud of divine glory alights on the meek (*Nedarim* 38a), while the arrogant cause the *Shechinah* to depart.

3 MORAL TRADITION

1 These questions have particular relevance in view of the attempts of modern scholarship to find in the 'Q' sayings collection an earlier kind of gospel free of the 'myths' that allegedly shaped the canonical Gospels: cf. Mack 1993.

2 There is some evidence of a continuing group of John's disciples – some were absorbed into the Christian communities (cf. Acts 18.24–19.5) – but it is the Christian community which has preserved his memory.

3 The issue of whether one should begin a study of 'New Testament ethics' with Jesus is well discussed in Hays 1997.

4 Cf. Goulder 1989: 273; Davies and Allison 1988: 304; Webb 1991: 175; Tuckett 1996: 113.

5 Cf. Betz and Riesner 1994: 143–7; VanderKam 1994: 168–70; Betz 1992: 205–14; and especially Taylor 1997: 15–48.

6 Cf. Mark 11.29–33; Matt. 21.23–27; Luke 20.1–8.

7 The text is further discussed below in relation to Jesus' ministry. See pp. 106–7.

8 Cf. McDonald 1993: 218–22; Hilton and Marshall 1988 *passim*.

9 This heading takes its cue from H. C. Kee's *Community of the New Age*, 1977.

10 To take our study further into the Gospels of Matthew and Luke would be to enter further into the realms of *Redaktionsgeschichte*, leaving behind our concern with the roots of the tradition. Thus Matthew and Luke represent a continuation of the basic issues that have occupied our attention, but in later settings.

11 On the use and alleged abuse of this pericope in the papal encyclical *Veritatis Splendor* 1993, cf. Moore 1994.

12 See Chapters 1 and 2.

13 The Oxyrhynchus Papyri were discovered about a century ago in Egypt and subsequently published by Grenville and Hunt. Three papyri relevant to this study are numbered as 11, 654 and 655.

14 The so-called 'Nag Hammadi library', one of the outstanding discoveries for biblical studies in the mid-twentieth century, includes the remarkable document found in the second codex from Chenoboskion which is described in an appended note as 'The Gospel according to Thomas'. Containing virtually no narrative, it should not be classified as a Gospel but, as it professes, a collection of 'hidden sayings' attributed to Jesus as source and to the disciple Didymus Judas Thomas as recorder. More than half the recorded sayings reflect the teaching of Jesus in the Gospels (predominantly Matthew and Luke, but John also scores well), and only 30 out of its 114 sayings do not resonate with the New Testament (Morrice 1997: 62).

15 These are helpfully set out in Valantasis 1997: 29–48, where the precise references will be found.

16 See Chapter 5, where the nature of community is discussed.

4 MORAL PERSONS

1 On the personal, cf. also Buber 1959, MacMurray 1961 and, more recently, Taylor 1989.

2 In preparing this chapter, I was greatly helped by auditing the 1996/97 Gifford lectures given at Edinburgh by Professor Richard Sorabji on 'Emotions and how to cope with them: what ancient thought has to teach us'. This section owes a debt to these lectures, particularly in relation to the interpretation of the emotions in Plato and the discussion of anger.

3 Again I acknowledge here a debt to Professor Sorabji's exposition.

4 For further etymological studies of these and other terms used in the New Testament to denote aspects of personal life, the reader is referred to Kittel 1964–74, *in loc*.

5 Cf. the discussion of Gnosticism and ethics in Chapter 3 above, also the Introduction, and the sources cited there.

6 Some suggest that Col. 1.15–20 may well be a pre-Pauline hymn, incorporated into the letter, presumably by the author. For a full discussion, see in particular Cannon 1983: 19–49. Most commentaries discuss the issue: e.g., Lohse 1971: 41–61; O'Brien 1982.

5 MORALITY, COMMUNITY AND SOCIETY

1 Some material in this chapter has already appeared in article form in McDonald 1997: esp. 8–15.

2 In this respect there is a parallel with Gnosticism, in which the 'soteriological ethic of brotherhood' (Jonas) was concerned to nurture the divine spark within each member. See Introduction and Chapter 3.

3 For a fuller discussion of Galen cf. Wilken 1984: 68–93.

4 The rabbinic schools, such as those of Hillel, Shammai and their successors, may perhaps be instanced as communities, since their

disciples formed distinctive groups bound together by a common purpose and outlook. Mention should also be made of the *haburoth* or fellowship groups which met for duty meals (e.g., the observance of a commandment, or a special event such as a betrothal, marriage, circumcision or funeral) and meals of a charitable nature to which all contributed. The question of their bearing on the disciple group that celebrated the last supper need not be discussed here. Cf. Jeremias 1966: 29–31.

5 A full translation of the document and an introduction to it is found in Laistner 1967: Appendix I, 75–122.

6 Elliott's full discussion (1982: 165–266) of 'the significance and function of the household within the strategy of 1 Peter' is worthy of careful study.

7 See in this connection the book in the present series by Deborah Sawyer, who shows in her contextual study that two theories of gender are evident in early Christianity: one underpinning the Aristotelian notion of natural order, and the other a more inclusive position, as in Plato's *grove of academe* – Sawyer 1996 *passim*.

8 That Christians were concerned about the manumission of slaves is seen in *Ad Polycarp* 4.3, Hermas, *Similitudes* 1.8, Hermas, *Mandata* 8.10 and other texts. The ecclesiastical common chests were sometimes used for this purpose. Cf. Harrill 1995 *passim*, and esp. 178–82. See also Kyrtatas 1987: 55–74.

6 MORAL EXCELLENCE

1 For a further exploration, cf. Finley 1962.

2 For a contemporary view of Socrates, cf. Vlastos 1991.

3 See our discussion in Chapter 5 above.

4 This is well illustrated in the work of Plutarch: consult, for example, Russell 1972.

5 For a magisterial study of Philo, see Wolfson's two-volume work published in 1948, and in particular his study of ethical theory, II: 165–321, which considers virtue in relation to commandments, the control of desire, prayer and repentance, and reward, and also offers a definition. For a study of Hellenistic Jewish piety, see Goodenough 1969.

6 See Chapter 3 above.

7 Some material incorporated in this chapter appeared in earlier form in McDonald 1997: 2–8.

BIBLIOGRAPHY

Allegro, J. (1956) *The Myth of Innocence*, Philadelphia: Fortress.

Anderson, H. (1985) '4 Maccabees', in J. Charlesworth (ed.) *The Old Testament Pseudepigrapha*, II, London: Darton, Longman & Todd.

Appleby, J. (ed.) (1996) *Knowledge and Postmodernism in Historical Perspective*, London: Routledge.

Armstrong, A. H. (1949) *An Introduction to Ancient Philosophy*, London: Methuen.

Auerbach, E. (1968) *Mimesis*, Princeton, NJ: Princeton University Press.

Baker, W. R. (1995) *Personal Speech-Ethics in the Epistle of James*, Tübingen: Mohr (Paul Siebeck).

Balch, D. L. (1981) *Let Wives be Submissive: The Domestic Code in 1 Peter*, Chicago: Scholars Press.

Barclay, J. M. G. (1991) 'Paul, Philemon and the dilemma of Christian slave-ownership', *New Testament Studies* 37.2: 161–86.

—— (1996) *Jews in the Mediterranean Diaspora*, Edinburgh: T. & T. Clark.

Barclay, J. M. G. and Sweet, J. (eds) (1996) *Early Christian Thought in its Jewish Context*, Cambridge: Cambridge University Press.

Barrett, C. K. (1963) *Reading Through Romans*, London: Epworth.

—— (1979) *The Community of the Beloved Disciple*, London: Chapman.

—— (1991) *The Epistle to the Romans*, London: A. & C. Black.

Barton, S. C. (1986) 'Paul's sense of place: an anthropological approach to community formation in Corinth', *New Testament Studies* 32.2: 225–46.

Barton, S. C. and Horsley, G. H. R. (1981) 'A Hellenistic cult group and the New Testament churches', *Jahrbuch für Antike und Christentum* 24: 7–41.

Bartsch, H. (1954) *Kerygma and Myth*, I, London: SCM.

Beare, F. W. (1959) *A Commentary on the Epistle to the Philippians*, New York: Harper.

Bellah, R., Madsen, R., Sullivan, W. M., Swidler, A. and Tipton, S. M. (1985) *Habits of the Heart: Middle America Observed*, New York and London: Harper and Row.

Best, E. (1969) '1 Peter and the Gospel tradition', *New Testament Studies* 16.95–113.

—— (1981) *Following Jesus. Discipleship in the Gospel of Mark*, Sheffield: JSOT Press.

Betz, O. (1992) 'Was John the Baptist an Essene?', in H. Shanks (ed.) *Understanding the Dead Sea Scrolls*, New York: Random House.

Betz, O. and Riesner, R. (1994) *Jesus, Qumran and the Vatican: Clarifications*, London: SCM.

Bickermann, E. J. (1945) 'The date of IV Macabees', Louis Ginzberg Jubilee Volume, New York: English Section, 105–12.

Bilde, P., Engberg-Pedersen, T., Hannestad, L. and Zahle, J. *Religion and Religious Practice in the Seleucid Kingdom*, Aarhus: Aarhus University Press.

Birch, B. C. (1995) 'Divine character and the formation of moral community in the Book of Exodus', in J. W. Rogerson *et al.* (eds) *The Bible in Ethics*, Sheffield: JSOT supp. series 207.

Blenkinsopp, J. (1977) *Prophecy and Canon*, Notre Dame, IN: University of Notre Dame Press.

Bockmuehl, M. (1996) 'Halakhah and ethics in the Jesus tradition', in J. M. G. Barclay and J. Sweet (eds) *Early Christian Thought in its Jewish Context*, Cambridge: Cambridge University Press.

Borgen, P. (1988) 'Catalogues of vices, the apostolic decree and the Jerusalem meeting', in J. Neusner *et al.* (eds) *The Social World of Formative Christianity and Judaism*, Philadelphia: Fortress.

Breitenstein, U. (1978) *Beobachtungen zu Sprache, Stil und Gedankengut des Vierten Makkabaerbuches*, Basel: Schwabe.

Briant, P. (1990) 'The Seleucid kingdom, the Achaemenid empire and the history of the Near East in the first millennium BC', in P. Bilde *et al.* (eds) *Religion and Religious Practice in the Seleucid Kingdom*, Aarhus: Aarhus University Press.

Brown, R. E. (1966) *The Gospel According to John*, New York: Doubleday.

—— (1982) *The Epistles of John*, New York: Doubleday.

—— (1986) *The Gospel of John and the Johannine Epistles*, Collegeville, Minn.: Liturgical Press.

Buber, M. (1959) *I and Thou*, Edinburgh: T. & T. Clark.

Büchsel, F. (1965) 'ἐπιθυμια', in G. Kittel (ed.) *Theological Dictionary of the New Testament*, III, Grand Rapids, MI: Eerdmans.

Bultmann, R. (1952) *Theology of the New Testament*, I, London: SCM.

Burkert, W. (1992) *The Orientalizing Revolution*, Cambridge, MA.: Harvard University Press.

Cannon, G. E. (1983) *The Use of Traditional Materials in Colossians*, Macon, GA: Mercer University Press.

Carrington, P. (1940) *The Primitive Christian Catechism*, Cambridge: Cambridge University Press.

Carroll, R. P. (1990) 'Eschatology', in R. J. Coggins and J. L. Houlden (eds) *A Dictionary of Biblical Interpretation*, London: SCM and Philadelphia: Trinity.

—— (1991) *Wolf in the Sheepfold. The Bible as a Problem for Christianity*, London: SPCK.

Cassuto, U. (1961) *A Commentary on the Book of Genesis I* (English translation), Jerusalem: Magnes Press, The Hebrew University.

Catchpole, D. R. (1987) 'The Law and Prophets in Q', in *Tradition and Interpretation in the New Testament*, Festschrift für E. E. Ellis, Tübingen: Mohr.

—— (1993) *The Quest for Q*, Edinburgh: T. & T. Clark.

—— (1996) 'Mark', in J. M. G. Barclay and J. Sweet (eds) *Early Christian Thought in its Jewish Context*, Cambridge: Cambridge University Press.

Charlesworth, J. H. (ed.) (1990) *Jews and Christians*, New York: Crossroad.

—— (1992) *Overcoming Fear Between Jews and Christians*, New York: Crossroad.

Chilton, D. B. (1979) *God in Strength. Jesus' Announcement of the Kingdom*, Friestadt: Plöchl.

—— (1996) *Pure Kingdom. Jesus' Vision of God*, Grand Rapids, MI: Eerdmans.

Chilton, D. B. and Evans, C. (eds) (1994) *Studying the Historical Jesus: Evaluations of the State of Current Research*, Leiden, New York, Cologne: Brill.

Chilton, D. B. and McDonald, J. I. H. (1987) *Jesus and the Ethics of the Kingdom*, London: SPCK.

Clines, D. (1995) 'Ethics as deconstruction, and, the ethics of deconstruction', in J. W. Rogerson *et al.* (eds) *The Bible in Ethics*, Sheffield: JSOT supp. series 207.

Coggins, R. J. and Houlden, J. L. (eds) (1990) *A Dictionary of Biblical Interpretation*, London: SCM and Philadelphia: Trinity.

Cohen, S.D. (1990) 'Religion, ethnicity and "hellenism" in the emergence of Jewish identity in Maccabean Palestine', in P. Bilde *et al.* (eds) *Religion and Religious Practice in the Seleucid Kingdom*, Aarhus: Aarhus University Press.

Cohn, N. (1993) *Cosmos, Chaos and the World to Come*, New Haven, CT and London: Yale University Press.

Colson, F. H. (1939) *Philo of Alexandria* (Loeb Classical Library), VIII, London: Heinemann and Cambridge, MA.: Harvard University Press.

Conzelmann, H. (1961) *The Theology of St Luke* (English translation), London: Faber.

Crossan, J. D. (1991) *The Historical Jesus. The Life of a Mediterranean Jewish Peasant*, Edinburgh: T. & T. Clark.

Cullmann, O. (1976) *The Johannine Circle*, London: SCM.

Daube, D. (1956) *The New Testament and Rabbinic Judaism*, London: Athlone.

Davies, M. (1990) 'Reader-response criticism, in R. J. Coggins and J. L. Houlden (eds) *A Dictionary of Biblical Interpretation*, London: SCM and Philadelphia: Trinity.

—— (1995) 'Work and slavery in the New Testament: impoverishments of traditions', in J. W. Rogerson *et al.* (eds) *The Bible in Ethics*, Sheffield: JSOT supp. series 207.

Davies, S. L. (1995) *Jesus the Healer*, New York: Continuum.

Davies, W. D. and Allison, D. C. (1988) *The Gospel According to St Matthew* (International Critical Commentary I), Edinburgh: T. & T. Clark.

Deeken, A. (1974) *Process and Permanence in Ethics: Max Scheler's Moral Philosophy*, New York: Paulist Press.

Derrett, J. D. M. (1988) 'Clean and unclean animals (Acts 10.15, 11.9): Peter's pronouncing power observed', *Heythrope Journal* xxix: 205–21.

Douglas, M. (1966) *Purity and Danger*, London: Routledge and Kegan Paul.

Downing, F. G. (1992) *Cynics and Christian Origins*, Edinburgh: T. & T. Clark.

Dungan, D. L. (1971) *The Sayings of Jesus in the Churches of Paul*, Oxford: Blackwell.

Dunn, J. D. G. (1982) 'The relationship between Paul and Jerusalem according to Galatians 1 and 2', *New Testament Studies* 28.4: 461–78.

—— (1988) *Romans 1–8*, Dallas, TX: Word Books.

—— (1990) 'Judaizers', in R. J. Coggins and J. L. Houlden (eds) *A Dictionary of Biblical Interpretation*, London: SCM and Philadelphia: Trinity.

—— (1991) *The Partings of the Ways Between Christianity and Judaism and Their Significance for the Character of Christianity*, London: SCM and Philadelphia: Trinity.

Elliott, J. H. (1982) *A Home for the Homeless. A Sociological Exegesis of 1 Peter, Its Situation and Strategy*, London: SCM.

Ellis, E. E. (1981) 'The silenced wives in Corinth (1 Cor. 14.34–35)', in E. J. Epp and G. D. Fee (eds) *New Testament Textual Criticism: Its Significance for Exegesis*, Oxford: Clarendon.

Engberg-Pedersen, T. (1990) *The Stoic Theory of Oikeiosis*, Aarhus: Aarhus University Press.

Epp, E. J. and Fee, G. D. (eds) (1981) *New Testament Textual Criticism: Its Significance for Exegesis*, Oxford: Clarendon.

Erikson, E. (1980) *Identity and the Life Cycle*, New York: Norton.

Esler, P. F. (1987) *Community and Gospel in Luke–Acts*, Cambridge: Cambridge University Press.

Fairweather, I. C. M. and McDonald J. I. H. (1984) *The Quest for Christian Ethics*, Edinburgh: Handsel.

Ferguson, J. (1958) *Moral Values in the Ancient World*, London: Methuen.

Finley, M. I. (1962) *The World of Odysseus*, London: Chatto.

Fiorenza, E. S. (1988) 'The ethics of biblical interpretation: decentring biblical scholarship', *Journal of Biblical Literature* 107/1: 3–17.

Fisher N. R. E. (1988) 'Greek associations, symposia and clubs', in M. Grant and R. Kitzinger (eds) *Civilisation of the Ancient Mediterranean: Greece and Rome*, 2, New York: Scribner's.

Fleddermann, H. T. (1995) *Mark and Q*, Leuven: Leuven University Press; Uitgeverij Peeters.

Fowl, S. E. (ed.) (1997) *The Theological Interpretation of Scripture*, Cambridge, MA and Oxford: Blackwell.

Fowler, J. W. (1981) *Stages of Faith*, San Francisco: Harper and Row.

Freyne, S. (1980) *Galilee from Alexander to Hadrian*, Wilmington, DE: Michael Glazier.

Friedrich, J., Pohlmann, W. and Stuhlmacher, P. (1976) 'Zum historischen Situation und Intention von Röm. 13.1–7', *Zeitschrift für Theologie und Kirche* 73: 149ff.

Furnish, V. P. (1968) *Theology and Ethics in Paul*, Nashville, TN: Abingdon.

—— (1973) *The Love Command in the New Testament*, London: SCM.

Gager, J. (1975) *Kingdom and Community: The Social World of Early Christianity*, Englewood Cliffs, NJ: Prentice Hall.

Gerhardsson, B. (1996) *The Shema in the New Testament*, Lund: Novapress.

Gibson, J. C. L. (1981) *Genesis 1*, Edinburgh: Saint Andrew Press and Philadelphia: Westminster.

Gill, R. (1991) *Christian Ethics in Secular Worlds*, Edinburgh: T. & T. Clark.

Goodenough, E. R. (1969) *By Light, Light: The Mystic Gospel of Hellenistic Judaism*, Amsterdam: Philo Press.

Goulder, M. (1989) *Luke – A New Paradigm*, Sheffield: Sheffield Academic Press.

Grenville, B. P. and Hunt, A. S. (1904) *New Sayings of Jesus and Fragments of a Lost Gospel from Oxyrhynchus*, London: Frowde.

Hadas, M. (1953) *The Third and Fourth Books of Maccabees*, New York: Harper.

Haenchen, E. (1982) *The Acts of the Apostles: A Commentary*, Oxford: Blackwell (2nd edn).

Hall, S. G. (1990) 'Gnosticism', in R. J. Coggins and J. L. Houlden (eds) *A Dictionary of Biblical Interpretation*, London: SCM and Philadelphia: Trinity.

Harrill, J. A. (1995) *The Manumission of Slaves in Early Christianity*, Tübingen: Mohr (Paul Siebeck).

Harris, G. (1991) 'The beginnings of church discipline: 1. Cor. 5', *New Testament Studies* 37.1: 1–21.

Hartman, L. 'Code and context: a few reflections on the paraenesis of Colossians 3.6–4.1', in B. S. Rosner (ed.) *Understanding Paul's Ethics*, Carlisle: Paternoster.

Harvey, A. E. (1981) *God Incarnate: Story and Belief*, London: SPCK.

Hasenstab, R. (1977) *Modelle paulinischer Ethik*, Mainz: Matthias-Grünewald-Verlag.

Hauerwas, S. (1981) *A Community of Character*, Cleveland, OH and London: University of Notre Dame Press.

Hawthorne, G. F. (1983) *Philippians* (Word Biblical Commentary 43), Waco, TX: Word Books.

Hays, R. B. (1997) *The Moral Vision of the New Testament*, Edinburgh: T. & T. Clark.

Hilton, M. and Marshall, G. (1988) *The Gospels and Rabbinic Judaism*, London: SCM.

Hoffmann, P. (1972) *Studien zur Theologie der Logien Quelle*, Münster: Aschendorff.

Honecker, M. (1990) *Einführung in die Theologische Ethik*, Berlin: de Gruyter.

Hooker, M. (1959) *Jesus and the Servant*, London: SPCK.

—— (1991) *A Commentary on the Gospel According to St Mark*, London: A. & C. Black.

Hooker, M. D. and Wilson, S. G. (1982) *Paul and Paulinism. Essays in Honour of C. K. Barrett*, London: SPCK.

Horsley, G. H. R. (1989) 'A fishing cartel in first-century Ephesos', in G. H. R. Horsley (ed.) *New Documents Illustrating Early Christianity*, 5, Sydney: Macquarrie University, Ancient History Documentary Research Centre.

Houlden, J. L. (1973) *Ethics and the New Testament*, Harmondsworth: Penguin.

Jacoby, H. (1899) *Neutestamentliche Ethik*, Königsberg: Thomas.

Jaeger, W. (1939) *Paideia: The Ideals of Greek Culture*, I, (English translation), Oxford: Basil Blackwell.

Jeremias, J. (1966) *The Eucharistic Words of Jesus*, London: SCM.

Keck, L. E. (1996) 'Rethinking "New Testament Ethics"', *Journal of Biblical Literature* 115/1: 3–16.

Kee, H. C. (1977) *Community of the New Age*, London: SCM.

—— (1980) *Christian Origins in Sociological Perspective*, London: SCM.

—— (1995) *Who Are the People of God? Early Christian Models of Community*, New Haven, CT, and London: Yale University Press.

Kittel, G. (ed.) (1964–74) *Theological Dictionary of the New Testament*, I–IX, Grand Rapids, MI: Eerdmans.

Kloppenborg, J. S. (1984) 'Tradition and redaction in the synoptic sayings source', *Catholic Biblical Quarterly* 46: 34–62.

—— (1987) *The Formation of Q*, Philadelphia: Fortress.

—— (1987a) 'Synoptic eschatology and the apocalypticism of Q', *Harvard Theological Review* 80: 287–306.

—— (1988) *Q Parallels*, Sonoma, CA: Polebridge.

Koester, H. (1982) *Introduction to the New Testament*, II, *History and Literature of Early Christianity*. Philadelphia: Fortress and Berlin/New York: Routledge.

—— (1995) *History, Culture and Religion of the Hellenistic Age*, New York and Berlin: Walter de Gruyter (2nd edn).

Kvalbein, H. (1997) 'The kingdom of God in the ethics of Jesus', *Studia Theologica* 51: 60–84.

Kyrtatas, D. J. (1987) *The Social Structure of the Early Christian Communities*, London and New York: Verso.

Laistner, M. L. W. (1967) *Christianity and Pagan Culture in the Later Roman Empire*, Ithaca, NY: Cornell University Press.

Lieu, J. M. (1990) 'Pharisees and scribes', in R. J. Coggins and J. L. Houlden (eds) *A Dictionary of Biblical Interpretation*, London: SCM and Philadelphia: Trinity.

Lightfoot, J. B. (1894) *St Paul's Epistle to the Philippians*, London: Macmillan.

Lillie, W. (1956) *The Law of Christ*, London: Hodder and Stoughton.

—— (1961) *Studies in New Testament Ethics*, Edinburgh and London: Oliver and Boyd.

Lim, T. H. (1997) *Holy Scripture in the Qumran Commentaries and Pauline Letters*, Oxford: Clarendon.

Lindbeck, G. (1987) 'The story-shaped church', in S. E. Fowl (ed.) *The Theological Interpretation of Scripture*, Cambridge, MA and Oxford: Blackwell.

Logan, A. (1996) *Gnostic Truth and Christian Heresy: A Study in the History of Gnosticism*, Edinburgh: T. & T. Clark.

Lohmeyer, E. (1956) *Der Brief an die Philipper, an die Kolosser und an Philemon*, Göttingen: Vandenhoeck & Ruprecht.

Lohse, E. (1971) *Colossians and Philemon*, Philadelphia: Fortress.

—— (1991) *Theological Ethics of the New Testament*, Minneapolis, MN: Fortress (2nd edn).

—— (1995) (first published in 1980) 'The church in everyday life. Considerations of the theological basis of ethics in the New Testament', in B. S. Rosner (ed.) *Understanding Paul's Ethics*, Carlisle: Paternoster.

Long A. A. (1974) *Hellenistic Philosophy*, London: Duckworth.

Louth, A. (1983) 'Allegorical interpretation', in R. J. Coggins and J. L. Houlden (eds) *A Dictionary of Biblical Interpretation*, London: SCM and Philadelphia: Trinity.

de Lubac, H. (1968) 'Spiritual understanding', in S. E. Fowl (ed.) *The Theological Interpretation of Scripture*, Cambridge, MA and Oxford: Blackwell.

McDonald, J. I. H. (1980) *Kerygma and Didache*, Cambridge: Cambridge University Press.

—— (1989) 'Romans 13.1–7: a test case for New Testament interpretation', *New Testament Studies* 35.4: 540–9.

—— (1993) *Biblical Interpretation and Christian Ethics*, Cambridge: Cambridge University Press.

—— (1995) 'New Testament interpretation in the context of Jewish-Christian dialogue', *The Edinburgh Review of Theology and Religion: Studies in World Christianity* 1.1: 26–40.

—— (1997) 'The crucible of Pauline ethics. A cross-cultural approach to Christian ethics-in-the-making', *The Edinburgh Review of Theology and Religion: Studies in World Christianity* 3.1: 1–21.

MacIntyre, A. (1995) *After Virtue: A Study in Moral Theory*, London: Duckworth.

McLuhan, M. (1962) *The Gutenberg Galaxy*, London: Routledge and Kegan Paul.

MacMurray, J. (1961) *Persons in Relation*, London: Faber.

Mack, B. (1988) *The Myth of Innocence*, Philadelphia: Fortress.

—— (1993) *The Lost Gospel. The Book of Q and Christian Origins*, San Francisco: Harper Collins.

Malherbe, A. J. (1983) *Social Aspects of Early Christianity*, Philadelphia: Fortress.

Mangey, T. (1742) *Philonis Judaei opera quae reperiri potuerunt omnia* (2 vols), London.

Manson, T. W. (1935) *The Teaching of Jesus*, Cambridge: Cambridge University Press.

Martin, R. P. (1976) *Philippians*, Greenwood, SC: Attic Press.

—— (1988) *James*, Waco, TX: Word Books.

Marxsen, W. (1993) *New Testament Foundations for Christian Ethics*, Edinburgh: T. & T. Clark.

Matera, F. J. (1996) *New Testament Ethics*, Louisville, KY: Westminster/John Knox.

Meeks, W. (1983) *The First Urban Christians: The Social World of the Apostle Paul*, New Haven, CT: Yale University Press.

—— (1987) *The Moral World of the First Christians*, London: SPCK.

—— (1993) *The Origins of Christian Morality*, New Haven, CT and London: Yale University Press.

Merklein, H. (ed.) (1989) *Neues Testament und Ethik*, Freiburg, Basle, Vienna: Herder.

Michael, J. H. (1928) *The Epistle of Paul to the Philippians* (Moffat Commentaries), London: Hodder and Stoughton.

Michaelis, W. (1935) *Der Brief des Paulus an die Philipper*, II, Leipzig: Deichert.

Michaels, J. R. (1988) *1 Peter*, Waco, TX: Word Books.

Moore, G. (1994) 'Some remarks on the use of scripture in *Veritatis Splendor*', in J. Selling and J. Jans (eds) *The Splendor of Accuracy*, Kampen: Kok Pharos.

Morrice, W. G. (1997) *Hidden Sayings of Jesus*, London: SPCK.

Moxnes, H. (1988) 'Honour and righteousness in Romans', *Journal for the Study of the New Testament* 32: 61–77.

Murray, R. P. R. (1990) 'Jewish Christianity', in R. J. Coggins and J. L. Houlden (eds) *A Dictionary of Biblical Interpretation*, London: SCM and Philadelphia: Trinity.

Neirynck, F. (1988) *Q Synopsis: The Double Tradition Passages in Greek*, Leuven: Leuven University Press.

Neusner, J. (1971) *The Rabbinic Traditions about the Pharisees before 70* (2 vols), Leiden: Brill.

—— (1973) *From Politics to Piety*, Englewood Cliffs, NJ: Prentice Hall.

—— (1979) *The Way of Torah. An Introduction to Judaism*, Belmont, CA: Wadsworth.

Neusner, J., Borgen, P., Frerichs, E. S. and Horsley, R. (1988) *The Social World of Formative Christianity and Judaism*, Philadelphia: Fortress.

Niccum, C. (1997) 'The voice of the manuscripts on the silence of women: the external evidence for 1 Cor. 14.34–35', *New Testament Studies* 43.2: 242–55.

Nock, A. D. (1972) 'The Gild of Zeus Hypsistos', in Z. Stewart (ed.) *Arthur Danby Nock: Essays on Religion and the Ancient World*, Oxford: Clarendon.

Nussbaum, M. (1986) 'Therapeutic arguments: Epicurus and Aristotle', in M. Schofield and G. Striker (eds) *The Norms of Nature: Studies in Hellenistic Ethics*, Cambridge: Cambridge University Press.

O'Brien, P. T. (1982) *Colossians, Philemon*, Waco, TX: Word Books.

O'Neill, J. C. (1975) *Paul's Letter to the Romans*, Harmondsworth: Penguin.

Osborn, E. (1976) *Ethical Patterns in Early Christian Thought*, Cambridge: Cambridge University Press.

Osborne, C. (1994) *Eros Unveiled*, Oxford: Clarendon.

Otzen, B. (1990) 'Crisis and religious reaction: Jewish apocalypticism', in P. Bilde *et al.* (eds) *Religion and Religious Practice in the Seleucid Kingdom*, Aarhus: Aarhus University Press.

Page, R. (1996) *God and the Web of Creation*, London: SCM.

—— (1997) 'God, natural evil and the ecological crisis', *Studies in World Christianity* 3.1: 68–86.

Parker, D. (1997) 'Ethics and the New Testament', *Studies in Christian Ethics* 10.2: 39–57, 62–3.

Parker, I. (1992) *Discourse Dynamics*, London and New York: Routledge.

Patterson, S. J. (1993) *The Gospel of Thomas and Jesus*, Sonoma, CA: Polebridge.

Pearson, B. A. (1986) 'Christians and Jews in first-century Alexandria', *Harvard Theological Review* 79: 206–16.

Piper, R. A. (ed.) (1994) *The Gospel Behind the Gospels. Current Studies on Q*, Leiden: Brill.

Plummer, A. (1919) *A Commentary on St Paul's Epistle to the Philippians* (International Critical Commentaries), London: Robert Scott Roxburghe House.

Polanyi, M. (1958) *Personal Knowledge*, London: Routledge and Kegan Paul.

—— (1959) *The Study of Man*, London: Routledge and Kegan Paul.

—— (1967) *The Tacit Dimension*, London: Routledge and Kegan Paul.

Quispel, G. (1975) *Tatian and the Gospel of Thomas*, Leiden: Brill.

von Rad, G. (1968) *Old Testament Theology* (English translation), Edinburgh: Oliver and Boyd.

Räisänen, H. (1986) *Paul and the Law*, Philadelphia: Fortress.

Rensberger, D. (1992) 'Love for one another and love for enemies in the Gospel of John', in W. M. Swartley (ed.) *The Love of Enemy and Nonretaliation in the New Testament*, Louisville, KY: Westminster/John Knox.

Rivkin, E. (1978) *A Hidden Revolution. The Pharisees' Search for the Kingdom Within*, Nashville, TN: Abingdon.

Robinson, J. A. T. (1952) *The Body*, London: SCM.

Robinson, J. M. (1971) *Trajectories Through Early Christianity*, Philadelphia: Fortress.

—— (1979) 'The discovery of the Nag Hammadi codices', *Biblical Archaeologist* 42: 206–24.

—— (1994) 'The Jesus of Q as liberation theologian', in R. A. Piper (ed.) *The Gospel Behind the Gospels. Current Studies on Q*, Leiden: Brill.

Rogerson, J. W. (1995) 'Discourse ethics and biblical ethics', in J. W. Rogerson *et al.* (eds) *The Bible in Ethics*, Sheffield: JSOT supp. series 207.

Rogerson, J. W., Davies, M. and Carroll R. (eds) (1995) *The Bible in Ethics*, Sheffield: JSOT supp. series 207.

Rosner, B. S. (ed.) (1995) *Understanding Paul's Ethics*, Carlisle: Paternoster.

Rowland, C. (1982) *The Open Heaven*, New York: Crossroad and London: SPCK.

—— (1988) *Radical Christianity*, Cambridge: Polity Press and Oxford: Blackwell.

Rowland C. and Corner, M. (1990) *Liberating Exegesis*, London: SPCK.

Rudolph, K. (1984) *Gnosis: The Nature and History of Gnosticism* (English translation), Edinburgh: T. & T. Clark.

Runia, D. T. (1993) *Philo in Early Christian Literature: A Survey*, Assen: Van Gorcum and Minneapolis, MN: Fortress.

—— (1995) *Philo and the Church Fathers*, Leiden, New York, Cologne: Brill.

Russell, D. A. (1972) *Plutarch*, London: Duckworth.

Sanders, E. P. (1977) *Paul and Palestinian Judaism*, Philadelphia: Fortress.

—— (1985) *Jesus and Judaism*, London: SCM.

—— (1990) *Jewish Law from Jesus to the Mishnah*, London: SCM and Philadelphia: Trinity.

—— (1993) 'Jesus in historical context', *Theology Today* 50.3: 429–48.

Sanders, J. T. (1975) *Ethics in the New Testament*, London: SCM.

Sawyer, D. F. (1996) *Women and Religion in the First Christian Centuries*, London: Routledge.

Schelkle, K. H. (1971–3) *Theology of the New Testament* (3 vols), Collegeville, MN: Liturgical Press.

Schmithals, W. (1965) *Paul and James*, London: SCM.

Schnackenburg, R. (1975) *The Moral Teaching of the New Testament*, London: Burns and Oates (2nd edn).

Schottroff, L. and Stegemann, W. (1978) *Jesus von Nazareth. Hoffnung der Armen*, Stuttgart: Kohlhammer.

Schrage, W. (1960) 'Zur formalethischen Deutung der paulinischen Paränese', *Zeitschrift für evangelische Ethik* 4: 207–33.

—— (1988) *The Ethics of the New Testament* (English translation), Edinburgh: T. & T. Clark.

Scobie, C. H. (1964) *John the Baptist*, London: SCM.

Scott, D. (1996) *Michael Polanyi*, London: SPCK.

Scroggs, R. (1979) 'The sociological interpretation of the New Testament (the present state of research)', *New Testament Studies* 26: 164–79.

Seeberg, A. (1996; orig. 1903) *Der Katechismus der Urchristenheit*, Munich: Chr. Kaiser Verlag.

Selling, J. and Jans, J. (1994) *The Splendor of Accuracy*, Kampen: Kok Pharos.

Selwyn, E. G. (1946) *The First Epistle of St Peter*, London: Macmillan.

Shanks, H. (ed.) (1992) *Understanding the Dead Sea Scrolls*, New York: Random House.

Shillington, V. G. (ed.) (1997) *Jesus and His Parables*, Edinburgh: T. & T. Clark.

Simon, M. (1986) *Verus Israel*, Oxford: Oxford University Press.

Smalley, S. S. (1984) *23 John*, Waco, TX: Word Books.

Smith, M. (1978) *Jesus the Magician*, San Francisco: Harper and Row.

Sordi, M. (1994) *The Christians and the Roman Empire* (English translation), London and New York: Routledge (2nd edn).

Spicq, C. (1965) *Théologie morale du Noveau Testament*, I–II, Paris: Lecoffre.

Sprott, W. J. M. (1958) *Human Groups*, Harmondsworth: Penguin.

Stacey, W. D. (1956) *The Pauline View of Man*, London: Macmillan.

Stanton, G. (1995) *Gospel Truth? New Light on Jesus and the Gospels*, London: Harper Collins.

Steiner, G. (1989) *Real Presences: Is There Anything in What we Say?*, London: Faber.

Stewart, Z. (ed.) (1972) *Arthur Danby Nock: Essays on Religion and the Ancient World*, Oxford: Clarendon.

Streeter, B. H. (1924) *The Four Gospels*, London: Macmillan.

Swartley, W. M. (ed.) (1992) *The Love of Enemy and Nonretaliation in the New Testament*, Louisville, KY: Westminster/John Knox.

Tarn, W. W. (1930) *Hellenistic Civilisation*, London: Edward Arnold.

Taylor, C. (1989) *Sources of the Self: The Making of Modern Identity*, Cambridge: Cambridge University Press.

Taylor, J. E. (1997) *The Immerser. John the Baptist within Second Temple Judaism*, Grand Rapids, MI: Eerdmans.

Telford, W. P. (ed.) (1995) *The Interpretation of Mark*, Edinburgh: T. & T. Clark (2nd edn).

Theissen, G. (1978) *The First Followers of Jesus*, London: SCM.

—— (1982) *The Social Setting of Pauline Christianity* (English translation), Edinburgh: T. & T. Clark.

—— (1992) *The Gospels in Context: Social and Political History in the Synoptic Tradition*, Edinburgh: T. & T. Clark.

Thomson, P. J. (1990) *Paul and the Jewish Law*, Assen/Maastricht: Van Gorcum and Minneapolis: Fortress.

Troeltsch, E. (1960) *The Social Teaching of the Christian Churches*, Louisville, KY: Westminster/John Knox.

Tuckett, C. M. (1986) *Nag Hammadi and the Gospel Tradition*, Edinburgh: T. & T. Clark.

—— (1988) 'Thomas and the synoptics', *Novum Testamentum* 30: 133–57.

—— (1996) *Q and the History of Early Christianity*, Edinburgh: T. & T. Clark.

Vaage, L. E. (1994) 'Q and cynicism: on comparison and social identity', in R. A. Piper (ed.) *The Gospel Behind the Gospels. Current Studies on Q*, Leiden: Brill.

Valantasis, R. (1997) *The Gospel of Thomas*, London and New York: Routledge.

VanderKam, J. C. (1994) *The Dead Sea Scrolls Today*, Grand Rapids, MI: Eerdmans and London: SPCK.

de Vaux, R. (1961) *Ancient Israel: Its Life and Institutions* (English translation), London: Darton, Longman & Todd.

Verhey, A. (1984) *The Great Reversal: Ethics and the New Testament*, Grand Rapids, MI: Eerdmans.

Vermes, G. (1961) *Scripture and Tradition in Judaism*, Leiden: Brill.

—— (1973) *Jesus the Jew*, London: Collins.

—— (1995) *The Dead Sea Scrolls in English*, Harmondsworth: Penguin (4th edn).

—— (1997) *The Complete Dead Sea Scrolls in English*, London: Allen Lane The Penguin Press.

Via, D. O. (Jr) (1985) *Ethics of Mark's Gospel in the Middle of Time*, Philadelphia: Fortress.

Vlastos, G. (1991) *Socrates: Ironist and Moral Philosopher*, Cambridge: Cambridge University Press.

Walzer, R. (1949) *Galen on Jews and Christians*, Oxford: Oxford University Press and London: Geoffrey Cumberlege.

Watson, F. (1986) *Paul, Judaism and the Gentiles. A Sociological Approach*, Cambridge: Cambridge University Press.

Webb, R. L. (1991) 'John the baptizer and prophet', *Journal for the Study of the New Testament Supplement* 5.62: Sheffield Academic Press.

Weber, M. (1965) *The Sociology of Religion*, London: Methuen.

Wibbing, S. (1959) *Die Tugend-und Lasterkataloge im Neuen Testament*, Berlin: Topelmann.

Wilken, R. L. (1984) *The Christians as the Romans Saw Them*, New Haven, CT and London: Yale University Press.

Wilson, R. McL. (1982) 'Gnosis at Corinth', in M. D. Hooker and S. G. Wilson (eds) *Paul and Paulinism. Essays in Honour of C. K. Barrett*, London: SPCK.

Wink, W. (1973) *The Bible in Human Transformation*, Philadelphia: Fortress.

—— (1984) *Naming the Powers: The Language of Power in the New Testament*, Philadelphia: Fortress.

Winter, B. W. (1991) 'Civil litigation in secular Corinth and the church: the forensic background to 1 Corinthians 6.1–8', *New Testament Studies* 37/4: 559–72; also in B. S. Rosner (ed.), *Understanding Paul's Ethics*, Carlisle: Paternoster.

—— (1994) *Seek the Welfare of the City*, Grand Rapids, MI: Eerdmans and Carlisle: Paternoster.

Witherington, Ben III (1988) *Women in the Earliest Churches*, Cambridge: Cambridge University Press.

Wolfson, H. A. (1948) *Philo. Foundations of Religious Philosophy in Judaism, Christianity and Islam*, I–II, Cambridge, MA: Harvard University Press.

Wright, N. T. (1996) *Jesus and the Victory of God*, London: SPCK.

Yoder, J. H. (1994) *The Politics of Jesus*, Grand Rapids, MI: Eerdmans (2nd edn).

Zandee, J. (1977) *'The Teachings of Silvanus' and Clement of Alexandria: A New Document of Alexandrian Theology*, Leiden: Brill.

INDEX OF REFERENCES

Other Writings

GENERAL INDEX